Praise for *Designing Across Senses*

"As the web becomes an overlay on our physical reality and everyday objects come alive with embedded intelligence, we must evolve new ways to interact with our technology. In this enlightening book, Park and Alderman not only demystify multimodal design to bring us closer to our machines, but they also make sense of the startling sensory experiences that keep us human."

DAVID PESCOVITZ,
RESEARCH DIRECTOR, INSTITUTE FOR THE FUTURE
AND CO-EDITOR, BOING BOING

"John and Christine have written a UX classic that will be referenced and pulled on and off the bookshelf for years to come. This book defines and sets the stage for multimodal design and sensory experiences we are experiencing today and designing in a not too distant future."

KELLY GOTO,
CEO AND FOUNDER, GOTOMEDIA

"Technology is breaking away from the screen, and this is the first book that addresses how voice, virtual reality, and other upcoming interaction models should be designed. Take a moment to feel this book. When it is in your hands, you'll find it insightful. When it's out of your hands, you'll miss it dearly."

GOLDEN KRISHNA,
DESIGN STRATEGIST AND AUTHOR,
THE BEST INTERFACE IS NO INTERFACE

Designing Across Senses

*A Multimodal Approach to
Product Design*

Christine W. Park and John Alderman

Beijing · Boston · Farnham · Sebastopol · Tokyo

Designing Across Senses

by Christine W. Park and John Alderman

Copyright © 2018 Christine Park and John Alderman. All rights reserved.

Published by O'Reilly Media, Inc., 1005 Gravenstein Highway North, Sebastopol, CA 95472.

O'Reilly books may be purchased for educational, business, or sales promotional use. Online editions are also available for most titles (*oreilly. com/safari*). For more information, contact our corporate/institutional sales department: (800) 998-9938 or *corporate@oreilly.com*.

Acquisitions Editor: Angela Rufino
Editor: Angela Rufino
Production Editor: Melanie Yarbrough
Proofreader: Amanda Kersey
Indexer: Lucie Haskins

Cover Designer: Randy Comer
Interior Designers: Ron Bilodeau and Monica Kamsvaag
Illustrator: Rebecca Demarest
Compositor: Melanie Yarbrough

February 2018: First Edition.

Revision History for the First Edition:

2018-03-07   First release

See *http://oreilly.com/catalog/errata.csp?isbn=0636920049500* for release details.

The O'Reilly logo is registered trademarks of O'Reilly Media, Inc. *Designing Across Senses* and related trade dress are trademarks of O'Reilly Media, Inc.

Many of the designations used by manufacturers and sellers to distinguish their products are claimed as trademarks. Where those designations appear in this book, and O'Reilly Media, Inc., was aware of a trademark claim, the designations have been printed in caps or initial caps.

Although the publisher and author have used reasonable care in preparing this book, the information it contains is distributed "as is" and without warranties of any kind. This book is not intended as legal or financial advice, and not all of the recommendations may be suitable for your situation. Professional legal and financial advisors should be consulted, as needed. Neither the publisher nor the author shall be liable for any costs, expenses, or damages resulting from use of or reliance on the information contained in this book.

978-1-491-95424-9

[LSI]

[*contents*]

[*Preface*]

What Is This Book About?

FROM THE KEYBOARD, MOUSE, and touchscreen, to voice-enabled assistants and virtual reality, we have never had more ways to interact with technology. Called *modes*, they allow people to enter input and receive output from their devices. These inputs and outputs are often designed together in sets to create cohesive user interfaces (UIs). These modes reflect the way our senses, cognitive functions, and motor skills also work together in sets called *modalities*. Human modalities have existed for far longer than our interface modes, and they enable us to interact with the physical world. Our devices are only beginning to catch up to us. We can now jump and move around in our living rooms to play a game using Microsoft's motion-tracking peripheral, Kinect. We can ask Domino's to deliver a pizza using the Amazon Echo.

We often use several modalities together in our daily activities, and when our devices can do the same, they are considered multimodal UIs. Most UIs are already multimodal, but because they're so familiar we don't tend to think of them that way. In fact, almost all designed products and environments are multimodal. We see a door and knock on it, waiting for it to open or to hear someone inside ask who it is. We use our fingers to type on a keyboard, and see characters appear on the screen in front of our eyes. We ask Siri a question and see the oscilloscope-like waveform to let us know we are being heard. We receive a phone call and feel the vibration, hear the ringtone, and see the name of the person on the screen in front of us. We play a video game and are immersed in sensory information from the screen, speakers, and the rumble shock controller in our hands.

Multimodal products blend different interface modes together cohesively. They allow us to experience technology the same way we experience our everyday lives: across our senses. Good multimodal design helps us stay focused on what we are doing. Bad multimodal design distracts us with clumsy or disjointed interactions and irrelevant information. It pulls us out of our personal experience in ways that are at best irritating and at worst dangerous.

As technology is incorporated into more contexts and activities in our lives, new types of interfaces are rapidly emerging. Product designers and their teams are challenged to blend modalities in new combinations for new products in emerging categories. They are being asked to add new modalities to the growing number of devices we use every day. This book provides these teams with an approach to designing multimodal interactions. It describes the human factors of multimodal experiences, starting with the senses and how we use them to interact with both physical and digital information. The book then explores the opportunities represented by different kinds of multimodal products and the methodologies for developing and designing them. Following this approach will develop multimodal experiences for your users. You will be able to deliver successful products that earn trust, fulfill needs, and inspire delight.

Who Should Read This Book

This book is for designers who are developing or transforming products with new interface modes, and those who want to. It will extend knowledge, skills, and process past screen-based appraoches, and into the next wave of devices and technologies. The book also helps teams that are integrating products across broader physical environments and behaviors. The senses and cognition are the foundation of all human experience, and understanding them will help blend physical and digital contexts and activities successfully. Ultimately, it is for anyone who wants to create better products and services. Our senses are the gateway to the richness, variety, delight, and meaning in our lives. Knowing how they work is key to delivering great experiences.

HOW THIS BOOK IS ORGANIZED

This book is organized into two parts. Part I covers the human sensory abilities, how they function, and how we use them to interact with both the physical world and with technology. It also describes the ways technology fits with human senses in new interface modes. Part II sets out the flexible process and methodology of multimodal design. Starting with product definition, it explains how to identify and assess possibilities for innovation. From there, it describes the considerations, activities, and deliverables that take a team from concept to launch. Sprinkled throughout the book are short sections about relevant products and technologies.

Part I: New Human Factors

Chapter 1 describes how sensing, whether by humans or devices, turns physical events into useful information. It describes modalities and multimodalities and how they shape human experience. It describes the difference between human modalities and device modes and how together they become interfaces. Finally, it looks at the new human factors: sensing, understanding, deciding, and acting—important experiential building blocks for designing any kind of product or service.

Chapter 2 delves further into the building blocks of experience and how they relate to more familiar design concepts like affordances and mental models. The chapter looks at how they are useful for understanding human experience and how they are applicable to multimodal design.

Chapter 3 looks at how our senses evolved to perceive the diverse types of matter and energy in the world around us. Designing interfaces requires an understanding of the user's senses and the powers, limitations, characteristics, and expectations that each sense carries.

Chapter 4 is about how cognition is organized by schemas, which lets us parse and analyze sensory information and then understand and learn from it.

Chapter 5 is about how our physical form and abilities shape our interactions, and the considerations they raise in product design.

Chapter 6 digs into modalities and multimodalities: specific patterns of perception, cognition, and action that enable our behaviors. It introduces a few rules of thumb for designers creating multimodal interactions such as respecting cognitive load, supporting focus, maintaining flow, and allowing feedback and validation.

Chapter 7 explains how to identify opportunities for innovation by assessing user needs and contexts and reframing current products and technologies.

Chapter 8 looks at cues, affordances, feedback, feedforward, and prompts: the palette of multimodal interactions. These elements of experience describe how people use physical information within an interaction.

Chapter 9 explores ways to use maps and models to frame opportunities, contextualize insights, and align project efforts to create effective multimodal experiences. It builds on existing deliverables like customer journeys and ecosystem maps, and introduces new ones like focus models.

Chapter 10 describes the interplay of physical design and technology capabilities during product development. It emphasizes the need to map interface modes to the required modalities within user behaviors, and compare different mappings across products.

Chapter 11 distinguishes layers of context as ecosystems and looks at how they affect product usage. It includes four types of ecosystems: information, physical, social, and device.

Chapter 12 encourages designers to think of the entire design process as prototyping. It describes deliverables that can be used to specify product characteristics and usage behaviors.

Chapter 13 describes different ways that products can be released and identifies how teams can minimize risk, maximize learning, and increase the chances of a successful product.

Why Write a Book About Multimodal Design

In the last few years, the development of interface technologies has accelerated, causing an explosion of products and the Internet of Things. Many new subdisciplines in design have emerged as a result: gestural interfaces like Kinect and Leap Motion, voice user interfaces (VUIs) like Siri and Amazon Echo, and virtual reality (VR) and augmented reality (AR) products like the Oculus Rift and Apple's ARKit. The rising use of sensors has also enabled automated interactions: wearables can detect whether you are biking or walking, doors can unlock based on proximity, the Nest thermometer can set your home to a comfortable temperature—not to mention driverless cars and consumer robotics. Designers and product teams are challenged to create all kinds of new experiences with these technologies. This has largely been following a technology-centric approach to creating experiences, driven by whatever the new technology can do.

Design, however, works best as a user-centered discipline, focused on what people can do. And the one facet of user experience that connects all these new types of interactions is the senses. It turns out that sensory experience is key to human experience. For all the bits in the world, we can only understand the information they hold when they are translated to physical information: a vibration we can feel with our skin, a sound we hear with our ears, or a pixel we see with our eyes. Our lives are rooted in our senses. We enjoy a dazzling sunset, beautiful music, and delicious food. We see the smile on the face of a loved one. We smile back to share our happiness. We experience joy and empathy through our senses. We understand the way the world works through them as well. If we are called user experience designers, then we should understand how people experience in the first place. And human experience starts with the senses.

Acknowledgments

Apparently it takes a village to write a book. It's impossible to name everyone who offered insight, ideas, and encouragement along the way. We'd like to especially thank Wes Yun, Cecil Odom, Mark Blanchard, and Kelly Goto for riffing with us—and helping us tell the difference between crazy good ideas and crazy bad ideas.

We'd like to thank our reviewers Frances Close, and Christy Ennis-Kloote for their patience and clarity.

Christine would like to thank her grandmother, Chung Ja Kim, and aunt, Sanghee Hui, whose strength and intelligence have provided a lifetime of inspiration, and who make her laugh so hard she cries.

John would like to thank his mother Barbara for overall gumption and *joie de vivre,* and Paul Cuneo for being so supportive.

We'd both like to thank the extended O'Reilly team including our editors, Angela Rufino, Melanie Yarbrough, Jasmine Kwityn, and Mary Treseler; and our agent Peter McGuigan.

Very special thanks to our dog Barnaby who kept our feet warm while we were writing and reminded us to go outside.

[1]

Returning to Our Senses

If a Tree Falls in the Forest...

BRAZIL BEGAN USING SATELLITE imaging to monitor deforestation during the 1980s. This was the first large-scale, coordinated response to loggers and ranchers who had been illegally clearing the rainforests, and it worked, for a time. To avoid being spotted, loggers and ranchers began working more discreetly in smaller areas that were harder to detect (see Figure 1-1).[1] This required a new approach to monitoring the forests.

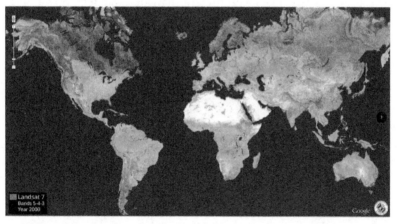

FIGURE 1-1.
A view powered by Google Earth Engine showing global deforestation

---

1   Gustavo Faleiros, "Looking Down on Deforestation: Brazil Sharpens Its Eyes in the Sky to Snag Illegal Rainforest Loggers," *Scientific American*, April 12, 2011, *https://www. scientificamerican.com/article/brazil-satellites-catch-illegal-rainforest-loggers/*.

Google Earth Engine and the Brazilian NGO, Imazon, worked together to create more powerful environmental monitoring capabilities. Their collaboration identified and mapped a much wider range of deforestation in much greater detail. With new analysis techniques for satellite imagery, they were able to classify forest topologies within the rainforest. This improved the accuracy of regional assessments, both for their contribution to the surrounding ecosystem and their vulnerability to human damage. They monitored the emergence of unofficial roads that marked new human activity. They modeled the environmental risks posed by agriculture, logging, and ranching to protected areas of the Amazon. They were also able to project future scenarios to help plan a more effective management strategy that balanced human land use with forest preservation.

The NGO, Rainforest Connection, takes a more on-the-ground approach to rainforest conservation in the Amazon, as well as in Indonesia and Africa. Networks of "upcycled," or refurbished, mobile phones are placed into solar-charged cradles, suspended high within the forest canopy (see Figure 1-2). The phones are reprogrammed to detect sounds associated with invasive activities, like motorcycles, logging trucks, or chainsaws. This cyberpunk-looking retrofitted beacon approach notifies residents and rangers who can respond immediately.

FIGURE 1-2.
One of Rainforest Connection's modified phones, placed to monitor sounds associated with illegal loggers (Source: Rainforest Connection)

Topher White, the founder of Rainforest Connection, described his first effort in Indonesia:

> We're talking hundreds of kilometers from the nearest road, there's certainly no electricity, but they had very good cell phone service, these people in the towns were on Facebook all the time...this sort of got me thinking that in fact it would be possible to use the sounds of the forest, pick up the sounds of chainsaws programmatically, because people can't hear them, and send an alert. But you have to have a device to go up in the trees. So if we can use some device to listen to the sounds of the forest, connect to the cell phone network that's there, and send an alert to people on the ground, perhaps we could have a solution to this issue...if you can show up in real time and stop people, it's enough of a deterrent they won't come back.

These digital sentinels in the sky and in the trees listen and watch over natural resources. They are powerful new tools that blend easily accessible sensor technologies with new data analysis capabilities to enable immediate response to illegal deforestation.

The same types of tools are also making city streets less mean.

The Sound of Violence

A bullet leaves the muzzle of a gun at between 3,500 and 5,000 feet per second. The speed of sound is 1,125 feet per second, making a gunshot a miniature sonic boom, audible for miles. For those unfamiliar with the sound, it might be confused for a tire blowout. For those who are familiar, it is a bleak reminder of how close and how commonplace lethal violence can be.

The effects of persistent gun violence on a community can be devastating. Trust erodes between law enforcement and citizens. Residents suffer from chronic fear-induced stress, more anxious all the time, and yet increasingly desensitized to violence. They often become resigned when violence does occur. The trauma to children is especially severe, with behavioral and learning difficulties that can impact the rest of their lives.

In 2016, the city of Cape Town, South Africa, adopted a new strategy to combat gun violence. An alert system, called ShotSpotters, was deployed in two areas of the city with high levels of gang activity. Using an array of microphones spread over 7 square kilometers, the system recognizes the sound of a gunshot, analyzes the sound to position its source, and then determines GPS coordinates. In under 60 seconds, the GPS coordinates are reported back to the Cape Town police, who can then send officers to within 2 meters of where the shot was fired (see Figure 1-3).

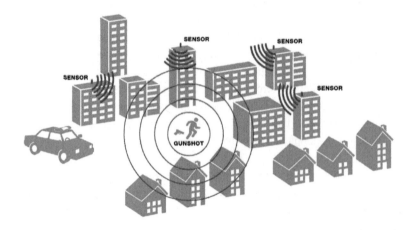

FIGURE 1-3.
ShotSpotters places sensors to monitor for gunshots and alert police (Source: ShotSpotters)

In one case, a gunshot was picked up and located by the microphone system. Per typical police response, a K9 unit—a trained dog and a police handler—was sent to investigate. On the spot, police noticed that two people saw them and immediately ran away, so they followed them to a nearby house. In the house they found and confiscated an illegal automatic 9mm gun, along with 64 rounds of ammunition and a magazine.[2] This immediate response became the norm.

Blending emerging smart city technology and trained Cape Town officers, the use of ShotSpotters was hugely successful. Within one month, the number of illegal gunshots dropped from 211 to 128. Within two

---

2   "Cape Town metro cops arrest 73 in crackdown," *Independent Online*, August 15, 2016, *http://www.iol.co.za/news/crime-courts/cape-town-metro-cops-arrest-73-in-crackdown-2057190.*

months it had dropped to 31, eliminating 85% of the gunshots fired. In total, 54 guns have been removed from the streets in 7 months—a figure that was previously only achieved over a 6-year period.[3]

Catching the shooters required large amounts of physical information to be collected, analyzed, and applied to action in real time: correctly identifying the sound and time of a gunshot, positioning its source in geographic space, knowing the location of the nearest K9 unit. Once on the scene, trained police dogs sought the scent of gunpowder. The police officers visually identified the suspects.

These stories are not just about policing or monitoring. They are also about the intersection of some of our oldest and newest sensory abilities and how we use them to understand and interact with our world. Vision originated under water as a patch of protein-based photoreceptors on a single-celled organism, during the Cambrian explosion hundreds of millions of years ago. Tracking dogs have been used since Roman times, and police dogs have existed for over a hundred years. A human has about 5 million scent glands, whereas dogs have 125 million to 300 million. Their sense of smell is up to 100,000 times better than ours.[4] Sound triangulation cross-referenced with GPS coordinates distributed via cloud-based analysis is relatively new, developed within the past decade. Technology can extend our natural sensory abilities, allowing us to see subatomic particles, to hear across a city, to keep watch over a continent, and to observe the farthest reaches of our universe. It lets us use our senses in ways we never have before, but it also relies on how we naturally use them in the first place. Understanding how our senses evolved, and how we use them now will help us as we design for new ways to use them in the future.

Experience Is Physical

Our senses gather the physical information that surrounds us. This information can't be Googled, but we use it all the time. We can tell it's morning by the light seeping through our curtains. We can tell what's

---

3   "Cape Town fights crime with drones, acoustic technology, and smartphones," *My Broadband*, January 25, 2017, *https://mybroadband.co.za/news/security/195448-cape-town-fights-crime-with-drones-acoustic-technology-and-smartphones.html*.

4   Peter Tyson, "Dogs' Dazzling Sense of Smell," *Nova*, October 4, 2012, *http://www.pbs.org/wgbh/nova/nature/dogs-sense-of-smell.html*.

for dinner by aromas coming from the kitchen. We grab our umbrellas when we hear the sound of rain. We laugh when we get a joke, and hopefully, we can tell when someone doesn't get the one we've just told. Aided by technology, we can tell that someone has just arrived at our front door, that our email was just sent, or that the truck in front of us is about to reverse (see Figure 1-4).

FIGURE 1-4.
Think about the way your senses work throughout the day. Sunlight can wake you. The smell of cooking can remind you how hungry you are. The sound of rain can delight or disappoint, depending on your plans.

David Eagleman is a cognitive neuroscientist who studies how human experience and the mind shape each other. He writes:

> Sealed within the dark, silent chamber of your skull, your brain has never directly experienced the external world, and it never will. Instead, there's only one way that information from out there gets into the brain. Your sensory organs—your eyes, ears, nose, mouth, and skin— act as interpreters. They detect a motley crew of information sources

(including photons, air compression waves, molecular concentrations, pressure, texture, temperature) and translate them into the common currency of the brain: electrochemical signals.[5]

Everything we know, do, and say happens through our senses—both the information we accumulate and how we act upon it throughout our day.

Unlike Tank in *The Matrix*, most of us can't do much with falling lines of machine code. The gazillions of bits of information on the internet must be translated to and from 1s and 0s into interfaces that we can physically experience. We can read text and view images, videos, and virtual worlds. We can hear sound alerts or speak requests to the latest speech assistants. We can feel the buzz of our phone in our back pocket, or the victorious rumble of the game controller in our hands as we blow up the last boss on the last level. We experience everything, whether physical or digital, natural or designed, through our senses.

Our senses are always on, sending a continuous stream of information through our nervous system to our brains. But a good deal of the time, we aren't aware of our senses at all. Think about what shoes feel like on your feet. You probably really haven't noticed them except when you put them on, unless they are uncomfortable. You probably didn't even notice what having feet felt like today until you read this just now (see Figure 1-5). Though essential to experience, we only notice a tiny fraction of the sensory information we gather.

---

5   David Eagleman, *The Brain: The Story of You* (New York: Pantheon Books, 2015, 41).

FIGURE 1-5.
Take a moment to feel your feet. When they are in shoes, we barely notice them. When we take off those shoes to walk barefoot through the grass, the wonderful sensation can completely take over.

At certain times, a single sensory experience, like a delicious taste or a beautiful piece of music, can consume us. At other times, we can tune out the monotonous conversation in front of us, or laser focus on the cutie giving us the eye from across a booming party. We can switch focus between different sensory experiences lightning fast: when we hear a sudden loud noise we turn to look. We shudder when a slimy fish touches our feet underwater. Sometimes we consciously choose where our attention is, and sometimes our reflexes take over.

[NOTE]

For the sake of clarity, the word *modality* will be used to describe human capabilities and the word *mode* will be used to describe device capabilities. They are often used interchangeably, but that would make this a very difficult book to read, let alone write. To add to the confusion, *multimodal* is used for describing both people and devices that have either multiple modalities or modes. We hope that this will be clear in context.

People Have Modalities

It isn't enough to simply sense the world around us. We need to extract meaning from this information and use it to make decisions and take action. Once light has been gathered on the back of our eyes by the retina, we interpret color, brightness, shapes, and movement. Because we have stereoscopic vision, we can also perceive distance. If we recognize a familiar face, we might smile and wave. If we recognize a snarling animal, we might back away.

It turns out that there are specific ways to interpret sensory information and apply it to our decisions and actions. We can recognize shapes visually and through direct contact, when we touch them. We don't generally taste or smell shapes to tell them apart (see Figure 1-6). Along the same lines, vibrations might not be the best way to provide IKEA furniture assembly instructions.

FIGURE 1-6.
Which of these chocolates is tarragon grapefruit, and which are cardamom nougat, or lavender vanilla? Our sense of vision works better for figuring out some things than others. Sadly, this book is not lickable, so you may never know.

The kinds of information we sense, the way we interpret that information, and the kinds of decisions and actions that can be based on that information are linked. Over the course of our lives, we develop patterns in how we use different sensory channels. These are called *modalities*. They are also known as *sensorimotor schema*. These modalities are usually described by their focal sense, like *visual, auditory,* or *haptic*. Vision relies on our eyes, audition relies on our ears, and haptics rely on our sense of touch and movement. Using these senses together is known as *multimodality*. Modalities shape the way we use sensory information to inform our behaviors (see Figure 1-7).

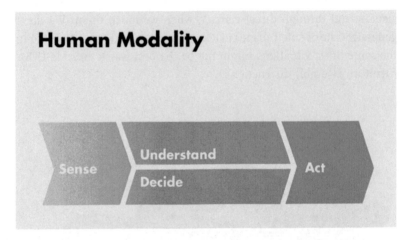

FIGURE 1-7.
A behavioral pattern using a set of perceptual, cognitive, and motor functions together

We are multimodal most of the time; very few human behaviors are *unimodal*. For example, walking down the street combines our sense of balance, vision, touch, and movement. Having a conversation combines the sense of hearing and vision, our ability to create speech, and perhaps also movements and touch if you tend to talk with your hands.

These combinations make our daily interactions possible. At a traffic light, we learn to step on our gas pedal when we see a green light. A yellow light makes us consider whether to step on the brake or not. We hear a kettle whistle and turn off the burner. We see a branch across our path, and we decide whether to jump over it or walk around it. We hear marimbas, and we pull out our phones to see who is calling. Our senses enable a wide range of behaviors, making us adaptive and responsive to the world, to each other, and to our devices. The more we use each multimodal combination, the stronger they become, forming the core behaviors, habits, and skills we use throughout our lives (see Figure 1-8).

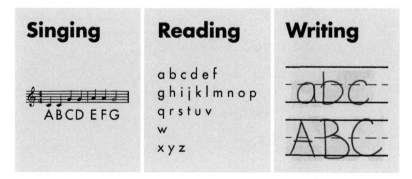

FIGURE 1-8.
Learning the alphabet through reading, writing, and singing (Modalities have been applied to education, where it is believed that some children have stronger visual, auditory, or tactile, kinesthetic learning styles. Teaching materials may include a mix of media to accommodate this.)

Devices Have Modes

Devices are now also becoming more adaptive and responsive. For a long time, the evolution of personal computing seemed somewhat steady: from the keyboard and mouse, to the feature phone, to the smartphone. Then it seemed to pick up the pace: tablets, Siri, the Nintendo Wii, XBox Kinect, Google Glass, the Nest thermostat, wearables, driverless cars, the Oculus Rift, Amazon Echo, and Google Home. It's reached an astonishing velocity (see Figure 1-9).

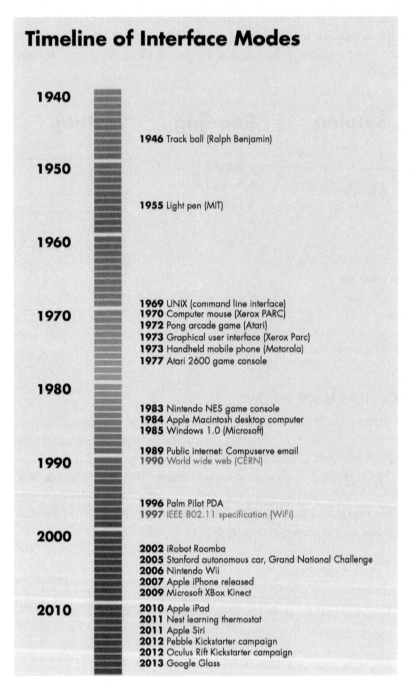

Timeline of Interface Modes

1940

1946 Track ball (Ralph Benjamin)

1950

1955 Light pen (MIT)

1960

1969 UNIX (command line interface)
1970 Computer mouse (Xerox PARC)
1972 Pong arcade game (Atari)
1973 Graphical user interface (Xerox Parc)
1973 Handheld mobile phone (Motorola)
1977 Atari 2600 game console

1970

1980

1983 Nintendo NES game console
1984 Apple Macintosh desktop computer
1985 Windows 1.0 (Microsoft)

1989 Public internet: Compuserve email
1990 World wide web (CERN)

1990

1996 Palm Pilot PDA
1997 IEEE 802.11 specification (WiFi)

2000

2002 iRobot Roomba
2005 Stanford autonomous car, Grand National Challenge
2006 Nintendo Wii
2007 Apple iPhone released
2009 Microsoft XBox Kinect

2010

2010 Apple iPad
2011 Nest learning thermostat
2011 Apple Siri
2012 Pebble Kickstarter campaign
2012 Oculus Rift Kickstarter campaign
2013 Google Glass

FIGURE 1-9.

The number of interface modes has kept pace with technical innovation, and has likely contributed to it as well

These different channels of interaction are called *modes* (see Figure 1-10). Similar to human modalities, they are developed around specific types of physical information. While multimodal interfaces have always been a part of user experience design, there have never been as many different kinds. Speech, touch, haptic, and gestural interfaces are now ubiquitous across laptops, smartphones, tablets, game consoles, and wearables. Virtual reality (VR) is growing across the gaming industry, and new types of products are entering our homes, cars, offices, and the streets of our cities. Devices can now use many different kinds of human behavior as input and provide feedback across a wide array of outputs.

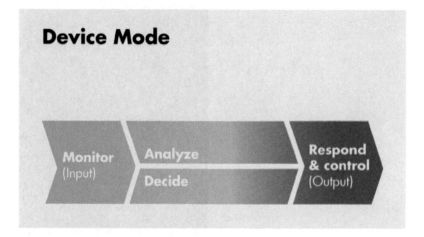

FIGURE 1-10.
The building blocks of device modes mirror those of human modalities

An example of this is force touch on Apple devices. When a user hard presses on an item, say an email header in their inbox, the taptic engine creates a "popping" haptic feedback, accompanied with a blurring visual effect. The touchscreen employs a number of force resistance capacitors to detect the amount of pressure that is being applied, the position, as well as the duration. Once the touch gesture is recognized, it provides various email features on the screen.

There can be many different modes for the same interaction, or multiple modes within a single interaction. In fact, the moment computing became *multimodal* (via the mouse, keyboard, and GUI) was when it really began to become accessible to everyone.

Think of using your screen or Siri to make a phone call. To call someone, you can tap out the phone number on the touchscreen. You can also ask Siri to make the call for you. You may have long-pressed the Home button to initiate Siri in the first place or have simply said "Hey, Siri" (see Figure 1-11).

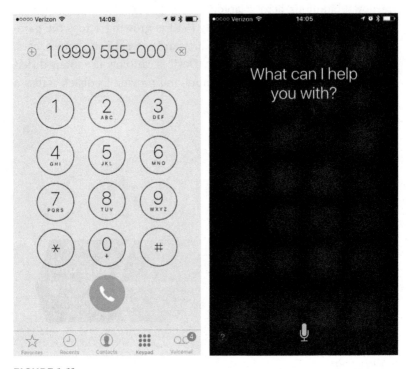

FIGURE 1-11.
You can use buttons to make a call yourself (left) or ask Siri to dial for you (right)

Human Modalities + Device Modes = Interfaces

Technology can now be embedded into any object or environment, seamlessly integrating into a wider range of our experiences. It can literally be incorporated directly into our bodies. Screens, locks, cars, glasses, and many other objects can now be considered *devices*, as they become connected and digital. The kinds of interactions we can have with these devices has expanded well beyond the clicks, swipes, and taps that we are accustomed to with screens. Approaching a door fitted with an August smartlock can unlock it, while walking away can lock it again (see Figure 1-12). Many fitness devices can tell the difference between walking, running, and biking, which trigger them to start tracking the activity. (Unfortunately, we still have to do our own exercising.)

FIGURE 1-12.
An August lock can open when it detects its owner

Our interactions with technology are being blended into the ways we already interact with the physical world, and product design teams are responsible for figuring out how. These types of interfaces, like *hands-free* or *eyes-free*, complement the physical activity they accompany. Many have existed for some time with simpler mechanical technologies. Turn signal in cars are augmented by clicking. We may not have the chance to glance at the blinking arrow on our dashboard, but we can hear that our signal is engaged by the sound.

In addition, these physical interactions may have many layers of information within a single sensory channel; VUIs are an example of this. *Prosody* is the intonation, tone, stress, and rhythm we use in spoken language. It expresses meaning and emotions beyond words. Changes in intonation and stress can indicate sarcasm. They can also change a statement to a question. For interaction design, prosody is important to designing voice interfaces, but it has equally powerful implications for all sound design. Game designers use prosody to great effect (see Figure 1-13). Background music speeds up to let players know that they are running out of time. Triumphant music often rises in pitch, while setbacks are marked with falling tones.

FIGURE 1-13.
The video game Vilmonic, like most others, uses tonal sound effects and short melodies to reinforce a sense of drama and narrative

It's also very common for people to use one sense to compensate for another. This behavior, known as *substitution*, allows us to use an alternative sensory modality when our usual modality is blocked or engaged. When it is dark, we put our hands out in front of us and shuffle our feet. We can no longer see obstacles in our path, so we feel them out. When it's loud, we may look at the movements of a person's lips more closely and may use more gestures to communicate. Many crosswalks use sounds to indicate changes in signal. Closed-captioning originated as way for people with hearing impairments to watch films and television; it is now a staple of sports bars where no one can hear a television at all. Substitution is a very common design strategy for accessibility: Braille, screen readers, and sign language remap information from one sensory modality to another. But it's common for all people to rely on other senses when they cannot use their typical modality for a task.

Our senses of vision and hearing are very closely tied together and we develop many multimodal behaviors between them. In multisensory integration, an effect known as *synchrony* emerges, where we try to align visual movement and auditory rhythms together. Our visual and auditory abilities reinforce each other, and increase our ability to predict each other better. Those 8-bit game sound effects aren't just retro cool. They help players learn to play and develop their skills more effectively. They reinforce the difference between a positive and negative event using some of the same cues used in spoken language. The audiovisual combination is particularly effective for timing or rhythm-based user activities. The combination of visual, haptic, and proprioceptive abilities—our senses of sight, touch, and movement—reinforce each other in creating spatial mappings of objects and environments. Much of screen-based design relies on this sensory integration in creating core interactions like navigation and browsing.

Much of interaction design relies on how each sense works individually and on abilities that emerge from how we integrate them together. Mapping sensory modalities to interface modes correctly can mean the difference between a cohesive experience and a disjointed one (see Figure 1-14). This integration can also help people learn new experiences more quickly and feel excited and delighted by them.

Modality plus Mode equals Interactions

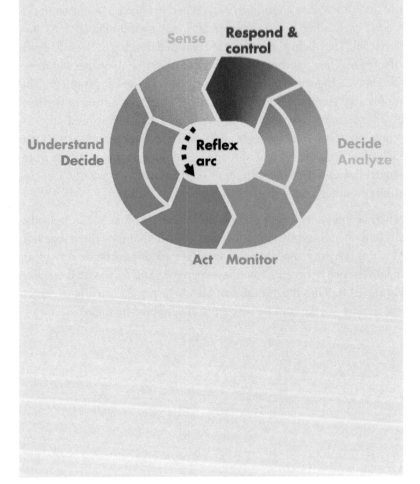

FIGURE 1-14.
Human modalities and device modes work together to create feedback loops, essential for effective interactions.

Physical Information: The New Data

We use physical information to guide all our experiences. We monitor air temperature with our skin to decide if we need a sweater. We use proximity to gauge when to reach for a doorknob as we are walking towards it. We hear the sound of an oncoming train and start shuffling toward the edge of the platform. Researchers estimate that the eye alone can capture 10 million bits of information per second.[6] We use a phenomenal amount of physical information to get through our day.

These kinds of physical information are making their way into interaction design through the expanding variety of sensors in devices. Ruggedized, miniaturized, and power-optimized for their use in smartphones, these components and technologies now easily cross over to new environmental and usage contexts. The research company CBI says that from 2004 to 2014, the cost of sensors fell to an average of $0.60 per unit: "Declining sensor cost is one of the main drivers of Internet of Things technology, and the proliferation of internet-connected devices in the built environment. Those sensors are allowing us to gather new data that was previously inaccessible."[7] In Teslas, they are used to help cars park themselves. Our ovens might use them to tell us that they have reached the correct temperature for lasagna. Smoke detectors monitor carbon monoxide—a gas that we cannot easily detect on our own.

The use of physical information expands the types of interactions we can have with our devices, and the kinds of functionalities that can be automated. Using sensor-based data to shape interactions is a substantial shift from forms, clicks, and other measurements of screen-based user behavior. Interactions can be more immediate, more contextual, and more dynamic. Physically rooted interactions can feel more intimate and private to the user, and impart a stronger sense of embodiment and identity. They also introduce considerations about how information is gathered and used.

---

6   Kristin Koch, et al., "How Much the Eye Tells the Brain," *Current Biology* 16, no. 14 (July 2006).

7   "80+ Startups Making Cities Smarter Across Traffic, Waste, Energy, Water Usage, and More," *CB Insights*, January 24, 2017, *https://www.cbinsights.com/research/iot-smart-cities-market-map-company-list*.

Sensor data is often a continuous stream of information, as opposed to a set of individual data points. That can require much more processing and analysis in order to extract meaning, and the meaning that's extracted can be more than a user bargained for. Biometric analysis can extract a person's identity from certain kinds of data, exposing them to cybercrime and immoral or illegal forms of bias. Compliance laws are particularly strict around health and identifiable information, with requirements about the type of data, how it is used, as well as where it is stored, and for how long. The way this information is managed will determine whether people trust the next generation of devices and the companies that make them.

The same types of privacy issues led to public concern about the ShotSpotters system.

"The microphones are only listening for gunshots. But, there have been a few cases where someone's voice was picked up by ShotSpotter's mics," says Oakland police officer Omega Crumb, who's responsible for much of the department's technology. He believes an incident in which an officer from the neighboring city of Fremont came to Oakland to serve a warrant was a case study in how valuable that recording can be.

"They get out to make the arrest and the suspect shoots the Fremont officer," Crumb recounts. "The suspect said when he went to court that he didn't know it was the police, they never said it. ShotSpotter was able to come in and pulled that sensor and you can hear them clearly saying, 'Freeze! Police,' And then you hear the suspect shoot. So that was a key one. That was a big one for us," says Crumb.

In another case in 2007, a shooting victim shouted out the street name of the person who just shot him—and that recording was used in court to convict the killer of second-degree murder.

This technology allows the police to record our conversations without our knowledge. The privacy concerns are obvious. "Are they maybe this terribly evil thing right now? No. Probably not," said Brian Hofer, now chair of the Oakland Privacy Advisory Commission, who worked with the city government to create a privacy policy for ShotSpotter. "Could they be? Sure, just re-program your software."[8]

In response to this, the CEO of ShotSpotters commented:

> It's a healthy conversation to have. We need to discuss the costs and benefits of these new technologies, and examine the trade-offs, not only in how the data is used, but if there is data leakage. We don't yet fully understand the trade-offs in the benefits or costs of using this kind of information on behalf of users. The security threats are just surfacing. We're going to find out what they are very rapidly.

The decisions that users and companies make together on these issues will not only shape our experiences, but our rights as well. Making these decisions explicit and transparent is vital.

Sensing, Understanding, Deciding, and Acting: The New Human Factors

The foundational tenets of user-centered design originated from research and design principles in the fields of marketing and industrial design: understanding user groups, designing for how something is used as well as how it looks, designing for real people across a variety of sizes, shapes, and abilities. These tenets had existed for almost a century. And then the computer came along and flipped the script. Very rapidly, designers needed to shift from how people *used objects* to how they *interacted with information*. Those interactions focused primarily on a single type of hardware: the screen. Much of what we know about usability is based on it. This shift was profound for designers, but its impact to our collective behavior was even more so. We now spend most of our waking hours with screens. For the last 30 years, the screen has risen in use until it completely dominated all of our interactions of any kind. We spend more time with screens than we do with other people, the outdoors, pets, or other kinds of tools. The only other thing

---

8   Andrew Stelzer, "Is this crime-fighting technique invading your privacy?", *Newsworks*, November 22, 2016, *http://www.newsworks.org/index.php/local/the-pulse/98667-is-this-crime-fighting-technique-invading-your-privacy.*

in your life that comes close to that much of your face time is your pillow. User-centered design helped create a screen-centered life for many people.

The rise of new interface technologies is poised to reverse that tide and redefine the role of technology in our lives. We know a great deal about how people consume information. The rise of sensor-based technologies is illuminating how we live with it. Information and interactions can be distributed across many kinds of device capabilities and in any physical object, environment, activity, or event. An input trigger could be the moment a person comes within a set physical location, such as with GPS or beacon devices, not just a direct interaction with a device interface. An output might be a text notification, or a fully automated behavior, like having your living room mopped. To create these kinds of interactions requires a new understanding of user behaviors.

A simple way to organize these new factors is by what we are doing with physical information during an interaction: how we sense, understand, decide, and act. These are the core building blocks to all multimodal experiences. We may not use all the blocks in every single experience and there is overlap and interplay between them. In other cases, they may form a response loop.

This particular model helps to break apart the kinds of design considerations that occur across the multiple modes of interactions. It also provides flexibility around how human modalities blend together and how different interface modes can be mapped to them.

SENSING

Perception is not just how we sense physical information, but how we become aware of, organize and interpret it. An example of perception is hearing: it is specially attenuated within the range of the human voice, which comes as no surprise. The physiognomy of our ears—the tympanic membrane, the malleus, incus, and stapes of our middle ear—is physically optimized to transmit those acoustic frequencies.

In the same way that standards for text legibility are well defined, the *sensibility* of other kinds of physical information will begin to become more firmly established. The use of speech technology introduces new metrics, like the number of utterances in a voice interaction, and confidence—the likelihood that a word was recognized correctly. Haptic interactions can be measured by pressure or force, vibration speed, and intensity. Traditional usability metrics are being applied to new types of experiences as well. Differentiation and recall, tests that can be used to measure the usability of icons, are also being used for haptic vibrations, sometimes called hapticons; these gauge how well a person can remember a vibration pattern or tell two different patterns apart.

Product development teams will need to be familiar with the anthropometrics that describe our sensory capabilities, like our field of vision, the range of human hearing, and the amount of force detectable by our sense of touch. We will also need to better understand how we process that information and apply it during physical activities.

UNDERSTANDING AND DECIDING

Cognition describes the processes we have in place to help acquire understanding and knowledge. An example of this is how the speed and accuracy of our reading ability play decisive roles in the design of road signage. At highway speeds, our ability to read a sign degrades rapidly because of how quickly we pass them, so the number of words must be limited. Our ability to recognize our exit and to make a turn off is also affected. To accommodate this, exit signs may need to be placed a full half mile before an exit to give us the time we need to process the information, make a decision, and execute it. These response times aren't just good design practice. They are federal regulation.

Executive cognition is part of this, which is how we use understanding to control our behavior. There are many different models of decision making in psychology, and probably no single right one. In a lighter example, there are many kinds of decisions when it comes to dessert. You can decide to have chocolate pudding instead of lemon cake, which is *preference*. You can decide that you really shouldn't have cake at all, which is *inhibition*. You can decide that you need cake right away, and begin to bake one, which requires *procedural* abilities. There are also different levels of decisions like buying a cake versus starting a bakery, and they require their own information, analysis, and sequence along the way.

ACTING

Action is to apply information (or sometimes not apply it) in the physical world. Our primary forms of action are physical movement and speech. Physical movement is spans basic skills like gripping objects and moving your eyes while scanning images, to more complex activities like paragliding, chopping vegetables, or playing electric guitar. Action encompasses not just the activities themselves, but how we acquire these physical skills. Repeating a physical activity over time can improve our ability to execute it. Repetition can also make it a more permanent and automatic part of our behavior: an ingrained habit like biting your nails or an expert skill like your tennis swing. This is especially relevant to augmented, assistive, and automated technologies, and understanding the ins and outs are critical to human safety. One example is the way we automatically move our eyes to focus them, a reflex called *focal accommodation*. Because we have no control over this reflex, it can interfere with the use of VR and AR headgear, causing dizziness and nausea.

Awareness during physical activities is idiosyncratic. There are some activities, like flossing our teeth, where we mentally check out and it's OK. It's easy for us to multitask and maybe watch a TV show at the same time. There are other activities where we want to check out, but shouldn't, like repeating a forklift maneuver for the 78th time today. The key is balancing engagement against cognitive limits.

Focus: The New Engagement

For the first time in 50 years, the number of fatalities from traffic accidents in the United States rose in 2015. This rise was widely attributed to distracted driving—using smartphones while at the wheel.[9] While adding turn-by-turn navigation to driving has fundamentally changed the experience, access to other features has also made it more dangerous. These dangers must be prioritized and carefully considered; a person's focal abilities must come first. Adding a new activity or modifying the current one can cause user errors or complete distraction. Engagement is not always what it's cracked up to be.

Conversely, focus is gaining prominence in interaction design. It's the ability to prioritize, organize, and delegate attention in a controlled but comfortable way. Reducing distraction is one part of this, but

---

9   Barb Darrow, "Distracted Driving Is Now an Epidemic in the U.S.," *Fortune*, September 14, 2016, *http://fortune.com/2016/09/14/distracted-driving-epidemic/*.

supporting the way our attention naturally works is another. Designing for focus also accounts for the duration of activity, fatigue, and other factors.

Flow is a state of mind first described by psychologist Mihaly Csikszentmihalyi. The writer Dana Chisnell describes it as being "'in the zone,' relaxed and energized at the same time. The outside world ceases to exist and time fades away. Awareness heightens and senses are charged, increasing productivity and creativity."[10] In physical activity—which is pretty much all activity—flow is the ideal state of performance. Perception, cognition, and action fuse into a seamless, effortless multimodal experience.

These flow states emerge as we develop "ways to order consciousness so as to be in control of feelings and thoughts."[11] And flow is necessary to accomplish many different kinds of daily activities. Just imagine throwing a ball to a dog. You do it pretty effortlessly. Now try to imagine calculating the distance, force, and trajectory mathematically, accounting for both the weight of the ball and your own arm. All of that complex calculation is already in the throwing action. You figured it out, you just didn't do it *consciously*. We need to be in a flow state to successfully complete many kinds of activities. Flow creates control from *non-aware* perception, cognition, and behavior. Counterintuitively, we can do certain things better when we aren't fully aware that we are doing them. This is the opposite of what most would consider engagement in interaction design, which is a high level of awareness.

Enabling focus in multimodal experiences is creating the right combination at the right time: filtering distraction, prioritizing and organizing aware engagement, allowing for flow—non-aware engagement, and even allowing for disengagement. Different kinds of multimodal experiences have different impacts to focus or require certain levels of focus to be effective. For example, reading can be difficult in noisy environments, especially if there is a great deal of spoken language in the background. When both our eyes and ears are trying to use the language-processing part of our brain, it can cause crossed signals. On the

---

10 Dana Chisnell, "Beyond Task Completion: Flow in Design," *UX Magazine*, October 7, 2011, *https://uxmag.com/articles/beyond-task-completion-flow-in-design*.

11 Mihaly Csikszentmihalyi. *Flow: The Psychology of Optimal Experience* (New York: Harper Perennial Modern Classics, 1990), 24.

other hand, some people tap their feet to music, accentuating *rhythm—* which is a special pattern recognition of its own. They might not even realize they are doing it, but it enhances the experience for them. Some modalities complement each other. Some conflict. It depends on a number of factors, like the person, the context, and the modalities.

Multimodality Makes a Wider Range of Human and Product Behaviors Possible

We have various systemic and cross-modal abilities to process the sensory information we gather. For example, our ability to detect rhythm spans audio and haptic patterns. Some of our sensory behaviors are *reflexive* or tied to involuntary or instinctive behaviors. A loud sound or bright light can trigger a startle response, where we might literally jump to attention to respond to what is happening. Mercedes-Benz takes advantage of this in one of its new safety features, called PRE-SAFE Sound. According to *Wired*:

> When a collision is detected, the car emits a static sound at about 85 decibels. This is loud enough to trigger the acoustic reflex that contracts the stapedius muscle in the middle ear to block out the sound, protecting the sensitive eardrums and other bits of the inner ear. This sound is not loud enough to cause hearing loss, but it protects the ear from the airbag deployment, which can emit a pressure wave in the 150–170 decibel range, which *can* damage hearing.[12]

People are able to combine their sensory abilities, analytical and decision-making processes, and physical skills in limitless ways. Product teams have only just begun to scratch the surface of how to combine modes in our technologies. The types of multimodal abilities and interfaces is as limitless as the kinds of experiences we can dream up.

---

12 Jordan Golson, "Mercedes Is Using Loud Static to Protect Fancy Ears in Crashes," *Wired*, July 13, 2015, *https://www.wired.com/2015/07/mercedes-using-loud-static-protect-fancy-ears-crashes/*.

How Multimodality Affects Design

CREATING USABILITY

All interactions rely on some aspect of human multimodality, though sometimes in unexpected, and even counterintuitive ways. We get used to the mostly silent, mostly rectangular presence of our phone in our pocket, except perhaps when we sit down on it funny (see Figure 1-15). We don't really notice the weight or size of it at all. Sometimes, if we are looking for our phone, we have to tap or rummage through all our pockets to find it, even though we *could* technically feel it in our pocket with the nerve endings in our skin. In a short amount of time, we forget the feeling of the seat we are sitting on and focus on the meal in front of us. Our eyes adjust to darkness, our sense of taste to a soup that's just a little too salty, or our skin to the temperature of a cold swimming pool. Over longer periods of time and repetition, we can fall asleep easily in a noisy city apartment, or drive less stressfully on a winding road in the dark. This phenomenon, known as *neural adaptation*, allows us to filter out repeated sensory stimulus. This frees our focus for new information that we can quickly compare to our existing expectations of an experience.

FIGURE 1-15.
Nothing gets between me and my notifications...or does it? Do you feel your phone in your back pocket every second of the day that it's there? Or just sometimes, like when it vibrates?

Neural adaptation is precisely why interactions like notifications and alerts work. Once we are accustomed to a certain noise level or the visual state of our laptop screen, we set a baseline sensory expectation called a *threshold*, and concentrate our attention within it. A sudden vibration or sound deviates from that baseline, and we automatically refocus our attention. We notice that sound and figure out how to respond. Our static screen has a flash of a different color and animation on it; we read the alert.

While we might think of engagement as one of the most important parts of user experience, it is partly our sensory ability to *disengage* that makes notifications effective. What allows us to refocus our attention is the *contrast* in sensory expectations to the new sensory stimulus. This can be triggered by activating an unused sensory channel, like a sound when it's quiet. It can be within the same sense that we are focused on, but by changing it: an animation or a shot of a vivid color when the visual field is static or monochrome. It can be by a different sensory channel, like a tap on the shoulder when we are concentrating on a book. What can be most effective is to use some combination of all of these.

The reverse can also work. Reducing or eliminating an expected stimulus can also redirect our attention. It can be unnerving when all conversation stops suddenly as we enter a room. We definitely notice. Eliminating the responsiveness of one button can redirect a person to seek one that does work. A dimming screen lets us know that our laptop is about to go to sleep. People automatically seek out and notice these changes, called *threshold events*. They anchor our experiences and form the boundaries and transitions between them (see Figure 1-16).

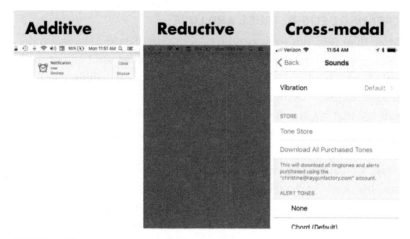

Additive	Reductive	Cross-modal

FIGURE 1-16.
The iPhone and MacBook use several different ways to interrupt our threshold, or baseline sensory experiences, to deliver notifications

Paradoxically, neural adaptation can eventually cause interactions to fail. Over time, we get used to certain types of stimuli, and start to tune them out—especially when they are overused or aren't immediately relevant. Since 1993, browser-based advertisements were usually in a banner near the top of a screen or down the righthand column. As a result, people developed banner-blindness; they stopped seeing banner ads on pages all together. They visually recognized the shape and position of the banners and filtered them out without reading them.[13] Because of this, internet advertising formats are an endless arms race between our brain's ability to filter out noise, and advertisers' efforts to regain our attention.

Neural adaptation is one of the many attributes of multimodality that can play a powerful role in creating effective user experiences. Most significantly, multimodality shapes how we learn from new experiences, how we focus and engage within experiences, and how that focus and engagement adapt over repeated experiences. It is a crucial component of multitasking, "expert" behaviors, and calm technology. It also underpins most design strategies for accessibility.

---

13 Jan Panero Benway. "Banner blindness: The irony of attention grabbing on the World Wide Web," Proceedings of the Human Factors and Ergonomics Society 42nd Annual Meeting (October 1998): 463-467.

CREATING DELIGHT, TRUST, AND LOVE

More than this, the senses and modalities are inextricably tied to perceiving quality and experiencing delight. When we shut a door made out of solid hardwood, there is something really satisfying about the weight, the slow swing, and the precise click of the bolt catching. We can tell that it's sturdier than a hollow particle board door by how it moves and the sound it makes (see Figure 1-17). Much of the delight of experiences is sensorial, whether an intoxicating perfume, a soulful song, a breathtaking view, or the lulling sway of a sailboat on a calm sea. It's poetic to describe delightful experiences across senses: a velvety bite of cake, a deliciously satisfied grin, a gentle caress as soft as a daydreamer's sigh. To take a less lyrical tack, there is a scientific basis to this. Delightful experiences are very often multisensory and multimodal, whether directly within the experience or by association with memories. We enjoy foods that have a pleasant texture in our mouth, scents that remind us of a spring hike through the woods, or a warm, fuzzy, squirmy, and ridiculously adorable puppy. We are more likely to feel an emotional response or connection to a multisensory experience. We also remember them for longer, recall them more clearly and easily, and are more likely to both desire and repeat the experience later.

FIGURE 1-17.
A hardwood door feels solid and satisfying

The senses are also how we create bonds of trust and intimacy with other people, with brands, and with the products we use. There are millions of search results that offer advice about how to pass the touch barrier on a date, underscoring how important it is to building human relationships (see Figure 1-18).

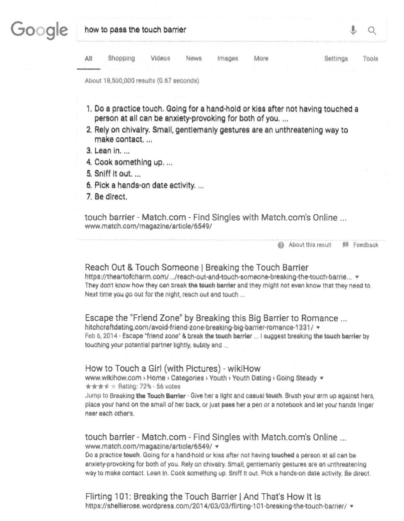

FIGURE 1-18.

Establishing physical contact has a dramatic impact to the intimacy within a relationship, and it might just get you to date #2

Both physical proximity and contact are a sign of trust; more frequent proximity and contact increase that trust. Results of a study on this topic revealed how even just a little bit went a long way in creating emotional bonds. Waitresses were instructed to lightly touch their patrons. "Surprisingly, the researchers found that the tipping rate of both male and female customers was significantly higher in both of the touching conditions than in the baseline no-touch condition (a phenomenon that has been labeled the "Midas touch" effect)."[14]

This crosses over into products as well. People are more likely to purchase items in a store if they can touch them and to feel a stronger affinity for brands with which they have had a physical interaction. For many, seeing and touching something "makes it real." We may have rational ideas and powerful emotions, but we validate them with physical evidence. It's only through our senses that people, places, and things become a part of our world and our lives. Touch, especially, is a two-way street. When we touch, we feel our own fingers as much as we feel the object we are touching. We can feel how cold our own hands are in the warm grasp of our friend. Touch is vital—not only because it affirms the emotional connection to others, but also of others to us. In his famous experiments with baby rhesus monkeys, Harry Harlow demonstrated that baby monkeys preferred a cloth-covered surrogate mother *without* food to a wire and wood surrogate *with* food (see Figure 1-19). Without a comfortingly touchable surrogate, the baby monkeys suffered adverse health conditions. It became crystal clear that touch is vital to our well-being and, in various stages of our life, our very survival.[15]

---

14 Alberto Gallace and Charles Spence, "In touch with the future: The sense of touch from cognitive neuroscience to virtual reality," (Oxford: Oxford University Press, 2014), 165–166.

15 Harry F. Harlow, "The Nature of Love," *American Psychologist* (1958): 673–685.

FIGURE 1-19.
Baby monkeys preferred soft, cloth covered surrogate mothers to those with only wire and wood, even when the soft mothers offered no food

On the flip side, people feel a strange sense of discomfort and exposure when they cannot physically affirm presence. A study conducted in 2014 in the UK explored the deep emotional attachment and bond between people and their mobile devices. Participants showed extreme levels of distress and anxiety when a phone was nonfunctional, damaged, or lost. They felt *protective* over their devices. "Phones were considered an extension of self," with an elevated desire to ensure the presence of the phone by touch or visual "checking." The researchers found that the physical proximity and constant physical and visual contact with the phone increased both the emotional bond that their owners felt for it and their own sense of security and control for themselves.[16] Though participants rationally valued the technology (the

---

16 Gisli Thorsteinsson and Tom Page, "User attachment to smartphones and design guidelines," *International Journal of Mobile Learning and Organization* 8 (2014): 201–205.

communication, information, and other conveniences that their smartphone provided), it was the physical affirmation of the device that made them feel secure—that the device was there and ready when needed.

According to Ralph Schiller, the CEO of ShotSpotters, the company's technology had a strong effect on trust and the sense of personal security within the community:

> Instead of a 10 or 20 percent response [based on citizen reporting], there is a 100 percent response to gunshots. The community feels that change. People begin to volunteer information; they become a part of their own safety. Their awareness changes the dynamics completely. They expect a response, and in turn it makes their police force more accountable to them. With both the community and the police force working together, it deters further gun violence, because bad actors expect a response. It denormalizes the violence. It sends the message that this isn't supposed to happen here. This isn't supposed to happen anywhere.

Press about the efforts also notes that greater trust between the communities and police "is leading to officers getting more on-the-ground information that supports the accumulation of the forensic data needed for prosecutions."[17]

The ability of devices to not only earn trust for themselves but enable other people to increase their trust of one another despite violent circumstances is a powerful testament to the kinds of outcomes that are possible.

Multimodal Design Is Cross-Disciplinary

While multimodal design seems to be unfolding in the new kinds of interfaces possible with technologies like natural language or emerging sensor-based interactions, it has always been a part of all design and tool use. The first cave painting required our creative ancestors to see the color applied to the cave wall, and to guide its application by touch. Product design accounts for both the visual and tactile experience of

---

17 Bill Corcoran, "Sensors help police curb gang violence in Cape Town," *Irish Times*, November 10, 2016, *https://www.irishtimes.com/business/sensors-help-police-curb-gang-violence-in-cape-town-1.2854954*.

objects. In fashion design, the *hand* of the fabric is the way that a fabric feels overall—texture, weight, the way it drapes and folds, its rigidity—how stiff a tightly woven wool coat can feel compared to the airiness of silk gauze (see Figure 1-20). Designers have always had to intuit these underlying principles of multimodality in the objects that they create. With the advances in both cognitive neuroscience and behavioral psychology, we can see more clearly why it works.

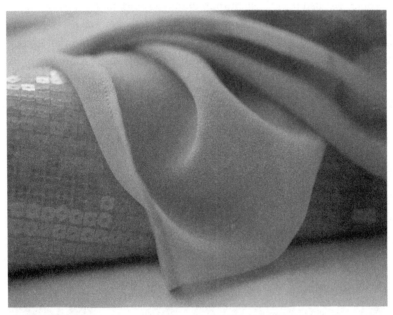

FIGURE 1-20.
The "hand" of a fabric is how it feels, and because our fingers and skin are so sensitive, clothing designers know that subtle details will not go unnoticed

As interaction blurs into existing design disciplines and spawns new hybrids—fashion technology, wearables, driverless cars, the connected home, and smart cities—blending multimodal experiences across interaction and existing physical design disciplines becomes increasingly important. We already have tactile relationships with the designed objects in our lives. Physical interactions that already exist can be incorporated into new delightful experiences. In the classic self-winding Rolex Oyster Perpetual watch, people shake their wrist to give the watch a few extra winds throughout the day to keep it running. In the Pebble watch, this gesture activated the backlight feature, bringing new meaning to an old habit.

Multimodal interactions can also improve the kinds of experiences that are already being delivered. We have automatic cognitive processes in our minds to read facial expressions and body language, and we notice how people stand, how they move when they speak. We read emotional cues in nonverbal communication. Being able to read each other's emotional cues is an important survival skill for the social creatures that we are, so we are constantly seeking them out when we look at other people. We also read those human emotions into inanimate objects, in a phenomenon called anthropomorphism. In automotive design, the overall look of the car is called its *stance*: how people can infer aggressive, playful, or relaxed faces and body positions in the geometry of its shapes (see Figure 1-21). People find emotional cues in the "posture" of their car.

FIGURE 1-21.
A car's stance adds personality and fosters attachment

It is also why the brightening and dimming of the sleep light on a MacBook could be so evocative. It matched the rise and fall rhythm of a sleeper's breath. It makes the state of sleep mode immediately recognizable. The computer isn't turned off at all, and will "wake up" when opened. It's why the shaking motion of a rejected password is endearing even though something went wrong. It looks a bit like a baby refusing a bite of food it doesn't like. These product behaviors appeal to our rational understanding of what is happening, but tap into subtle body language cues that we already know. In cognitive neuroscience, mirror neurons are understood to fire both when we act or feel an emotion, and when we observe someone else performing the same act or feeling the same emotion. We may even have tense the same muscles. It's possible that these emotive behaviors in products cause the same mirroring, eliciting empathy for our products. You get an unconscious sense that a computer needs sleep, recharge, and to let its processors cool down. This is actually good for the device, and more than just rationally understanding it, you feel it. You get a sense that bad passwords taste yucky for your computer, so you try to enter your password more carefully the next time. You feel responsibility for the well-being of the device, and treat it more carefully. And it is true—our devices need us to care for them, as much as we need them to function for us. Displaying it as if it were an emotional need—not just a pragmatic set of instructions in the user manual—changes the feeling and urgency dramatically.

These interactions don't just show love for people, they ask for it in very charming ways. Along with everything else, our senses allow us to express and feel love. And people do love giving love as much as they love receiving it. We're funny that way.

Summary

The senses are the (only) ways that we have of experiencing the world. Understanding how they work is key to designing new interfaces. They can also be extended by technology, with sensors that can go places, stay alert, and perceive things that we can't. These design methodologies expand upon existing practices and introduce some new ones. Both the human capacity and device capability for multimodal combinations and activities is near limitless.

[2]

The Structure of Multimodal Experiences

"Our personal worlds are constructions built by our brains using the raw materials of the senses—raw materials that are greatly modified during the construction process."

—FAITH HICKMAN BRYNIE IN *BRAIN SENSE* (2009)

WHILE THE TITLE USER experience designer implies that designers create experiences for people, it might be more accurate to say that people construct experiences for themselves. As the saying goes, "Beauty is in the eye of the beholder." And not just beauty, but functionality, clarity, and reliability. If you want to be very literal, they aren't just in our eye. They are also in our skin, distributed across the surface of our bones, within our spines, and definitely a bunch of it is up in our heads.

Designers, magicians, and filmmakers tap into many aspects of this construction process to great effect. Our eyes can differentiate hundreds of frames per second, but we can extrapolate continuous movements at much lower speeds, which allows us to enjoy stop-motion animation and animated gifs. Many graphical user interfaces, or GUIs, use the metaphor of the desktop as a way to organize information (see Figure 2-1). This relies on a process known as *assimilation*, our ability to reuse mental models across new types of information. We have already learned how a physical desk works; this existing mental model helps us to understand how to use a computer's operating system more easily. Another perceptual phenomenon, known as *amodal completion*, allows us to see objects as a whole, even if sections aren't directly visible. This is used to create visual effects in screen-based navigations such as sliding panes and parallax. It's also how the sawing-a-person-in-half trick works.

FIGURE 2-1.
The Mac operating systems use visual metaphors

When we experience the physical world, we mostly need to figure out what is going on and what to do next. We are highly flexible and adaptive creatures, so it comes as no surprise that how we figure stuff out is also. We pull together our many different perceptual, cognitive, and physical abilities to come up with the appropriate response from one moment to the next. Our minds and bodies develop some shortcuts along the way to make it easier. Our product experiences are no different, and we figure out how to use devices and develop usage patterns and shortcuts in the same way.

The Human Slice of Reality: Umwelt and Sensibility

The way we experience the world is largely based on anticipating what we need, whether that anticipation is hardcoded into our body's sensory mechanisms or softcoded by our own expectations built up by learning and doing. We all experience the world in different ways, and this diversity is even greater across species. Several types of snakes can sense heat in pits around their lips, which they use to zero in on prey while night hunting. Dolphins have twice as much hearing processing-power as humans and use it to locate objects underwater—something that most land animals can't do there. A dog's sense of smell is 100,000 times better than our own, and they use it to read emotions, which we can't really do anymore. Like many devices, eels detect a range of the electromagnetic spectrum that most animals can't. They use this ability to detect the proximity of other creatures. Each of these sensory abilities allow those that have them to access to a unique slice of physical information that shapes the way they interact with their environments.

The idea of a biological foundation for how we perceive the world as individuals and species is called *umwelt*, in theories articulated by Jakob von Uexküll and expanded by Thomas A. Sebeok and others. The word umwelt literally means "environment," and Uexküll's basic idea is that a being lives in a sensory world that reflects the things that can help it live and flourish.

Described by the psychologist James J. Gibson as *affordances*, the ability to identify usefulness in our environments was applied to design by Donald Norman, usability expert and author of *The Design of Everyday Things* (Basic Books). We perceive the different possibilities of interaction with objects and environments. But perceiving those interactions is also deeply tied to how we understand them. Most people rely on their sense of vision to navigate their surroundings. We can't use hearing for navigation the way a dolphin does, or use smell to recognize each other in social interactions the way a dog does. Our umwelts define the range of interactions that are *sensible* by us, and in which senses we use for what purpose. These is true not just for humans, but for all living things (see Figure 2-2).

Umwelt
How it affects sensing distance

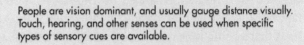

People are vision dominant, and usually gauge distance visually. Touch, hearing, and other senses can be used when specific types of sensory cues are available.

Light and color degrade rapidly underwater, making vision less useful at greater depths. Dolphins use echolocation—their hearing instead of vision, to construct almost holographic information about the space and objects around them.

Dog nostrils are specially shaped to give them a constant sense of smell, uninterrupted by exhalation. This allows them to detect variations in the strength of a smell relative to its source.

Electric eels send out a low voltage electromagetic signal to help them navigate underwater and to locate prey.

The iPhone antennae gather and transmit electromagnetic signals to communicate over several wireless protocols, including Bluetooth, WiFi, GPS, UMTS, GSM, and NFC. While GPS seems like the natural protocol for measuring distance, the others can also be used in tandem with location networks like iBeacon.

FIGURE 2-2.

A slice of the umwelts of a human, dolphin, dog, eel, and iPhone; all have particular senses that inform their "worldview"

Assembling Multimodal Experiences: Schemas and Models

The *mental model*, also introduced to design by Donald Norman, should be familiar to product designers. It is the internal model that people build of an object to understand what it is and how it works. Many human capabilities are developed through patterns that emerge over repeated experiences. In psychology, the concept of *schemas* is used to describe patterns in thought or behavior. *Models* are used to describe internal representations of external objects and events, built through repeated experiences. There is some overlap between these two concepts and how they are applied. There are many types of schemas and models, and they are used across all aspects of human behavior. We have a *body schema*, a map of ourselves in space that allows us to walk around without bumping into things and is integral to hand–eye coordination. Modalities and multimodalities are considered types of schemas, which are patterns in how we use our perceptual, cognitive, and physical abilities together. So while we couldn't use a keyboard without a mental model of the layout and behavior of the alphanumeric keys, we couldn't type without our body schema either. We would not be able to use a word processing application if we were not able to integrate language, typing, and reading into a single activity. That is multimodality.

While we use schemas to organize and interpret our existing knowledge and behaviors, we create them to be able to handle new information and experiences effectively. They give rise to our expectations and skills, and they shape our ability to focus within an experience. Schemas are understood to be living structures—they evolve and expand with us over time. And like all working models, some become more permanent, validated over repeated experiences. Others continue to evolve, for experiences that are less common, new, or complex. Schemas and models emerge to make human experience manageable (see Figure 2-3). Design patterns mirror this aspect of human behavior, emerging to make interfaces manageable. Our senses at their best work invisibly, as we synthesize and systematize sensory data, and create automation in the form of skills and habits that we can perform without thinking about them. Good design, like our own senses, does the same.

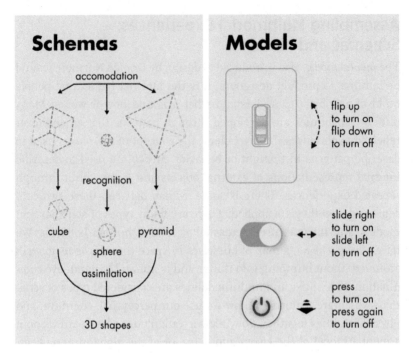

FIGURE 2-3.
Schemas affect how we perceive, recognize, and remember related things; design patterns follow mental models to make interaction consistent and manageable. If all power switches worked completely differently from each other, we would have to relearn them every time we used one.

The Building Blocks of Multimodal Experience

Sensing, understanding, deciding, and acting can be thought of as the building blocks to all our multimodal abilities. They are organized with schemas into cohesive bodies of knowledge and behaviors. In a very simplified example, combine language comprehension with vision, and you have the ability to read. Combine language with hearing, and you have listening. Combine language together again with hand movements, and you have writing or typing. Combine language with vocal cord and mouth movements, and you have speech. It also works for accessibility. Combining touch again with language in a different way allows for Braille reading and typing. Combine vision again with language, and it allows for sign language. Over time and practice, we develop patterns in how we use these different building blocks together and can use them more and more effortlessly (see Figure 2-4). These patterns are called modalities, and when we use multiple sets of senses together, they are called *multimodalities*.

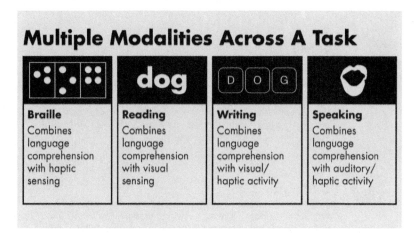

FIGURE 2-4.
Human communication spans multiple multimodalities: there are many different ways to communicate the same idea

Each of the building blocks of our abilities contributes in some way to how we develop our multimodalities, and they all strongly influence the design of products. Our senses delimit the kinds of physical information we can experience (see Figure 2-5). This is where *sensibility* guidelines like legibility and audibility come into play. Our eyes can only distinguish shapes up to a certain size and distance. Our ears can only hear within a certain range of volumes and pitches. Our cognitive abilities are gaining more attention as part of product design. *Cognitive walkthroughs* are a research practice that examine the roles of memory, language comprehension, and the ability and methods people use to assess different factors in decision making. They are gaining widespread usage in product design. Decision making is a special area of interest. There are many different models of decision making, because there are many different kinds of decisions we make—from accepting a friend request to how to get around a puddle. Certainly, our physical abilities have always informed design. All the important controls on a car dashboard must be within arm's reach of the driver and usable with only one hand. Computer desks are now often adjustable in height to allow our elbows and wrists to be at comfortable angles to prevent repetitive stress injury.

Building Blocks of Experience

Sense
We gather information via light, chemicals, and mechanical energy that has significance to our experiences. We can't do much with raw sensory stimuli, and have evolved to interpret them as colors, movements, sounds, smells, as well our own physical state. Together our eyes, ears, nose, and other sensory organs gather more information that we really need, and we developed sensory filters and focus to prioritze it.

Understand
Once we have acquired information, we must determine its significance, apply it to our behavior, and align it with what we already know and remember. Modalities and other patterns in our thoughts and behaviors work as templates for filtering, organizing, and using information, often based on specific activities.

Decide
Using information gathered from our current state and previous experiences, we use information to motivate ourselves, control our behaviors, and to identify choices and select among them. There are many kinds of decision making, ranging from those that happen instantly without our awareness, and those that take a great deal of time and consideration. Our decisions are shaped through the integration of goals, choices, expected outcomes, and rewards.

Act
Based on the information we gather, we create intentions, which are fulfilled through physical movement or speech. When activities are repeated, we develop implicit memory for them, and they become skills. Our physical abilities are often measured by ease and proficency during performance, level of effort required, specialized expertise, as well as whether we can repeat them as needed.

FIGURE 2-5.

Sense, understand, decide, and act can be considered the building blocks of experience

Parity: From Senses to Sensors

While device modes and human modalities are similar in some ways, they are very different in others (see Figure 2-6). This comparison, called *parity*, examines the overlap between abilities. In some cases, overlap is necessary, like being able to see the color range of a screen. In other cases, the difference extends our own abilities, like how expanded spectrum telescopes can help us understand the different kinds of energies emitted by the sun and stars that we can't see with our eyes alone. In many cases, human ability exceeds technological capability—human fine movement being one of them. So for now, we still have to put away our own groceries.

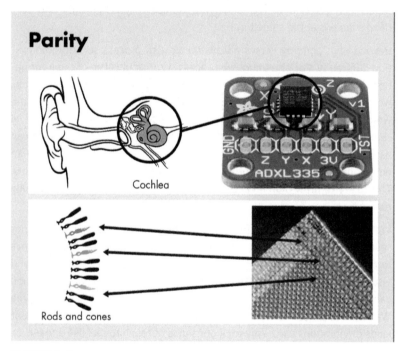

FIGURE 2-6.

The human cochlea and an accelerometer, a human eye and camera's photo-optic array: each has advantages, disadvantages, and interesting properties

It's remarkable that the cochlea in the inner ear works similarly to an accelerometer in detecting orientation and balance: a liquid that remains level with the ground can move across the x, y, and z axes. Unlike us, however, spinning an accelerometer fast won't make it dizzy. Vision, however, is different. We can easily detect a much wider color range, or gamut, than the typical camera. Seeing a beautiful landscape with our own eyes is much more vivid and colorful than a camera could capture or a screen could display, not to mention the wind in our hair and the smell of freshly fallen snow. With that said, we definitely cannot see 100,000 frames per second, like high-speed cameras. Certain cameras can detect ultraviolet and infrared light—outside our own visible spectrum. However, within our spectrum we have much better dynamic range; we can see very bright light and very deep shadows at the same time.

Beyond physiognomy versus hardware, we also process sensory information differently. For one thing, we process surprisingly little of the information that our senses detect. While we can see a whole page of text at once, we can really only read one word at a time. We remember very few of the words we read a few days later, though we can extrapolate higher level summaries and meaning very easily. In comparison, a computer's RAM can easily hold all the words of one page at once and in fact all the pages of an entire book. Computer storage memory can hold an exact copy indefinitely. The ability to draw high level conclusions, however, has not yet been fully realized.

We have many automatic processes for sensory *analysis*, and we cannot seem to turn those off either. Each of the modalities provides different ways to extract knowledge from sensory data. For example, conversations and visual imagery can carry a lot of information in a way that a haptic vibration cannot. The Taptic Engine, a haptic system in Apple's iPhones and Apple Watches, takes advantage of this imprecision (see Figure 2-7). Different kinds of vibrations can easily trick our sense of touch to feel like a real click of a physical button that moves, as in the iPhone, or to feel like a tap on the wrist, as with the Apple Watch.

FIGURE 2-7.
Earlier iPhones, with their Taptic Engine home button, took advantage of our haptic imprecision to create the illusion of mechanical and human contact

We aren't very good at distinguishing different kinds of movement in touch—we are much better at detecting variations in surface texture. These variations in our sensory abilities define whether information can be presented in one sensory channel or another. They also determine what kinds of sleight-of-hand design tricks that a designer can get away with.

Summary

Our minds and senses continually work together so that we are able to coherently experience the world. Psychology studies the ways we perceive what is happening, understand how it relates to us, decide which of the many options afforded by our context are right for us, and how we will proceed. All this is important information for designers. Sensing, understanding, deciding, and acting can be considered the building blocks of multimodal experiences. The chapters that follow will go deeper into them and explore how to use them to work together.

[3]

Sensing

HUMAN BEINGS ARE MARVELOUS perceptual, cognitive, and biomechanical creatures. We filter and process millions of pieces of sensory information every moment. We weave that information into a constantly updating view of ourselves, the people around us, and everything else in the world. What we think of as the five senses—vision, hearing, touch, taste, and smell—are not what we think. They are actually multiple forms of perception working together. Riding our little round spaceship through the universe, we are bombarded with energy and atoms across four dimensions. And yet, human experience is not as elemental. We feel warmth and see color. We taste pizza and smell jasmine. The bridge between the realm of science and what we actually experience is our senses.

The Three Main Categories of Stimuli

Our bodies evolved to perceive things that had some significance, and therefore needed to be accounted for and possibly acted upon. The things that trigger the sensations we experience are varied, but fall into three basic types (see Figure 3-1).

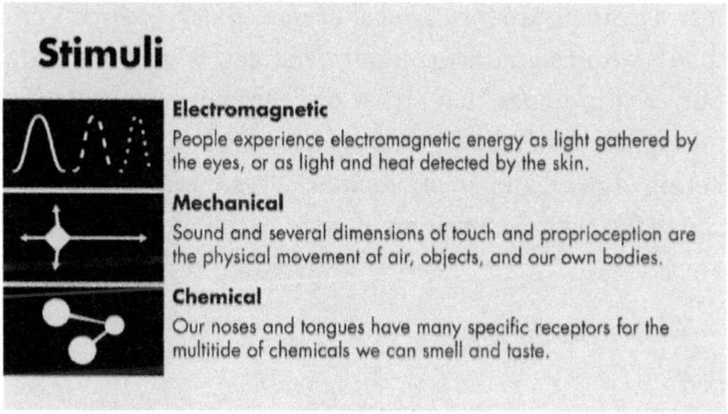

Stimuli

Electromagnetic
People experience electromagnetic energy as light gathered by the eyes, or as light and heat detected by the skin.

Mechanical
Sound and several dimensions of touch and proprioception are the physical movement of air, objects, and our own bodies.

Chemical
Our noses and tongues have many specific receptors for the multitide of chemicals we can smell and taste.

FIGURE 3-1.
There are three basic categories of stimuli that our senses perceive

ELECTROMAGNETIC

Vision is the ability to detect frequencies of electromagnetic waves and interpret them as light and color. The strength of the wave, or *amplitude*, is perceived as lightness and darkness. The span of the electromagnetic spectrum that we see is called the visible spectrum. Ultraviolet and infrared fall just outside either end of what humans (and most other creatures) are able to see. Heat, experienced through touch, is also a form of electromagnetic energy.

The photon is the component of light as well as all other electromagnetic radiation. Its properties, such as the quality of behaving sometimes like a wave and sometimes like a particle, continue to amaze and perplex scientists. (A fun fact is that humans and other animals carry a photochemical response that is similar to how solar panels work. The difference: we use it to get a tan, by creating melatonin.)

CHEMICAL

We are able to detect the presence of many chemicals as they pass through the nose or over the tongue. This response is based on direct contact between molecules and receptors. We have plenty of delightful perfumes and delicious foods, but no significant interfaces based on chemical senses. Our skin can detect some chemicals to a degree, though not in a very broad or sophisticated way. This is mainly through hot, cold, or tingly responses to stimuli such as chili oil, menthol, eucalyptus, and so on. This is caused by temperature receptors, normally stimulated by hot and cold, being triggered by compounds in plants that probably developed them as protection.[1]

MECHANICAL

Physical touch and hearing are mechanical events. Touch is direct contact with our body, while sound is generally indirect. Waves of air are funneled by our ears to bones that strike the eardrum, causing tiny hairs inside to wiggle. Other bodily senses are mechanical, such as balance, the feeling of pain, and *proprioception*, a lesser-known but very important sense that tracks the position of body parts, movement, and level of effort.

---

1 David J. Linden, "How We Sense the Heat of Chili Peppers and the Cool of Menthol," *Scientific American*, February 4, 2015, *https://www.scientificamerican.com/article/how-we-sense-the-heat-of-chili-peppers-and-the-cool-of-menthol-excerpt/*.

No matter which type of stimulus triggered a sensation, our sense apparatus converts it to electrochemical signals, and those signals are processed by the brain, where the information, if noticed, is shaped by the mind into coherent experiences.

Defining the Senses: Dimension, Resolution, and Range

Touch is made up of several types of sensory receptors that detect information about warmth and coolness, texture, pressure, and more. It generally requires direct contact, or even movement against something, in order to work. Vision, on the other hand, detects only light, and at a basic level requires only that the eyelids remain open to receive it. Despite sensing just one thing, it can detect many aspects of it in fine detail, such as millions of colors, precise movements, and complex forms. While color and intensity fade away across distance, and outlines get smaller until they disappear, this might happen very slowly. We can see something across thousands, even millions, of miles. When there is little light pollution, a good portion of our entire galaxy is visible to the naked eye. We can see stars, nebulas, and other objects that are light years away. The sense of touch, on the other hand, drops instantly to nothing when we lose direct contact (see Figure 3-2).

FIGURE 3-2.
Our eyes can see flowers a few feet from us, or stars billions of light years away. To untrained eyes, the flowers and stars may appear very similar; it takes time for us to learn how distance and size affects the way things look.

These examples illustrate dimension, resolution, and range. *Dimension* describes the types of stimuli that a sense detects. The many dimensions of touch include warmth, texture, and pressure, whereas light is the single dimension of vision. *Resolution* is the level of detail and amount of information within the stimuli, which is low for most of our sense of touch (it varies across our bodies, with fingers being among the standout exceptions) but incredibly high for vision and hearing. We can process a large amount of visual and auditory information with very fine detail. On the other hand, it is difficult to tell the exact temperature through touch. *Range* is the variation in the stimuli that can be sensed. For example, we are able to see many colors and differentiate subtle grades of light and darkness. Though our precision in detecting temperature is low, we can experience a range from between freezing up to about 140° or 150° Fahrenheit, where we stop feeling heat and start feeling pain.

> **[TIP]**
>
> The word *focus* is used to describe how we delegate our attention to different aspects of our experience. When it is used to describe sensory abilities, it will be described as *sensory focus*. When it is used to describe modal or multimodal abilities, it will be described as *modal focus*.

Sensory Focus: Selecting, Filtering, and Prioritizing Information

Each of our sensory abilities can process different kinds and amounts of information. Together, our senses provide us with a superabundance of information. To use it, people need to figure out which bits of information are important or urgent, which are unreliable (like trying to figure out colors in low light conditions), and which are most relevant to our immediate decisions and actions. In design, this is incredibly important, because it determines what people notice and what people miss, what people can remember and what causes confusion. Within each sensory ability, we delegate attention, called *sensory focus*, figuring out which things to apply and to remember, and we ignore the rest. How we do this is very much dependent on the sense, the context, and our immediate objectives. We have many different ways to focus within vision: we can track a movement with our eyes, focus on specific objects at various visual depths, or examine a particular detail very finely, and we do so with a high level of awareness. Our sense of touch is less aware: we use it automatically for regular physical movement but tune out a great deal of haptic information unless we experience discomfort. We tune out the sensation of clothing on our skin, ambient temperature, and even the chair that we are sitting on, because it is not immediately pertinent. Within hearing, we can focus to identify connections and groupings across sounds like harmonies or rhythms, or to isolate one sound source in particular. Sensory information surrounds us constantly. While our senses receive all of it, we filter out most of it.

Test Drive Sensory Focus

Here's a little exercise: pick a new song that you have never heard, and listen to it.

Now, try to perform the following tasks:

1. Pick out the beat of the song.

2. Find the quietest and loudest notes of the song.

3. Count the length of the song in seconds. (Don't peek at the track length.)

You might have had to listen to the song three different times—once for each individual task. It's very difficult to do all three simultaneously. Even though it's the same sensory data and the same sense, you were seeking different types of information. The last exercise might have even forced you to block out the rhythm of the song, especially if the tempo did not fall on seconds. Sensory focus allows people to select both a sense and then to attenuate to various slices of sensory information within that sense. It can be difficult to split focus across different kinds of sensory information—even within the same sense—when higher levels of concentration or analysis are required.

Reflexes

We have many patterns of response that require no awareness and which happen immediately, known as reflexes. Many of these are innate, but they can also be learned and refined over time.

When hit on the knee, your leg responds with a kick before you've fully "sensed" the blow and certainly considered it. This is an example of an innate reflex, stimuli that send signals on a different path to speedier action than traveling through the higher functions like the brain for cognitive processing. In some cases, it may work its way to cognition through a secondary, slower path. That can sometimes leave us with the feeling, "How did I do that?" as if for a moment, we had been granted superpowers. This quicker path is known as a *reflex arc*—for instance, going directly to the spinal cord to send a reaction signal to motor neurons. Some reflex actions are also affected by cognition. A flash shined in your eyes will automatically trigger your pupils to constrict, but if shined in one eye and not the other, the level of constriction will depend on which eye, whether seeing light or dark, is topmost in consciousness.[2]

When creating sensory experiences, it's a good idea to pay attention and not accidentally trigger an unwanted reflex or automatic response. Fight or flight, also known as the startle response, can be brought on with a sense of danger, like from too many loud noises. Many of our reflexes can be traced back to the way our senses and nervous systems evolved. In an odd twist of evolution, our most automatic functions are sometimes our most primitive. In contrast, automation technology is usually a more advanced capability.

Our Senses and Their Unique Properties

Each sense is a combination of stimuli, plus physical and mental processing, that provides a specific stream of information about our experiences. It's increasingly common to examine the amount of information (resolution) and range of the senses for interaction design. These factors determine the types of design elements used in an interface mode, as well as the characteristics of these elements.

Vision

As bilateral creatures, we very often have mirrored pairs of anatomy. We have two eyes, two ears, and two nostrils, but hopefully not two left feet. The small distance between our eyes working in sync allows us to perceive spatial distance and to see in three dimensions. Two types of photoreceptive cells in the retina, cones and rods, detect photons and react by sending a signal along the optic nerve and then deeper into the brain for processing. There are usually three types of cones sensitive to lightwaves that roughly correspond to red, green, and blue. While our eyes are fixed inside our head, they can move inside their sockets, allowing us rapid tracking and precision movement. This is

---

2 Marnix Naber, Stefan Frässle, and Wolfgang Einhäuser, "Perceptual rivalry: Reflexes reveal the gradual nature of visual awareness." PLoS ONE (June 2011). *https://doi.org/10.1371/ journal.pone.0020910.*

important for reading, scanning, spotting and following objects, and having a consistent view of the world despite any other moves our bodies make. We have a blind spot, where the optic nerve enters the retina. Our vision curves at the edges much like a photograph taken with a fisheye lens, because our eyes are spherical. We also lose color perception away from the center of our vision. The tip of our nose is visible to us all of the time. Yet we don't often perceive these discrepancies in our visual field; we think we see seamless and distortion-free visual field with an even distribution of color (see Figure 3-3).

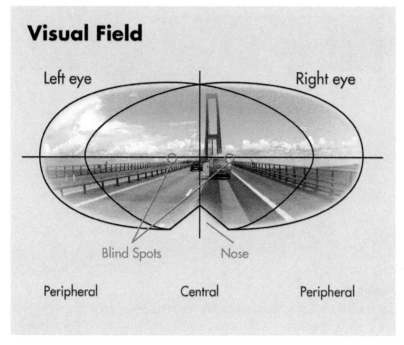

FIGURE 3-3.
The visual field that our eyes see is different than the resulting image our mind creates by smoothing over the blind spots and uneven distribution of color

Some important characteristics of vision include the *visual field*, which is what our eyes take in, usually measured by degrees. The field for healthy human eyes is typically 60° toward the nose, 107° outward, 70° up, and 80° down. You can measure your visual field by looking straight forward and stretching your arms out horizontally until your hands disappear. Do the same vertically and you have a personalized measurement. When it comes to film and TV screens, the *aspect ratio* describes the visual field created for viewing (see Figure 3-4). Some popular formats are 16:9 (HDTV), 4:3 (NTSC video and "four thirds" photography), 3:2 (35mm film), or 2.35:1 (Cinemascope). For obvious reasons, screen design is informed greatly by the visual field, and the overlap between the visual fields of each eye inform the way 3D and stereoscopic technologies work.

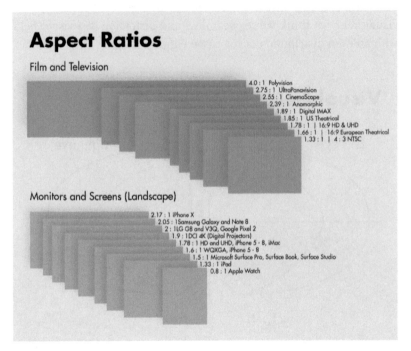

FIGURE 3-4.
Different theories about how to simulate the visual field, efficiences in film and video usage, as well as overall device experience have led to the proliferation of aspect ratios

Vision also helps us to know which way is up, and plays a big role in balance. It is the foundation of written and printed communication; the visual lexicon of letters and numbers enable imaginative and precise description of our most complex thoughts. Some nuanced abilities are made possible by visual processing: facial recognition, spatial and volumetric measurement, estimating the speed of a moving object, and calculating our own trajectory through space by using environmental anchors like the horizon or the sun.

As our dominant sense, at least 50% of sensory processing is used for vision, equal to all the other senses combined. Neurons devoted to visual processing take up a full 30% of the cortex.[3] Because we process so much, vision takes longer to perceive, even though light is the fastest moving thing in the universe. In return for that cognitive expense, we get an incredibly rich moving picture of the world around us. We can see brightness, colors, shapes, and movement—four parallel image processing systems that work in unison. The range of shades we see from light to dark can also allow us to perceive depth and form. Though the number of colors we can see varies between individuals, as well as over lifetimes, it is in the millions. We can tell what time it is by gauging the quality of sunlight, view the trees to stay on the path where we are walking, and keep watch over a fading campfire by pale moonlight.

There are many reasons that vision takes so much processing. A big one is that we're doing a lot more than just detecting shapes, light, color, and movement. We are analyzing, matching, sorting, recognizing, remembering, judging, reacting, and more. While it's true that we might tell a lot by the character of a voice, or quality of a particular smell, we simply see with greater nuance and breadth, both because of the body's equipment and through cultural training. Being set to process so much information so well, vision is very useful for absorbing abstract data, as we do with reading, data visualization, and iconography. We can also close our eyes, thus stopping most visual stimulus. None of our other senses has such an immediate on/off switch. Table 3-1 contains the human factors of vision.

---

3   Denise Grady, "The Vision Thing: Mainly in the Brain," *Discover*, June 1, 1993, *http:// discovermagazine.com/1993/jun/thevisionthingma227*.

TABLE 3-1. The human factors of vision

DIMENSIONS	Photons (light)

RANGE	*Vision requires a clear line of sight with no obstruction in the light paths.*
	
	Brightness
	    Measurements vary based on application: lumens, lux, foot candles
	    Presence or absence of photons emitted or reflected from objects. There are varying recommended ranges of ambient light for visibility during certain activities.
	
	Color (spectrum)
	    400–700 nanometers
	    +10 million colors (gamut)
	
	Visual field
	    Approximately 70° above, 80° below, and 170° outward
	
	Distance/visual acuity
	    We can see objects resting on the surface of our eyes and stars billions of miles away.
	    20/20 vision describes being able to see at 20 feet what most people can see at 20 feet.

RESOLUTION	*High degree of resolution across vision, with highest ability in the center of the visual field, decreasing outward.* Smallest object discernible is 0.4 nm (about a human hair).
FOCUS	Eye movement coordinates each eye together, as well as with our bodily movement. We calibrate vision with vestibular and proprioceptive inputs to form a kind of optical image stabilization system. Pupil dilation controls the amount of light entering our eyes. Because the area of our eyes that offer very high resolution is relatively small, *saccades*, or rapid movements of both eyes, allow us to gather more data and build a richer understanding than a fixed gaze. Focal accommodation allows our eyes to change shape to focus at different visual depths.

REFLEXES	We have a blind spot, where our optic nerve interrupts our retina. The brain fills in the blank with a guess at what should be there.
	We blink to keep our eyes moist and to clean and protect them.
	Pupil dilation is correlated to many different human behaviors, like concentration, sexual attraction and arousal, and surprise.
	Startle response, also known as fight or flight, may be triggered by sudden, loud, or unexpected sounds or movements. Correlated to other senses.
	Miscoordination between our sense of balance and vision can cause dizziness and nausea.
	Awkward position or rapid movement visual stimulus can cause eye strain, forcing the eye muscles to hold a difficult position for long periods or fatigue through constant movement.
ACCESSIBILITY	Vision loss is measured using visual acuity. Approximately 64% of Americans require some form of vision correction, while 3% of the population experiences vision loss. Vision deteriorates with aging.
ADDITIONAL PROPERTIES	Form is the visual ability to recognize shapes, outlines, and volumes.
	Movement is the visual ability to recognize changes in the position of objects. This is often measured in frames per second (fps) for video technologies or milliseconds for response times.
	Night vision is lower in humans than many other animals. It makes use of rods instead of cones concentrated at the edges of our retina, Thus, night vision is best just outside of the direct center of our field of vision.

VISUAL INTERFACES

As our dominant sense, most design tends to be based on vision. The bulk of media is made to be seen, whether with words, images, shapes, or all three. Screen-based interaction design reflects that reality. The field of graphic design is one of interaction design's most prominent influences. It addresses typography, colors, visual space, and images, bringing with it subdisciplines like iconography and data visualization. Motion-based media like film and animation bring the element of time into visual design. Interaction design extends these techniques in many ways. Much of interaction design could be described as the addition of haptic interfaces to visual media: the keyboard, mouse, and touchscreen greatly expanded the direct actionability of words, images, and graphics beyond just being able to turn a page.

Hearing

Hearing takes advantage of the fact that the air around us carries pressure in waves of vibrations. We perceive the variation of those vibrations in interesting ways. We perceive pitch and harmonics, and we can selectively focus listening, whether on a bird in a forest of activity, or one person speaking in a room filled with voices. (This last one is called the "cocktail party effect.") Because we have two ears separated by a distance, we also have *binaural* hearing, allowing us to position the source of sounds in 3D space. While air is by far the most commonly experienced vibration, we can also hear waves conducted through most any form of matter, as when swimming underwater, putting our ear to the ground, or using devices that use our bones to conduct sound waves.

Hearing is the next highest resolution sense after vision. Through language and music, it is tied to some of our most intellectual and creative pursuits. However, when you break it down, a violin concerto, a line of Shakespeare, or the burbling of a stream is really a bit of air getting smooshed in space between the source and our ears. Sound is perhaps most immediately tied to self-expression. Vocalization is one of our earliest communication capabilities. For obvious reasons, hearing is deeply tied to language ability, as well as a big part of what's known as *paralanguage*—nonverbal communication like sighs, facial expressions, gestures, the clearing of the throat, as well as the nuanced tones of words being spoken, known as *prosody*. Table 3-2 contains the human factors of hearing.

TABLE 3-2. The human factors of hearing

DIMENSIONS	Air compression waves (sound)
RANGE	Frequency/pitch 20–20,000 hertz (Hz) Cycles per second of air compression waves Amplitude/volume 0–130 decibels (dB) Degree of change in air pressure
RESOLUTION	*High degree of resolution in frequency and volume. We can easily distinguish minute differences in pitch and volume when we hear them in a series. It is much harder when a single sound is played alone.* We can also hear timbre, which encompasses additional qualities of sound like distance, reverberation, and vibrato. These terms are often used to describe human voices and musical instruments.
FOCUS	We can hear multiple sounds together, as in the different instruments in an orchestra. We can single out individual sounds from many different sounds, known as "selective auditory attention" or "cocktail party effect."
REFLEXES	At high volumes, the ear stops responding to sounds to prevent ear damage. Startle response, also known as fight or flight, may be triggered by sudden, loud, or unexpected sounds or movements. Correlated to other senses.
ACCESSIBILITY	Hearing loss is measured in dB and deteriorates with aging. Approximately 20% of all Americans have some form of hearing loss.

ADDITIONAL PROPERTIES	Binaural hearing allows us to perceive the position of objects in space relative to our own.
	Paralanguage is a broad term for nonverbal communication, and prosody is one type that describes the tone, stress, and other carriers of meaning.
	Lower-range sounds can also be felt as vibrations.

Auditory Interfaces

For designers, focus and cognition are key factors of designing for the experience of sound. Because carrying information in the form of speech is cognition-intensive, the pace at which it is delivered and the usefulness to the immediate setting are important. Google Maps, for instance, is careful to deliver turning directions just in time and to not overload the user with information that would be difficult to remember.

Early uses of sound were to carry simple messages over a distance. People figured out pretty fast that sound was a great way to capture other people's attention even when they were busy. Sirens on emergency responders' vehicles, loud alarms to scare intruders or mobilize building inhabitants in a fire, and church bells or calls to prayer basically function as a form of public broadcast. This is probably because hearing is our fastest sense. Milder, more personal uses of sound, such as telephone rings and mobile message alerts, are meant to alert but not alarm people. Many of these sounds are still throwback designs to the metal bells in church towers and telephones or steam horns on trains. Even beeping is a throwback to the simplest electronic speakers, with limited ability to reproduce more natural sounds. The way we are alerted by sound does not need to be so retro. Recent sound design has become more inventive, as with subways in Osaka that play a distinctive song at the arrival at each station. Passengers, who often fall asleep in their commute can easily recognize the unique melody for their home station and wake up when they hear it.

Beyond alerts, functional sound design often plays a supporting role, inviting or—even more commonly—confirming actions. On telephones, the dial tone indicated a functioning system and called for action. As digital interactivity replaces analog, confirmations are becoming more widespread, as with the customizable shutter click sounds for your camera. Because sound is used to supplement other senses—usually sight—it is particularly common in helping blind or visually impaired people, as with sound-augmented crossing signals, or the spoken names of train stops to help not only those commuters without sight, but those whose line of sight might be obscured.

Videogames make strong use of sound, both as an interactive element and a narrative one. An interesting subgenre of video game, "without video," meant to be played with eyes closed, was represented by the Papa Sangre franchise and its spin-offs, like The Nightjar, narrated by Benedict Cumberbatch (see Figure 3-5). It was based on sound, using binaural audio to deliver a sense of place, momentum, and action, while game play consisted of gestures detected by the phone's accelerometer, and controller buttons on the otherwise blank screen. These kinds of explorations carved out new, useful (and entertaining!) territory not only for gaming but for audio and haptic interactivity.

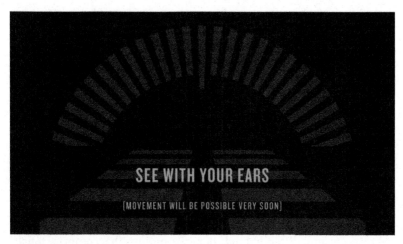

FIGURE 3-5.
The game The Nightjar puts players on a disabled spacecraft where key life support systems have failed. A loss of vision heightens the psychological horror of gameplay, which is primarily auditory and haptic.

The rise of voice-based interactions, like the Amazon Echo, Apple Siri, and Google Home and Google Assistant promise a more robust place for voice. Limitations still exist—particularly with hearing—because the technology cannot reproduce the human ability of cocktail party effect in noisy environments. Language adds to the already information-dense realm of sound by adding abstraction of thoughts, concepts, questions, descriptions, as well as *paralanguage*, to convey additional nuanced meaning. While speech is a motor capability—the ability to create vocal cord vibration and coordinate our mouths, tongues, and lips to create specific *phonemes*, it's common to think of voice technology as an auditory interface, because we take our speaking skills for granted.

The quick arrival and acceptance of tools like Amazon's Alexa and Apple's Siri show the huge progress that's been made in the last few years in the ability to process human language and convincingly respond. But just like R2D2 demonstrated by conveying meaning with wordless tone and rhythm, paralanguage and prosody can be a powerful tool for sound designers.

Touch (Somatosensory or Tactile Abilities)

The sense of touch, also known as our somatosensory abilities, includes the ability to feel movement, objects, temperature, and pain. We have nerve endings that are sensitive to all those things and that can sense edges, light, moisture, temperature, and even certain chemicals, like peppermint or chili oils. These nerve endings cover our skin and are also in our muscles, joints, organs, circulatory system, and even across the surface of our bones. These all generally require direct contact with an object or close proximity, where intermediaries like air, water, or nearby objects can relay the stimuli. Even if it can seem like we are detecting temperature over a distance, it's really because the temperature is coming to us. We also discern many haptic stimuli through movement and friction: we need to run our hands over something to feel its texture or have it moved across our skin, like a loofah.

There are several different kinds of nerve endings that comprise touch. Merkel discs detect fine shapes, details, and edges. Ruffini endings detect finger position and movement, Meissner's corpuscles detect light touch, and Pacinian corpuscles detect vibration and pressure. As science writer John M. Henshaw says in his book, *A Tour of the Senses*, "Touch sensitivity can be quantified in terms of how much distance between two stimulation points is necessary to recognize them as separate points."[4] In the places where that sensitivity is greatest, our fin-

4 John M. Henshaw, *A Tour of the Senses: How Your Brain Interprets the World* (Johns Hopkins, 2012), 160.

gertips, scientists have determined that we are able to feel a bump corresponding to the size of a very large molecule, depending on the type of surface where the bump occurs.[5]

Sensing the world through our skin and touch is constant, even if on a non-aware level. Our sense of "being in our skin" and "on solid ground" is rooted in our feelings of environmental stability. However subconscious, touch plays a big role in how we regulate our physical comfort within a given situation or environment. Deeply focusing on the sense of touch is not common, but once there, researchers have found that it is harder to shift away from a tactile modality than from an auditory or visual modality.[6] It is also strongly tied to guiding our physical and motor skills. Certain abilities, like grip, are dependent on it, as well as detecting slippage, when we are losing our grip. Much of that occurs below the level of awareness, especially if all is going well and working reliably. The sense of touch is one of our most adaptive: we can quickly tune out consistent sensations. But when something changes, we quickly snap out of autopilot. Table 3-3 contains the human factors of touch.

---

5   KTH The Royal Institute of Technology. "Feeling small: Fingers can detect nano-scale wrinkles even on a seemingly smooth surface." *ScienceDaily*. *http://www.sciencedaily.com/ releases/2013/09/130916110853.htm* (accessed February 3, 2018).

6   Alberto Gallace and Charles Spence, "In Touch with the Future: The Sense of Touch" from *Cognitive Neuroscience to Virtual Reality*, (Oxford, UK: Oxford University Press, 2014), 148.

TABLE 3-3. The human factors of touch

DIMENSIONS	Temperature
	    Measured in Fahrenheit, Celsius, or kelvin
	
	Pressure (force)
	    Measured in newtons (N)
	    Often described by characteristics like soft, firm, quick, sustained
	
	Vibration
	    Can be measured by frequency and decibels but is sensed in the same way as pressure
	
	Texture
	    No standard of measurement
	    Often described by characteristics like smooth, rough, regular, irregular
	
	Moisture
	    No standard of measurement
	    The presence of liquid
	
	Chemical
	    Certain chemicals, like menthol or chili oil, can be felt. They can also cause histamine response or allergies, like nickel or urushiol—the oil in poison ivy.
	
	Electrical
	    We can feel an electric shock on our skin.

RANGE	*Touch requires direct contact. Some forms of touch, like texture, also require movement.*
	
	Temperature
	    Skin can be damaged below 32°F and at temperatures of 111° F and above.
	
	Vibration
	    Varies by frequency and amplitude
	
	Texture
	    As small as three microns
	
	Chemical
	    Varies
	
	Electrical
	    No known ranges, but electrocution has occurred from currents as low as 42 volts.

RESOLUTION	*Resolution varies across the the body. Touch is highest resolution on our lips, tongue, fingers, face, and genitals.*
	
	Temperature
	    Often measured for comfort, generally between 64° and 70°F
	
	Vibration
	    Often measured by intensity, duration, or rhythm
	
	Texture
	    Wide range of qualities
	
	Chemical
	    Varies
	
	Electrical
	    Because it's generally an unpleasant sensation, we don't often try to discern detail from electrical currents, except perhaps to see if a 9V battery still works.

FOCUS	Because touch has multiple dimensions, people can focus on a single dimension, area of their body, or "seek" out a haptic sensation, like feeling out aches and pains after a workout.

REFLEXES	Haptic reflexes are very closely tied to our motor reflexes.
	Goosebumps or shivers to cold or strong emotions
	Sweating to heat
	Withdrawal reflex from pain sensations
ACCESSIBILITY	Tactile accessibility is closely tied to physical or motor accessibility.
ADDITIONAL PROPERTIES	Pain is related to touch, though not exactly the same thing. *Nociceptors* are the types of cells that sense much of the same things as the other touch receptors but are usually only triggered at extremes. Long-term stimulation makes them more sensitive, as opposed to most other nerve cells that lose sensitivity. The message is usually clear: something is wrong; fix it.
	Itching and tickling are specialized sensations related to pain that can produce the desire to scratch, rub the source, or to laugh and squirm away.

HAPTIC INTERFACES (TACTILE, PROPRIOCEPTIVE, AND VESTIBULAR)

The word haptic describes the combination of the tactile, proprioceptive, and vestibular systems together. (Proprioceptive and vestibular abilities are described later in this chapter.) Most interfaces—whether for computing or mechanical products—are haptic. It shouldn't be too surprising, as our hands have the most robust blend of sensory and motor capabilities. They are a part of some of most complex physical interactions with objects and environments. In many cases, our proprioceptive capabilities take dominance, with tactile and vestibular playing supporting roles in the experience. Used in tandem with vision, these capabilities are described as *hand-eye coordination,* which is far and away the most common type of direct physical interaction. Touchscreens, mice, and keyboards are haptic interfaces. So are wrenches, paint brushes, knives, and other mechanical technologies. The inventor of VR, Jaron Lanier, captures the breadth of what haptics encompasses:

Haptics includes touch and feel, and how the body senses its own shape and motion, and the resistance obstacles. It's surprisingly hard to define the term precisely because there are still mysteries about how the body senses itself and the world. Haptics is at the very least how you feel that a surface is hot, rough, pliant, sharp, or shaking—and how you sense stubbing a toe or lifting a weight. It's a kiss, a cat on a lap, smooth sheets, and corduroy desert roads. It is the pleasure of the sex that made us all and the pains of the diseases that end us. It is the business end of violence.[7]

Game designers have very often been the drivers of innovation in haptic interfaces for computing technologies. This is because game design often creates deeply immersive experiences that completely subsume physical reality, pulling user behaviors into a virtual world. That same desire for complete visceral engagement is driving similar work within virtual reality. Some early controllers were gun-shaped to simulate the experience of shooting. The Nintendo Wii and XBox Kinect technologies were a leap forward in haptic technologies. Using sensors, the Wii moved away from realistic controller objects to realistic control movements, allowing users to swing the controllers in the same way they would swing a tennis racket and a baseball bat or throw a bowling ball. The XBox Kinect explored gestural interfaces that use various cameras to track body position and movements. It ran into the issue that people have much finer proprioceptive and motor control in their fingers and faces than in their whole arm, and game players experienced some difficulty in executing and maintaining precision gestures. The sensor technologies of the XBox and Nintendo Wii are now applied across a wide range of automated and assistive consumer technologies.

Early uses of haptics, sometimes called *fly-by-wire*, included servomechanisms added to the steering wheels on ships and cars, the control yokes of planes (see Figure 3-6) and space exploration vehicles. Before power steering, the wheel of a ship had direct mechanical control of the rudder, which in turn had direct contact with the water. This created a feedback loop, allowing captains to feel the resistance from water currents and to adjust accordingly. This was similar to the yoke and wing flaps on planes, which had contact with air currents. Power

---

7   Jaron Lanier, *Dawn of the New Everything: Encounters with Reality and Virtual Reality,* (New York: Holt, 2018), 123.

steering augmented steering strength, but it took away that environment feedback and reduced steering accuracy. Simulating that direct increases sensitivity.

FIGURE 3-6.
Wind speed and drag are forces that affect the body of a plane and are not normally experienced through touch. Incorporating them into the steering yoke as haptic feedback can make it easier to pilot.

Smell (Olfactory Ability)

The ability to sense the chemical makeup of our immediate environment emerged long ago in the evolutionary chain. While it's hard to speak of firsts, even bacteria can detect nearby chemicals. Smell travels more deeply into our brain than the other senses, going directly to the olfactory bulb instead of being translated and relayed by the thalamus.[8] Science is still debating the exact number, but our noses have around

---

8   Tom Stafford, "Why can smells unlock forgotten memories?" BBC Future, March 2012. http://www.bbc.com/future/story/20120312-why-can-smells-unlock-memories.

350 types of smell sensors, and each of those can detect around 30 different odors.[9] Odorants must be present and attach to one of those sensors.

While it has been superseded by other senses, the deep tie to our past is part of what makes smell important. Smell is powerful not only for emotions, but is also closely associated with long-term memories, well-being, and sense of place. It takes a lot for sound and vision to nauseate us, and that is usually through symbolism or a mismatch between senses like vision and proprioception. It alone can do it immediately, through odors like rotten eggs, vomit, or excrement. Smell is deeply tied to hunger, sexual arousal, and comfortable or uncomfortable physical intimacy. Table 3-4 contains the human factors of smell.

TABLE 3-4. The human factors of smell

DIMENSIONS	Chemical
RANGE	Smell requires a chemical to be present in air that we can inhale through our nose.
	Threshold describes when a scent can be detected or recognized, which varies by chemical. Measured in concentration (parts per million or billion) and suspension medium (air, water, fat).
RESOLUTION	Though resolution varies by chemical, a wide variety of smells can be detected simultaneously, making smell a high-resolution sense.
	Odor is a large component of flavor, and both odors and flavors are often described by their source (orange, chocolate, cedar).
FOCUS	Little is understood of the role that smell plays in aware behaviors. It can play a large role in non-aware behaviors, like hunger, sexual arousal, and comfort.
REFLEXES	Revulsion response describes negative emotional and physical reactions like disgust, nausea, or a general sense of threat to well-being and health.

---

9   John M. Henshaw, *A Tour of the Senses: How Your Brain Interprets the World* (Baltimore: Johns Hopkins, 2012).

ACCESSIBILITY	No known accessibility issues, though loss of the sense of smell can diminish appetite, sexual drive, and pleasure, as well as indicate ailments.
ADDITIONAL PROPERTIES	Strong smells can be overwhelming. Smell is closely tied to memory.

OLFACTORY INTERFACES

The filmmaker John Waters experimented with adding scratch-and-sniff cards labeled "Odorama" as an added element to his film *Polyester*. Somehow that really didn't give olfactory interfaces much traction with the general public. Smell is sometimes used as a warning, and odorless gases like those in our stoves have an added chemical, mercaptan, to alert users of a leak.

While smell is not really used to create interfaces, it is increasingly popular as an aspect of service design and branding. Many companies like Krispy Kreme and Subway bake their goods on the premises during opening hours. The heat dissipates the smell better, tempting people to come inside and taste their goods. Retail and hospitality are increasingly using branded scents to differentiate themselves and to create positive associations for their customers. In one experiment, the sales of Hershey's products from vending machines tripled when a chocolate scent strip was attached to their exteriors.[10]

Taste (Gustatory Ability)

Taste was, until recently, thought of as the four elements of salty, sweet, sour, and bitter. Then recently a fifth, the savory taste of *umami* was added to the mix. A good reminder that individual senses rarely function alone, these five elements still leave us far from the luscious complexity of a ripe papaya, a fried chicken sandwich, or a bubbly and slightly charred pile of gruyere cheese melted over a cup of onion soup. That's because our receptors for taste, smell, touch (for texture), and probably several others such as the feeling of hunger work together to create the experience called *flavor*.

10 Karen Ravn, "Sniff . . . and spend," *Los Angeles Times*, August 20, 2007, *http://articles. latimes.com/2007/aug/20/health/he-smell20*.

The buds on our tongues, called papillae, respond to chemical stimuli. Contrary to popular belief, the specialized buds for each of these do not appear to be clustered on our tongues by type, but spread evenly. As the two senses that detect chemical stimuli, taste and smell work very closely together, with smell detecting airborne particles and concerned with solids. Our sense of taste is uniquely reserved for interaction with things we put in our mouths. These interactions are primarily focused on the pleasure and delight of eating. Table 3-5 contains the human factors of taste.

TABLE 3-5. The human factors of taste

DIMENSIONS	Chemical
RANGE	Taste requires direct contact with papillae, therefore the longest physical distance for taste is the distance we can stick out our tongues. (Be careful of frozen poles and triple dog dares.) • Sweet • Sour • Salty • Bitter • Umami
RESOLUTION	Taste is low resolution, until coupled with smell and other senses to create flavor.
FOCUS	We have the ability to isolate tastes and concentrate on them singly, as well as in combination. Taste is primarily associated with the activity of eating.
REFLEXES	*Revulsion response* describes negative emotional and physical reactions like disgust, nausea, or a general sense of threat to our well-being and health. People may spit out something that causes this response, strongly associated with things that may be harmful to ingest.
ACCESSIBILITY	No known accessibility issues, though loss of the sense of taste can diminish appetite and pleasure.
ADDITIONAL PROPERTIES	Strong tastes can be overwhelming.

GUSTATORY INTERFACES

Most of the experiences associated with taste are tied to eating or preparing food. These are intended to make the experience more delightful or, in the case of consumables like medicine or vitamins, less unpleasant. The authors are unaware of any kinds of interfaces that are designed around the sense of taste, though there is a tentative new product category of IoT devices called "ingestibles." These focus primarily on the ability of devices to withstand the stresses of our digestive system, rather than how the devices taste—so far.

Sixth Senses and More

Beyond the five commonly known senses, we have our sense of time; balance; our sense of movement and our position in space, known as proprioception; our proximity to other objects and people; and other forms of perception that shape our ability to interact with the physical world. We also have a range of senses devoted to internal perception, detecting states like hunger, satiation, muscle soreness, and body temperature (see Figure 3-11). Despite being usually taken for granted, these senses are surprisingly important. Take away the sense of balance, for instance, and people are close to incapacitated.

TIME AND RHYTHM

While we often refer to the "sense" of time, it is an awkward fit among the other senses. There is no main stimulus or equivalent sensor. It's helpful to look at the ability to measure the passage of time as a sense, and one that, like the others, arises out of a several parts working together.

The sense of time is closely tied to the sense of rhythm, which can be looked at as time perceived as a repeating pattern. A sense of time is a very important functional capability. It allows us to anticipate events, carry out complex tasks that involve multiple parts working together, and set or keep a pace in walking and other activities. This can be momentary personal rhythm that sets the pace for a jog, or longer periods such as 24-hour cycles, known as circadian rhythm. They can also be interpersonal events, as when we get into a conversational back-and-forth, or "turn taking." As a species, we play endlessly with rhythm and sound, which can feel fundamental to how we experience life. As Igor Stravinsky said, "music is the best way we have of digesting time."

We have mentioned the cocktail party effect, whereby someone can pick out and listen to one voice in a crowd. Research suggests that rhythm plays a strong role in that effect, driving our ability to anticipate words based on the familiar cadence of speech. Time may play another role in helping us hear where a sound is coming from by recognizing which ear received the sound first.

PROPRIOCEPTION AND THE VESTIBULAR SYSTEM

Proprioception is one of our most automatic senses, and one of which we have the least awareness. It is an internal sense that lets us perceive things like body and parts position, joint position, and how much effort we expend in a physical task. It is informed by proprioceptors in muscles, tendons, and joints. It also informs our position in space.

The ear is not just responsible for hearing. It also contains the cochlea, which monitors our orientation, guiding balance and movement. This system plays a strong supporting role in vision since, as a part of the vestibulo-ocular reflex, it syncs the movement of the head with compensating eye movement to retain a clear image. It also coordinates with other systems, even surprising ones like breathing and circulation, that adjust to body position (see Figure 3-7).

Summary

The world is made of diverse matter and energy that our senses have evolved to perceive in unique ways and for particular purposes. While the senses carry limitations—some going back to their origins—they have also evolved to work together for newer purposes. What we think of as perception is usually two or more sensations blended to bring about unique types of understanding, called modalities. To create effective interfaces requires understanding the abilities, limits, characteristics, and expectations encompassed by the senses.

Proprioception

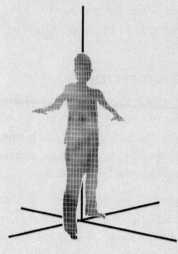

Egocentric

We use our own body as a primary reference point for determining distance and space. For example: "I have tucked the pencil behind my left ear," "The notepad is on my lap," and "My coffee is on the table to my right.."

Non-egocentric

Objective measurements are often a starting point, parsed into a subjective understanding or action. For example: "San Francisco is 381 miles north of Los Angeles; which is too far far to walk," or "The Empire State Building is 1,454 feet tall; it will take a long time to climb that many stairs."

Time & Rhythm

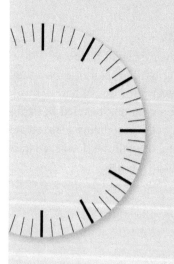

Egocentric

Like space, we experience time using the present moment as an anchor: "I should eat lunch soon," or "It was cloudy in Houston yesterday." Rhythm allows an individual to coordinate their own senses and action together, or to coordinate to other people or events.

Non-egocentric

Similarly, objective time and rhythm are also a starting point for subjective activity, though we rely on them more heavily than spatial references. We can internalize these starting points for a period of time, like the beat of a song for dancing or sunrise for our wake times. Without re-exposure to that reference point however, we can come off the beat.

FIGURE 3-7.
Proprioception and time

[4]

Understanding and Deciding

OUR ABILITY TO UNDERSTAND and decide stems from our need to delegate the effort and attention it takes to get by. So we store, organize, and sequence everything we've learned and done to make it as accessible and usable to ourselves as possible. This allows us to instantly respond to unfolding experiences. One metaphor that illustrates this is the culinary concept of *mise en place*. A French phrase, it roughly translates to "everything in its place." It describes the way chefs arrange their tools, ingredients, tableware, and working spaces in anticipation of the number of orders and how they need to be prepared (see Figure 4-1). There might be a dessert station, where all of the desserts are assembled. In this case, all of the dessert ingredients, dessert plates, and preparation tools are arranged in one area of the kitchen, within reach of the dessert chef. This allows the chef to fulfill orders rapidly as they come in; he or she can assemble any one of the menu items without leaving the station or rummaging for that darned scraper.

FIGURE 4-1.
Mise en place describes a well-staged working area, here with prepped vegetables and condiments

Human cognition is organized around the present moment like mise en place; mostly we need to understand what is going on and what is going to happen next. Our memory, sensory and motor skills, reflexes, and attention are structured to support that. We protect ourselves from the amount of information we experience, minimize and optimize our ongoing efforts, and prepare for new information and experiences as we go along. Like mise en place, we create efficient and repeatable patterns in thought and activity—the schemas and models as described earlier—to help us get a handle on our experiences.

The term *satisficing*, coined by the economist and scientist Herbert Simon in 1956, neatly combines two words, "satisfy" and "suffice," to describe how we do just enough to meet our needs. Cognitive processing in the brain is one of the most resource intensive biological processes that our bodies can perform. So to conserve energy, we default to using the bare minimum. As usability expert Steve Krug noted in the title of his book, "Don't make me think!" isn't just a good usability rule; it's a core survival instinct. We experience a complete and contiguous reality, but in fact, our minds try to filter out as much as possible on two levels: from our conscious awareness or from any awareness at all. And unlike in the London Underground, we don't seem to mind the gaps at all.

Because individual senses are imprecise and limited, cognition allows us to make decisions and act, despite imperfect or incomplete information in a highly dynamic environment. We can contextualize, filter, and prioritize information rapidly, then apply it meaningfully, with the least amount of effort possible. Simply put, it makes our behaviors *adaptive* and *responsive*. We are also capable of processing information in an astonishing variety of ways. Rough calculations put our memory at somewhere upward of 1 petabyte, or 1,000 terabytes, of information. For comparison, the entire Library of Congress is 250 terabytes. Despite being built to use our informational and analytical capabilities as frugally as possible, individual cognition is still a pretty impressive feat. One person's brain can store information at the same order of magnitude as the entire internet.[1]

---

1   "Memory capacity of brain is 10 times more than previously thought," *Salk News,* January 2016, *https://www.salk.edu/news-release/memory-capacity-of-brain-is-10-times-more-than-previously-thought/.*

The Foundations of Understanding: Recognition, Knowledge, Skills, and Narratives

There are several theories about the schemas and models that people develop—how we structure and internalize information and experiences. Each is a different kind of mise en place: a way to organize our knowledge and abilities to fit our needs. We are not born with these abilities; rather, we start to develop them at a very early age, and continue through the rest of our lives. There are four that are most relevant to product design (see Figure 4-2).

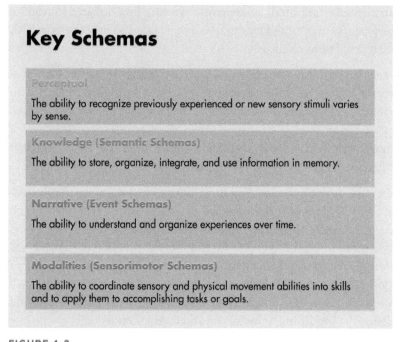

Key Schemas

Perceptual

The ability to recognize previously experienced or new sensory stimuli varies by sense.

Knowledge (Semantic Schemas)

The ability to store, organize, integrate, and use information in memory.

Narrative (Event Schemas)

The ability to understand and organize experiences over time.

Modalities (Sensorimotor Schemas)

The ability to coordinate sensory and physical movement abilities into skills and to apply them to accomplishing tasks or goals.

FIGURE 4-2.
While there are other schemas, these four are key to product design

Perceptual schemas exist across all of our senses and help us extract meaningful information from sensory data. For example, we experience sound as a big undifferentiated mess, all the air waves funneled together onto our eardrum. We automatically try to separate that one big audio stream into individual sources by listening for similarities in sound as well as spatializing the position with our binaural hearing. We can instantaneously recognize and distinguish the wind blowing from a police siren from puppy hiccups.[2] We can visually recognize individual objects, even when their forms overlap. We automatically organize distance into foreground and background, which helps us understand which objects are in front of, or behind, one another. We can calculate the trajectory of moving objects and follow them with our eyes. These are just a few examples of the organizational systems that exist within all of our sensory modalities.

Semantic models help us organize meaning into knowledge. These kinds of models include linguistics and the use of symbols, like iconography or data visualization. Navigations, color codes, and information architectures are kinds of semantic systems that designers create to help people understand how to use an interface and how to accomplish their goals through its use.

Modalities and *multimodalities* encompass the way we develop sensory and physical skills, coordinating them to be able to interact with physical objects and environments. They are also known as *sensorimotor schemas*. In product design, these schemas inform the creation of interaction models, gesture systems, controller elements, and product behaviors.

Event or *operational models* help us figure out continuity (the consistency of experiences over time) and causality (the relationship between cause and effect). We are born storytellers, and we experience events over time as narratives. As Donald Norman observed, "People are innately disposed to look for causes of events, to form explanations and stories."[3] In design, these models are employed to help create feedback loops, structure task models and flows, identify design patterns, and define the beginning, middle, and end of experiences.

There are many other kinds of schemas and models that work together. People have varying aptitudes across abilities: some people don't have a very good sense of direction, some are much stronger with math than words, and others are very good at reading the emotional states of

---

2   Matthew Kennelly, "Buck Has the Hiccups," YouTube video, 0:15, April 27, 2015, *https://www.youtube.com/watch?v=6QslV86odco.*

3   Donald Norman, *The Design of Everyday Things* (New York: Basic Books, 2013), 55.

others. Two things to keep in mind are that we are constantly developing or refining models and schemas, and we are mostly doing it without being aware of it all.

One important integration for designers to understand is tool use: this activity integrates our mental model of objects, our body schema, and our modalities. As cognitive researchers have noted, our minds experience tools as an extension of our bodies, as if they were our fingers, arms, or toes:

> After using a mechanical grabber that extended their reach, people behaved as though their arm really was longer ... It's a phenomenon each of us unconsciously experiences every day, the researchers said. The reason you were able to brush your teeth this morning without necessarily looking at your mouth or arm is because your toothbrush was integrated into your brain's representation of your arm...What's more, study participants perceived touches delivered on the elbow and middle fingertip of their arm as if they were farther apart after their use of the grabbing tool.[4][5]

When we use tools, our minds treat them as if they were a part of us. We imbue them with our own abilities to sense the world around us, to perform tasks, and to express ourselves. We feel the roughness of a piece of paper through the vibration of a pencil. We extend prosody to our musical instruments, and it feels a bit like singing or speaking, infusing sound with emotion, humor, urgency or calm. Designers may believe that devices extend human capabilities with useful features. The reverse is also true: tools become more useful when we can extend ourselves and our body schemas into them.

---

4   Angelo Maravita and Atsushi Iriki, "Tools for the body," Trends in Cognitive Sciences 8, no. 2 (2004): 79-86. *http://dx.doi.org/10.1016/j.tics.2003.12.008.*

5   "Brain Sees Tools as Extensions of Body," Live Science, June 22, 2009, *https://www.livescience.com/9664-brain-sees-tools-extensions-body.html.*

Aware and Non-Aware: Fast and Slow Thinking

Life fluctuates between the familiar and the unknown, which is why we have two types of understanding and deciding, described by the Nobel Prize–winning psychologist and behavioral economist Daniel Kahneman as *System 1* and *System 2*, respectively, fast and slow thinking:

> System 1 operates automatically and quickly, with little or no effort and no sense of voluntary control. System 2 allocates attention to the effortful mental activities that demand it, including complex computations. The operations of System 2 are often associated with the subjective experience of agency, choice, and concentration.[6]

We try to experience as much as possible through System 1, fast thinking. It encompasses most of the experiences in life that could be described as automatic, effortless, or routine. Once we understand how our front door opens, we just open it. After we have learned how to brush our teeth, we can do it while thinking about what shoes we are going to wear for our client meeting. System 2, or slow thinking, activates in situations that introduce uncertainty, unpredictability, complexity, risk, or novelty. It also allows for higher-level decision making, like problem solving, setting goals, challenging physical tasks, or planning future activities. These take more concentration and effort.

When designers think of engagement, it would probably resemble System 2. However, most of human experience falls within System 1. As Kahneman writes, "In the unlikely event of this book being made into a film, System 2 would be a supporting character who believes herself to be the hero."[7] Similar to Kahneman's supporting character, much of interaction design has elevated the status of aware attention to the hero of product design, and much of the performance of interaction design is measured to that level. This seems odd, since we are built to actively avoid as many of those kinds of experiences as possible. Some of our most successful experiences—the ones that are foundational to

---

6   Daniel Kahneman, *Thinking, Fast and Slow* (New York: Farrar, Straus and Giroux, 2011), 20.

7   Kahneman, *Thinking, Fast and Slow*, 31.

our daily lives—are the ones that most quickly and easily become invisible to us. As experience designers, we must recognize that most of what we create should not demand awareness from users.

We experience products and devices using both fast and slow thinking. Physical typing skills, knowledge of the alphabet, and click or touch commands become a part of non-aware behaviors, and we can take them for granted. When our focus is fed up, it allows higher-level goals to become achievable, like writing an email, snapping that hilarious photo, or beating a personal best on a favorite game level. New interfaces that feel "intuitive" and easy to use often tap into this non-aware knowledge and ability. In addition, what we perceive as a single task is very often already *multitasking*, combining multiple non-aware tasks together, or combining non-aware tasks with a single aware task. From that perspective, much of daily human activity would really be considered multitasking. Multitasking between two aware tasks is very difficult and quickly impairs the performance and success of each task significantly. Thus, the level of awareness required by each task is an important consideration when integrating them.

Agency: Balancing Self-Control and Problem Solving

Self-control and problem solving are related forms of cognition, though this may not be immediately obvious. "Several psychological studies have shown that people who are simultaneously challenged by a demanding cognitive task and by a temptation are more likely to yield to temptation."[8] One of these studies asked its participants to memorize a list of seven digits for a few minutes. They were then given the choice between "a sinful chocolate cake" and a "virtuous fruit salad" (see Figure 4-3). Those who had performed the memorization task were much more likely to choose the chocolate cake. Other studies in this vein demonstrated the interdependence of self-control, problem solving, and personal choice.[9]

---

8 Kahneman, *Thinking, Fast and Slow*, 41.

9 Kahneman, *Thinking, Fast and Slow*, 40.

FIGURE 4-3.

Reading about psychology and interaction design is challenging. Now would you prefer this chocolate cake or watermelon?

Self-control is often described as the ability to regulate attention, emotion, and effort. Performing a physically strenuous task requires suppressing the feelings of pain or aches we feel in our body. Solving an analytical geometry requires maintaining focus. Choosing healthy foods for dinner requires resisting temptation. While these tasks seem unrelated, they draw from the same pool of cognitive energy. This is not a metaphor. They all cause similar drops in blood glucose.[10] Like physical energy, mental energy can be depleted and restored. This phenomenon, known as *ego depletion*, is linked to *cognitive load*, our ability to solve problems and make decisions.

It's strange to think of it this way, but our senses of personal agency and free will come from the same part of ourselves as our ability to complete a physics assignment. When we aren't appropriately challenged, we may also not feel very fulfilled. When we cannot plan goals for ourselves, we feel aimless. Our sense of identity, of who we are, emerges from the kinds of problems we solve, the kinds of choices we make, when we show determination, and when we give into our impulses. Like sunken treasure, we find what is valuable, rewarding, and meaningful within the fluid depths of reasoning, desire, and choice.

There is a however, a subtle difference between external reward and what people find intrinsically rewarding. Gamification taps into this, by giving structure to the ways people align self-control with problem solving and goal completion. Companies are delving deeper into behavioral economics—the psychology of motivation and habit formation—to understand how technology and products become a part of

---

10 Kahneman, *Thinking, Fast and Slow,* 43.

users' lives. Tying longer term personal goals more directly to immediate tasks empowers users to complete tasks more quickly and to feel a greater sense of reward.

Motivation, Delight, Learning, and Reward: Creating Happiness

How will users react to a product? How will they learn to use it? What will persuade them to keep using it after the first moments of novelty wear off? Motivation and learning play a large role.

Psychologist B.J. Fogg's behavioral model stresses three core motivators (sensation, anticipation, and belonging), each with a pair of opposites: pleasure and pain, hope and fear, and acceptance and rejection.[11] By coordinating them, and focusing on smaller, easier behaviors, more sustained changes can happen over time.

There is a common mistake of expecting devices to move us toward the achievement of longer-term changes or even continued use, when they are not equipped to do so. They are much better at creating immediate motivations and delight and facilitating flow states. By doing those, habits may change and more permanent behaviors may be established. Toe dippers may become regular users.

The notion of happiness quickly gets into philosophical questions, and Morten L. Kringelbach and Kent C. Berridge use philosophy as an opening to discuss the topic in *The Neuroscience of Happiness and Pleasure*: "Since Aristotle, happiness has been usefully thought of as consisting of at least two aspects: *hedonia* (pleasure) and *eudaimonia* (a life well lived). In contemporary psychology, these aspects are usually referred to as pleasure and meaning, and positive psychologists have recently proposed adding a third distinct component of engagement related to feelings of commitment and participation in life (Seligman et al. 2005)."[12]

---

11 B. J. Fogg, "B. J. Fogg's Behavior Model," accessed January 20, 2018, *http://www. behaviormodel.org.*

12 Morten L. Kringelbach and Kent C. Berridge, "The Neuroscience of Happiness and Pleasure," Social Research 77, no. 2 (2010): 659.

Therefore, there are three levels of happiness: immediate delight (usually something based on senses, aesthetic stimulation, or interest); flow states (around activities and our ability to stay focused and achieve them); and gratifying longer-term changes (like changing behaviors to become better at a skill or developing a good habit).

The delight that we get from sensory and mental stimulation is usually short term. Flourishes like a cool animation, an interesting sound, or a clever phrase are fun and fleeting. That stimulation can, however, be used as a path to deeper change, like flow states and habits. Of course, those habits can be good or bad, and result in changes that range from better health to the epidemic of continuous partial attention caused by twitch-checking our phones and Facebook hundreds of times a day.

Learning is also a form of deeper change, creating cognitive patterns, rather than behavioral ones. To design learning experiences, it is important to motivate action that results in a valuable reward. The trick is to clearly demonstrate that the action caused the reward. Psychologists believe that learning works like memory, with the added factor of contingencies. As psychologists Peter Lindsay and Donald Norman put it, "The problem facing the learner is to determine the conditions that are relevant to the situation, to determine what the appropriate actions are, and to record that information properly."[13]

Summary

Patterns in sensing, thought, and behavior result in the development of models and schemas. These allow us to allocate our limited attention and cognitive resouces to the experiences that really matter. There are multiple theories about the kinds of models and schemas we develop, and how we develop them.

Cognition can be split between non-aware and aware, which align with psychologist Daniel Kahneman's System 1 and System 2 thinking. Many designs aim to create engaging experiences (i.e., ones that are very aware), but non-aware experiences are much more common and may be more appropriate. The relentless grab for attention has succeeded in sapping users' focus. Designing for reliable non-aware experiences that restore focus is ripe for exploration.

---

13 Peter H. Lindsay and Donald A. Norman, *Human Information Processing* (New York, Academic Press, 1977), 499.

[5]

Acting

MOVEMENT IS ONE OF the more complex acts of coordination between our senses, bodies, and intellect. Unlike many sculptors, Michelangelo carved in exquisite detail but left pieces deliberately unfinished. Partially complete, these works look like real human straining to be freed from a block of solid Carrera marble. Dancer Trisha Brown and basketball player Stephen Curry are sculptures in motion, pushing the envelopes of creative expression and athletic prowess (see Figure 5-1). And just how exactly do we get cereal in our mouths while reading the newspaper, not once looking down at the bowl or the spoon? Incredibly, we perform these types of physical feats with the least awareness. The saying goes that you never forget how to ride a bike. But it's fair to say that you don't consciously remember either.

FIGURE 5-1.
A typically athletic (and aesthetic) performance by the Trisha Brown dance company (Set and Reset, 1996; photo by Chris Callis)

Highly developed physical abilities bring the contrast between knowledge and awareness into high relief: we know how to do many activities very well, but we may not have the faintest awareness of how we know. "The best way to mess up your piano piece is to concentrate on your fingers; the best way to get out of breath is to think about your breathing; the best way to miss the golf ball is to analyze your swing."[1] Much of physical activity lies within the realm of *implicit memory*, knowledge that our brain stores but cannot consciously access.

These physical abilities don't start out as implicit memory. We develop many of them over time. It takes many months for a child to learn how to sit up, crawl, and then walk. We may also develop variations in these skills. For tying shoelaces, some people might learn the bunny ear method. Others might learn swoop and loop. It also takes time to develop the physical skills to use interfaces—typing being one of the most challenging. Much of interaction design relies on this implicit memory of physical movements. Gestures like tapping and pinching are really common manual gestures beyond screens, understandable on the first try. On the other hand, a more complex video game might dedicate a few introductory levels just to practice and memorize different button combinations. The ability to speak takes years to develop, distributed across understanding speech, developing motor control over our lips, tongue, and the vocal folds in our throats, the rules of grammar, a robust vocabulary, as well as the social etiquette of conversation. Calling this kind of user interface "natural" might be a misnomer: Most people have spent decades acquiring linguistic abilities through rigorous training and education.

About Anthropometrics

Our size and shape help define our physical abilities. This is already very well understood, and *anthropometrics*, the measurement of people, has long been a part of design. From the tolerance of high G-force on pilots and astronauts, to how age affects our grip on vegetable peelers, the catalog of human measurements is as varied as the kinds of physical tasks we undertake. Common activities like sitting, gripping manual tools, and getting soup into our mouths are very well-understood

---

1 David Eagleman, *Incognito: The Secret Lives of the Brain*, Reprint Edition (New York, Vintage, 2012): 56.

design problems that have been solved countless times over millennia. Sensors are a relatively new product technology. There are many different kinds that can be applied to everyday activities, and we are still in a largely experimental stage, figuring out how to make them valuable and usable in products. Part of this is understanding the complex link between our physical attributes and sensory abilities.

For example, 20/20 is a standardized relative measurement used to describe visual acuity. It means that a person can see what a "normal" person can see from 20 feet away. The ophthalmologist Heinrich Kuechler came up with this standard measurement of vision in 1843. Eye exams have evolved greatly in the last century, and has expanded to include new dimensions of vision and several types of eye movement. A check-up may now also evaluate peripheral vision, accommodation (the ability to shift visual focus via contraction of the ciliary muscle), movement (the ability to detect movement in the visual field), eye muscle performance (the ability of both eyes to work together and coordinate movement), and tests for blind spots.[2]

These new tests reflect a better understanding of vision and how deeply integrated our sensory and physical abilities really are. Focal accommodation and eye movement have a tremendous impact on head-worn devices, like AR and VR headsets. The precision of manual dexterity and the shape and size of our fingers play a strong role in touchscreen interactions, particularly on small screens like smartwatches. Designers humorously call this the "fat-finger" problem. The differences between the movement of walking and running are used in fitness trackers that recognize and measure exercise. These kinds of human measurements go far beyond just our various sizes and shapes nd deeper into how we incorporate our senses and physical movements into everyday activities.

THE ORIGIN OF ANTHROPOMETRICS

In the 1950s, the industrial designer Henry Dreyfuss conducted a study across over 2,000 people to obtain the face and neck measurements needed to design the Model 500 telephone for Bell Labs. He solidified this work into two personas, Joe and Josephine (see Figure 5-2):

2   "Eye Exam," Mayo Clinic, accessed January 20, 2018, *https://www.mayoclinic.org/tests-procedures/eye-exam/*.

They are a part of our staff, representing the millions of consumers for whom we are designing, and they dictate every line we draw … They react strongly to touch that is uncomfortable or unnatural; they are disturbed by glaring or insufficient light and by offensive coloring; they are sensitive to noise, and they shrink from disagreeable odor … Our job is to make Joe and Josephine compatible with their environment.[3]

FIGURE 5-2.

Top: The Model 500 phone; bottom: the personas Joe and Josephine, works created by industrial designer Henry Dreyfuss (sources: top—R Sull, Dhscommtech at English Wikipedia, Creative Commons Share Alike)

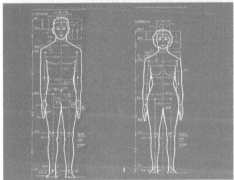

---

3   Henry Dreyfuss, *Designing for People* (New York: Allworth Press, 2003), 24.

Two members of Dreyfuss' staff expanded on this initial work to create the Humanscale design tools: a set of three scales using rotary wheels to create a range of measurements for human size, movement, strength, including for those with physical disabilities. This shifted from consolidated averages to ranges across audience segments, or cohorts. The scale broke out measurements indexing from a small woman to a large man, with special sections broken out for the elderly, disabled, and children. The tools included a wide range of anthropometrics, including measurements like height, weight, and arm and leg length. They added basic sensory and movement metrics, like sight line (10°), slumping (degree of not sitting up straight, 1.6" for men, and 1.4" for women), left-handedness (10% of population), glasses (30% of population at the time), and physical disability (15%–20% of population) (see Figure 5-3). Many of the measurable traits identified then are still common today, though the specific measurements have changed. Now we know that about 64% of the American population requires some form of vision correction.[4]

FIGURE 5-3.
The Humanscale design tools by Henry Dreyfuss offered a handy, comprehensive way to design for common ranges of human attributes

4   "Vision Facts and Statistics," MES Vision, accessed January 20, 2018, *https://www. mesvision.com/includes/pdf_Broker/MESVision%20Facts%20and%20Statistics.pdf.*

As design curator Ellen Lupton noted, this set of guidelines reflected a broader social movement to overcome diverse physical limitations:

> The Humanscale project responded to the UNIVERSAL DESIGN movement. In the late 1960s and early 1970s, the newly vocal disability community compelled designers, builders, manufacturers, and lawmakers to accommodate the needs of a greater diversity of bodies. Humans face physical limitations throughout their lives, from childhood through the aging process. Some disabilities are permanent and others are temporary, but all are exacerbated by poor design decisions.[5]

Task Performance

A key aspect of physical activity within interaction design is performance: the ability to execute a specific behavior. This is well understood in existing human factors for product design and architecture, and mechanical design in products like cars, appliances, and tools. Key metrics include physical ability, mobility, and appropriate response times. A simple example of this would be the number of times a phone rings before it is forwarded to voicemail. That number is based on the estimated time it takes for someone to locate their phones and make a decision about answering.

Other metrics address accuracy and repetition. These track whether people can successfully complete a physical action and whether they can repeat it for as long as needed. Typing on a tiny mobile phone keyboard, or any keyboard for that matter, can be cumbersome, especially when editing text. Features like autofill, autocorrect, and magnifying glass help to mitigate the small size of keys and text on screens, which can be much smaller than the contact area of our fingertips on a touchscreen. A similar feature emerged for the XBox Kinect, which required a user to hold their hand over an option to select it. Without a tap or click to verify selection, this gesture helped avoid incorrect selections in the interface. These kinds of features, which range between helpful and irritating, speak to the level of physical precision expected in some of our

---

5 Ellen Lupton, *Beautiful Users: Designing for People* (Princeton, Princeton University Press, 2014), 26.

interfaces. The increase in repetitive stress injuries like eye strain and carpal tunnel syndrome also point out that over time, the repetition of high-precision movement can be unhealthy (see Figure 5-4).

FIGURE 5-4.
High precision interface, such as that required by a mouse, can have unhealthy effects over the long term

Repetitive daily usage is one of the most challenging types of interaction to design. It's not uncommon for people to type hundreds or thousands of characters or click dozens or hundreds of buttons a day, every day, for a significant portion of their lives. It's not hard to imagine that the number of keystrokes we type could approach or exceed the number of breaths we take. Over the course of our lifetimes, we exert more muscular force by simply holding up the weight of our own fingers and arms than by lifting any external objects.

From that perspective, it's easy to understand how significant these small physical activities can be.

Nonverbal Communication

There are all kinds of estimates about how much communication is nonverbal. It seems to vary widely between cultures, relationships, and individuals. Following World War II, the U.S. Department of State committed deeply to international diplomacy and deepening ties with newly formed allies around the world. In order to communicate effectively across cultures, a special research team was assembled to better understand cultural norms and customs. From this body of work emerged the study of paralanguage headed by George Trager, kinesics headed by Ray Birdwhistell, and proxemics by Edward T. Hall. *Paralanguage* describes the nonlinguistic elements of verbal communication, like prosody, intonation, and utterances like gasps or sighs. *Kinesics* is the study of movement and gesture in communication—both alone and as modifiers of spoken language. *Proxemics* is the study of physical proximity and how people define the usage of physical space.

Kinesics explores the way physical movement is used in communication. These kinds of physical movements are not commonly used as part of interaction design, because they vary as widely as the verbal languages spoken, and the same gesture can mean wildly different things across cultures. For example, a thumbs up in American culture roughly means "OK." In the Middle East, it can be an offensive gesture.[6] (It's still unclear whether its use in emoji will continue or erase the split.)

Social relationships are strongly correlated to the physical distance between people. With voluntary proximity, the closer people stand, the more familiar they are with each other. (Emphasis on voluntary: this does not really apply in densely populated areas, or to the person who fell asleep on your shoulder during a flight.) People are sensitive to physical proximity and establish zones of personal and shared space (see Figure 5-5).

With the rising use of gestures in interaction, it is important to be sensitive to unintended meanings of gestures. Proximity-based technologies, like beacons, GPS, and Bluetooth technologies, are impacted by how people perceive the line between personal and social interactions, especially where privacy is a concern. It can feel at best awkward or at worst invasive and unsafe when spatial boundaries are mismatched to the nature of the experience. Touchless payment, like Apple Pay or Samsung Pay, happen over inches, which is well within the range of personal control. At farther ranges, however, it would feel strangely exposed.

---

6   Brendan Koerner, "What Does a 'Thumbs Up' Mean in Iraq?", *Slate*, March 28, 2003, *http://www.slate.com/articles/news_and_politics/explainer/2003/03/what_does_a_ thumbs_up_mean_in_iraq.html.*

Proxemic Ranges

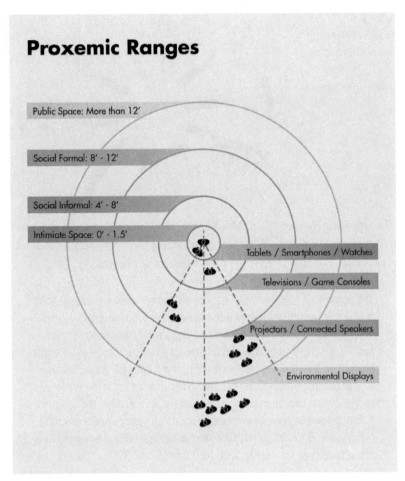

FIGURE 5-5.
Proxemic ranges contribute to user expectations for interactions

Precision Versus Strength

Our hands and feet have more individual tendons, joints, muscles, and nerves than our arms and legs. In contrast, our arms and legs have many times more bone density and muscle mass. Together, these specializations within anatomy give us strength and precision. Hand tools often reflect this balance between grip strength and control, used for a single or small range of actions. In contrast, interface controllers generally require less grip strength and allow a wider range of movements and hand or finger positions to be more versatile (see Figure 5-6).

FIGURE 5-6.

Hand tools balance grip strength and control, usually for a small range of interactions

The Grasping Hand, by C.L. MacKenzie and T. Iberall, details the ways that different hand positions and grips affect the possibilities for interaction and how that is affected by the design of objects:

> The amount of force you can generate depends on the way you hold it—the grip employed brings into play different muscle groups, which in turn differ in their force generation and sensory resolution capabilities. Power grasps are designed for strength and stability, involving the palm as well as the fingers. The form of the handle invites a particular kind of grasp: the hand's configuration determines the strength versus precision that can be applied. Maximum forces can be in the range of 5 to hundreds of Newtons. Precision, or pinch, grasps are less strong, generating up to 25% of the force, and are characterized by apposition of the thumb and distal joints of the fingers.[7]

Trade offs like these are common across many of our movements. We flex our legs and feet differently when we are balancing on uneven terrain versus trying to jump as high as we can. We make different faces when trying to read romantic poetry in a foreign language versus trying to chomp to the center of a Tootsie Pop in one go. This also applies to device interactions. Narrower smartphones allow a user to use one hand to maintain their grip of their phone while also typing with their thumb. Good chef's knives balance the weight of the handle against the weight of the blade to increase control of slicing movements. Power steering in cars and other vehicles emerged because in stopped or slow

---

7   Christine L. MacKenzie and Thea Iberall, *The Grasping Hand* (Amsterdam; New York: North Holland, 1994).

driving conditions, it was difficult for drivers to turn the steering wheel with enough force and control simultaneously. With the XBox Kinect in particular, the strain of holding up the entire weight of both arms demonstrated that fatigue in strength movements made them difficult to repeat. Fatigue in precision movements emerged more as a loss of control and degradation of accuracy (see Figure 5-7).

FIGURE 5-7.
Design for repeated precise movements must account for potential degradation of control and accuracy over prolonged use, caused by muscle fatigue

Inferring Versus Designating Intent

Many new smart products use automated technologies that are triggered by physical actions. The Dyson hand dryer starts when a person dips their hands between the blowers. In this case, it is *inferring* the user's intention to dry their hands. Occasionally this might not be the case—for example, when an article of clothing or a purse brushes through the opening or it's being wiped dry. However, it's uncommon that it is accidentally triggered, called a *false positive*, and the nuisance factor is low.

Palm rejection technology on Apple touchscreen devices is the opposite and assumes that resting your hand on a screen is unintentional, perhaps the product of habit or a tired wrist. However, if you wanted to make a finger-painted turkey it would also reject your palm print, defying generations of grade school tradition. This is called a *true negative*, when an intended action is not recognized. For now, real finger-painting will remain that much more accurate, messy, and satisfying. (Which is not to say that it wasn't already.)

Assisted or automated interactions blend the physical activity of a task with the trigger that activates device functionality. Stepping onto a scale triggers weighing. Approaching an automatic door causes it to slide open. Interactions that infer intent require thoughtful consideration of the user behavior that signals intent. Is the trigger behavior common across many different activities? Is it important to task performance? Do people have different methods or styles that could affect triggering? (See Figure 5-8.)

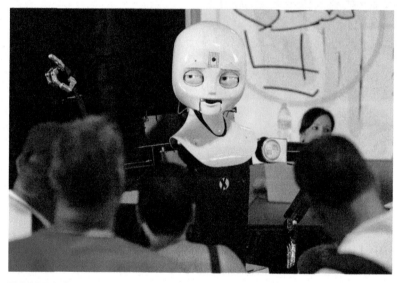

FIGURE 5-8.

Inferring intentions and responding appropriately is part of appearing lifelike and being useful, as demonstrated by this robot from the Office of Naval Research (source: U.S. Navy photo by John F. Williams)

A waving gesture "wakes up" the XBox Kinect. Gestures are tied to screen-based target areas. There is a specific set of gestures that *designate* specific commands. Because the Kinect accepts such a large range of physical movements as part of its overall interaction, it requires that certain commands be unique and deliberate to reduce the possibility of accidental commands and to distinguish between system commands and more general game play. This principle applies to the "wake words" for voice assistants as well. "Alexa," "Echo," and "OK, Google" are somewhat uncommon words or in everyday household conversation. Alexa, in particular, is a fairly uncommon name and will probably begin to decline even more.

Between inferred and designated intents, a great deal of consideration goes into the behaviors that become part of an interaction and whether that will interfere with everyday life. Common words and gestures can mean many things or nothing at all, so it can be challenging to rely on them for device functionality. A person may open their refrigerator door to find something to eat, to check if they have milk, or when the air conditioning is broken, to cool off on a hot day. The cost of a wrongly inferred intention can range from trivial to lifethreatening.

Summary

The ability to engage in tasks and activities is called acting. It involves using our bodies to accomplish something within their surrounding context. Some abilities we are born with, or soon develop, and others take effort to learn. For many, the highest level of learning a task is achieved when we forget that we are even doing it. Interfering with those non-aware activities can create unexpected distractions. Acting is also the way we demonstrate intent, so sensing and inferring what a user hopes to accomplish is an important and often nuanced part of interactivity. As the boundaries between an interface and an activity are blurred, designers must weigh how they complement and interfere with each other.

[6]

Modalities and Multimodalities

Test Drive Modalities

Here's a little exercise: take a sensory inventory of where you are right now. Look, smell, touch, feel, flex. Take a sip of your delicious and refreshing beverage, if you have one. Take a minute or two to take it all in. This information will be used to perform some tasks on the following page. Don't peek ahead!

Now, try to perform the following tasks:

1. Count the number of blue objects nearby.

2. Name the directions that light is coming from.

3. Identify the position of the loudest sound source.

4. Describe the texture of the closest object to you.

5. Determine whether your clothing still smells like laundry detergent (or fabric softener).

6. Sit up straight and relax your shoulders.

There is a good chance that you missed a lot of this information in your initial scan.

But more importantly, did you feel different? You probably needed to use your senses in a different way than you might have anticipated. Observing the light or colored objects may have led you to taking in more of their surface details. Listening for sound may have given you a greater sense of distance and space. You might notice how your frame of mind tends to shift with each different task.

The way we use our senses, the kinds of information we can parse, and what we are trying to accomplish are tied together. The first exercise requires the identification of color, and the unique items in the room. The second exercise combines matching our own position relative to light sources with our ability to discern brightness. The last exercise focuses inward to what our bodies are telling us about our posture. All that sensory information and much, much more was already there. We just didn't notice we needed it. Before Google Maps, our senses were already giving us just-in-time information. We adapt how we gather and use sensory information to apply it to the task at hand. These shifts also occur during non-aware activities. This link between purpose and sensory focus helps us filter out irrelevant information and turbo boosts the acquisition of the information we need.

The cognitive processes tied to each sense can also be activated simply by focusing on the sense itself. Using one sense over the other can change the way you think about and respond to an experience. This happens all the time. We shift between modalities, using the set of sensory, cognitive, and physical abilities that are best suited for what we are experiencing and need to accomplish. We easily switch attention from one sense to another, or from observing one type of phenomenon to another. Like a TV, modal focus allows us to change channels.

Modality

The word *modality* is used in other contexts, including music, logic, and grammar. It sometimes means one way of perceiving a type of stimuli, as in *the visual modality*. That's close to what we mean when we talk about an individual sense, and honestly, the line between them can be a little fuzzy. In this book, a modality is a pattern of sensory cognitive, and motor behaviors established to accomplish specific tasks.

Modalities: How We Use Our Senses

Modalities are patterns developed over the course of our lives—some are common, and some are unique to more specialized or personal abilities. Their existence can partially explain "having a good feel" for something, as if you already knew how to do it or just picked it up quickly. Modalities are not just the ability to see or hear, but include how we use that information. For example, while we are walking, we look around at different focal lengths, using our vision to help maintain balance, assess our speed, avoid obstacles, and find our way. This is different from how we use vision when hand writing a letter, following the movement of a writing tip at close focus. We need to guide a pen in the shapes of letters, to evenly space and align them, and check spelling and punctuation. Both of these activities rely on vision in completely different ways (see Figure 6-1). Modalities extend beyond sensing to how we derive information from a stimulus and how we apply it to thoughts and actions.

FIGURE 6-1.

How we see—our focus, intention, and what we notice—are quite different depending on whether we are walking or writing

People who experience visual loss may use their sense of proprioception and touch for obstacle detection with a walking stick as well as for reading and writing, with braille and keyboards. We can apply modalities flexibly. We have many different ways of sensing the objects, environments, and events around us. For example, we can hear wind, feel it on our skin, or observe it rustling the leaves of trees. But when we fly a kite, we experience wind by feeling the kite string pull in our grip and how the kite moves above our heads. And while wind is normally invisible, we can watch a weathervane from indoors, where we have no direct contact with the wind at all. The flexibility of our modalities becomes especially powerful when we create and use tools, devices, and other kinds of equipment. It allows us to interpret the behaviors of technologies and physical objects beyond our own sensory abilities. Many can use the sound of a hollow or solid hammer strike to know whether they will really anchor a nail or not. Chefs use their sense of touch to determine if a steak's interior is a pliable rare or a springier medium-well.

Think back to when you were learning how to drive a car. It took time to develop a visual sense for speed, when to accelerate and decelerate, and to anticipate obstacles. It took practice to learn when to look around and over your shoulder and to use the rear and side-view mirrors when turning or switching lanes (see Figure 6-2). Getting onto a highway for the first time was probably one of the most frightening parts of learning to drive. It required developing a sense of timing to estimate the speed and distance of oncoming traffic, as well as your own car's speed. Once this modality was developed, it could be adapted to driving other kinds of vehicles. As new modalities form, they become a more permanent part of our experiential toolkit we can then apply across similar activities.

FIGURE 6-2.
Using the sideview mirror to merge into oncoming traffic requires learning and practice to gauge car speed and direction in a reversed image

Everyone has their own distinct sets and preferences across modalities, relying on some more than others. Within a single activity, different people may prefer different modalities. Some are better at language comprehension via reading and writing. Some prefer listening. Still others prefer conversation—speaking reinforces understanding. Like our sizes, shapes, and physical abilities, there is variation across modalities. In all cases, we depend on them to coherently experience and interact with the world.

TYPES OF MODALITIES

The dominant sense of a modality is most commonly used to describe it (see Table 6-1). While smell and taste, respectively, the olfactory and gustatory modalities, are a meaningful part of human experience, they are not yet significant in creating interfaces.

TABLE 6-1. Key interface modalities

VISUAL	Based on our sense of sight
AUDITORY	Based on our sense of sound
HAPTIC	Based on the sense of touch and movement
PROPRIOCEPTIVE (KINESTHETIC)	Based on the sense of our own movement, and orientation. *Proxemics*, is a subset of this, focusing on presence and relative spatial distances.

We Shape Our Modalities, and They Shape Us

Vision is the most processing intensive sense, therefore the visual modality is complex. It consists of separate, innate systems for shape, color, and movement. There are also systems that combine learned and innate: recognizing faces and reading emotional cues are patterns that run deep. We have a large part of our brain devoted just to faces—we use the shapes of the eyes, nose, and lips, as well as their spacing. While we are born with these abilities, and start developing them as soon as we open our eyes, we can only attain accuracy through repeated use. Even less innate is the ability to read, but with practice our eyes sweep quickly across and down pages, effortlessly melding spatial order and tiny little glyphs into new ideas, new worlds, and beloved characters. We are born with our senses and the instinct to build modalities with them. Which modalities we build depend on our circumstances and choices.

As we develop modalities, they become a more permanent part of how we experience—literally. Scientists discovered visible differences in the size of London cab drivers' brains:

> In the drivers, the posterior part of the hippocampus had grown physically larger than those in the control group—presumably causing their increased spatial memory. The researchers also found that the longer a cabbie has been doing his job, the bigger the change in that brain region, suggesting that the result was not simply reflecting a pre-existing condition of people who go into the profession, but instead resulted from practice.[1]

These highly developed modalities can start to become a larger part of our lives. People who have developed an ear for music start hearing melodies in the way raindrops fall or rhythms in the click-clack of a train on its track. Inspiration and delight aren't just found out there in the world through luck. We build up our ability to discover them.

Attributes and Abilities of Modalities

Modal focus is the ability to select and prioritize the most important information about a task or activity. This establishes a feedback loop: sensing relevant information sharpens focus, which in turn sharpens the senses. Some neuroscience researchers describe focus as a "process that gives rise to a temporary change (often enhancement) in signal processing."[2]

Filtering enables us tune out the stimuli which aren't important, and usually accompanies modal focus. Our brains are very good at this: it's also called *selective filtering* or *sensory gating*. Being able to filter prevents us from being overwhelmed by too much irrelevant information. It helps us keep the story straight and reduces response time and effort. The downside is that it can let expectations become biases. We start to miss things because we're not expecting them.

1   David Eagleman, *The Brain: The Story of You*, Vintage, 2015, page 46.

2   Alberto Gallace and Charles Spence, *In Touch with the Future: The Sense of Touch From Cognitive Neuroscience to Virtual Reality*, Oxford University Press, 2014, page 147.

Calibration allows us to stabilize our sensory abilities and limits even when contexts or abilities change. Sensory processing can be somewhat fluid, and unique capabilities emerge as we need them. Put on prismatic glasses that show the world upside down, and after about four days, the brain will flip the image upright. Our cognitive processes are constantly tweaking our senses to make our experience of reality understandable and actionable. Since an upright image is easier to understand, that's what our brains go with. *Neural adaptation* describes how our senses can do things like block out stimuli after a period of exposure. The flipped image takes a while, but other responses are much quicker. Our eyes adjust to the amount of light in a room, as well as the color balance. We stop feeling the smooth tabletop where our arm is resting, or hearing the chugging sounds of an air conditioner. *Motion sickness* can occur when we are unable to calibrate our sense of movement to what we see.

Applying Modalities to Design

We develop modalities to help us understand our world, to interact with it, and to fulfill our needs. The use of smartphones has expanded the way we communicate with writing to include emojis, GIFs, videos, and photos. We now converse *pictorially* (see Figure 6-3). Some might say that this is a devolution in communication, but images are a higher resolution form of visual communication than text. We can actually convey more meaning this way. Devices can change which modalities we develop, and create new ones for us to learn.

Choosing one modality over another may improve an experience. Certain modalities are linked to specific analytical skills or physical abilities, allowing us to respond more effectively. For example, we have some of the fastest response times to spoken conversation but can more easily absorb dense information visually. We filter out a great amount of haptic information, but this also allows us to multitask across complex and automatic physical activities. The kinds of modalities that are used within an experience can enable or hinder successful interactions.

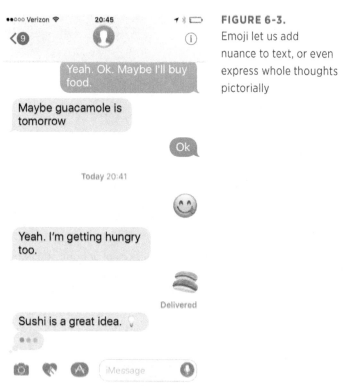

Different people have different proficiences and preferences across modalities. The majority of Americans require corrective lenses of some kind. Vision and hearing universally degrade with age. Some people have more strongly or easily developed modalities than others. Some people experience temporary injuries or illnesses. Some bars are really noisy and you need closed captions to be able to follow the basketball game. Our relationship to our sensory and physical abilities varies between people, over the course of our lives, and sometimes from one moment or place to another. Disability is not an issue for a small minority of people, but something everyone experiences in some form or degree.

Multimodalities

Woke up, fell out of bed,
Dragged a comb across my head
Found my way downstairs and drank a cup,
And looking up I noticed I was late.
Found my coat and grabbed my hat
Made the bus in seconds flat
Found my way upstairs and had a smoke,
Somebody spoke and I went into a dream.

— "A DAY IN THE LIFE," JOHN LENNON/PAUL MCCARTNEY

As the Beatles observed, daily life requires shifting between activities quickly and fluidly.

The reason is simple: our days are fluid sequences of actions and experiences, requiring countless thoughts, decisions, and actions. You wake up with some serious bedhead, and have to use much more product that usual. The coffee is too hot, and you have to wait before you can drink it. And this morning, you can't just walk to the bus stop. You need to run like there's medals involved. Life is filled with details and minor adjustments that we make on the fly, and having multimodal abilities allows us to manage them. Besides, all animals are multimodal. Apparently, staying alive means you have to keep track of a bunch of different stuff.

The use of technology relies deeply on our multimodal abilities and how we can develop them in specific ways. We wouldn't have been able to develop technologies without them in the first place. Using technology, however, is not natural or innate. One of the earliest films was of an approaching train. Some viewers jumped out of the way, believing they were about to be struck. Their eyes were deceived. Riding a bike is a continual flow of pedaling, balancing, and steering combined with scanning the road and listening for other bikers and cars. We look at our phones, listen to notification alerts, and mostly manage to keep our grip on them when our hands are wet. Some of these multimodal abilities have a bigger learning curve. Once we develop them, however, the level of focus and effort required can drop dramatically. We don't just come with autopilot; we create new autopilot programs all the time across myriad activities. These shortcuts provide rich playgrounds for things like optical illusions, surprise, and playfulness, but can also result in certain types of perceptual and cognitive bias. For designers to create magical experiences, ease and utility must be balanced against creating false or misguided expectations.

Trusted Version and Performance Optimization

A glass of water is a mass of complexity and possibility through the lens of phenomenology (see Figure 6-4). It is cold, it is wet, it is definitely half full. It was not on the table yesterday, and it needs to go in the dishwasher before bedtime. It can be moved, drunk, spilled, shattered, and if you are a well-informed Boy or Girl Scout, it can be used to start a campfire. It can then be used to put that fire out.

FIGURE 6-4.
A glass of water, but you probably knew that already

How do we know it's there? How do we know all this stuff about it? How do we know what we can do with it? This is where multimodality becomes useful. While we have multiple senses, they have their limitations. Being able to sense different things allows us to understand a wider range of experiences. It also allows us to use different senses together in the same experience. Our senses validate each other, ensuring that we have a reliable perception of reality. If we smell or taste vodka, then we know that it wasn't water like we thought.

VALIDATION

As observed by neuroscientists Barry E. Stein and M. Alex Meredith, *"cross-modal matching* is using information obtained through one sensory modality to make a judgement about an equivalent stimulus from another modality."[3] Sensory impressions that fit together are judged to be more reliable. Validation allows us to confirm what we are experiencing. When simultaneous sensory stimuli support each other, we pay more attention, we remember them better, and for longer. Our minds judge them to be reliable, and therefore give them higher priority in attention and memory. When simultaneous stimuli conflict, we may pay more attention to understand what is wrong, or experience confusion. We might try to focus more sensory attention to understand and resolve the conflict, or dismiss the stimuli as unpleasant sensory noise. Cross-modal techniques are believed to be particularly effective in learning experiences.

In interface design, cross-modal stimuli are constructed: integrated code triggers the simultaneous display of pixels, emission of sounds, and haptic feedback. They have to be deliberately matched together to simulate natural cross-modal experiences, like sound with animation or a visual effect with haptic vibration. Our sense of rhythm spans vision, hearing, touch, and proprioception and plays a strong role in how we align cross-modal stimuli. But the mind is a little forgiving. Misalignments of up to a few hundred milliseconds between stimuli are passable. More than this causes the mind tends to perceive separate events or dismiss one or more of the misaligned stimuli as noise.

INTEGRATION

Multisensory integration describes how different senses are synthesized into a coherent, multidimensional reality as it unfolds. The combination of taste and smell into the experience of flavor is one example. Audiovisual integration is one of our best-understood experiences across multiple design media. Vison in combination with the vestibular system allows us to keep our balance as we walk. Integrating modalities is fundamental to our most basic activities. One sense can prime the other to be prepared for what happens next, a type of response loop

---

3 Barry E. Stein and M. Alex Meredith, *The Merging of the Senses*, MIT Press, 1993.

known as *feedforward*. This allows people to prepare their attention and physical response before something happens. Watching someone's lips as they speak enhances the cocktail party effect.

Neuroscientific research conducted by Stein and Meredith shows that in humans and other species, an experience that involves two or more senses is judged by our brains as being more important and is therefore perceived more intensely:[4]

> Multisensory integration...is ubiquitous, and even animals with such seemingly exotic sensory apparatus as an infrared system (pit vipers) or an electroreceptor system (some fish) combine these inputs with those from more commonly represented modalities such as vision to provide an integrated world view.[5]

The sum is often greater than the sensory parts, as Stein and Meredith elaborate: "The integration of inputs from different sensory modalities not only transforms some of their individual characteristics, but does so in ways that can enhance the quality of life. Integrated sensory inputs produce far richer experiences than would be predicted from their simple coexistence or the linear sum of their individual products." They note that it's a pattern that seems to exist across all species, from unicellular organisms to higher primates: "We know of no animal with a nervous system in which the different sensory representations are organized so that they maintain exclusivity from one another."

In design and the arts, this richness makes delightful experiences possible. At a concert, the pounding bass gives the music kinesthetic impact—we feel it as much as we hear it. It might just get you to start moving your feet. Drivers of sports cars dislike too much shock absorption because haptic sensations enhance their perception of driving. In fact, many performance luxury cars are designed to accentuate this sensorial experience. People are not very good at gauging higher speeds visually, but we feel the rumble of the engine, feel the nervy swing into a tightly hugged turn, hear the engine's throaty growl as we shift gears. All of these sensory cues create an impression of power and speed. None of them have any bearing on acceleration.

---

4   Stein and Meredith, p.15.

5   Stein and Meredith, p. xi.

A SINGLE PRIORITIZED SENSE OR MANY TOGETHER?

Some multimodalities are simple, like a chain of sensation, action, and reaction. Others are more complex, sometimes deceptively so:

Across one main sense

The primary sense may be used across multiple modalities. You see movement, shift your gaze, focus in the area of movement, and watch to see what unfolds as you decide to walk closer, keeping vision as the main priority in each part of the sequence. Three different activities: noticing movement, identifying the source of movement, and maintaining observation require you to use vision in different ways, and rely on different cognitive processes.

Across multiple senses

You start to prepare dinner. You see and feel that the oil and pan is hot, so you drop minced garlic into it and affirm the decision by watching the oil bubble and hearing it sizzle. Your sense of timing is confirmed by watching and smelling, and you see that it's time to add garbanzos. And so on, as multiple modalities inform and guide successive sets of senses working together.

HOW MULTIMODALITY SHAPES OUR ACTIVITIES AND EXPERIENCES

"You don't perceive objects as they are,"[6] says neuroscientist David Eagleman. "You perceive them as you are." Two people can be in the same place and experience very different things. The differences arise from what we bring with us. Along with our memories and habits, much of what shapes an experience depends on the emphasis placed on various senses during each moment, as well as what we are trying to accomplish.

Imagine two people standing a few feet from each other on a crowded city street one morning. Woman A, who lives in the city, is waiting for a taxi to go to an appointment. Woman B, a visitor, is waiting to meet a childhood friend who lives there. Both women are visually scanning the busy streets. Both are looking for something, but everything from their postures to their faces shows them to be in very different modalities. Woman A is looking out for yellow cars and lighted signs and

---

6 David Eagleman, The Brain.

trying to confidently establish the curb territory as hers in case of competing commuters. Woman B is scanning faces, hoping not to look too conspicuous, trying to identify what may be a familiar face, and which may also be exhibiting the same type of expectant scan. Her senses are active, but not sharply focused, because she's not sure what will signify the arrival of her friend. She listens for her name. She keeps an eye on her phone. She glances at taxis, in case her friend arrives in one. Woman A, meanwhile, is much more focused and expert at her task. Her eyes are intent. Her spatial sense functions peripherally to perceive competition, and has vaguely noticed B as a possible, minor threat. Her arm is ready to shoot up when she sees a potential cab.

Very different experiences of the same moment and context.

In order to design for each of those women, we need to understand their purposes and expectations.. The multimodalities they use play a large part in both.

Attributes and Abilities of Multimodalities

Multimodalities are complex and varied. To support them, there is no particular checklist that covers each case. But there are common attributes and abilities that provide starting points for design.

FOCUS

Multimodalities structure focus by prioritizing important information and filtering out what's irrelevant. Despite this, suppressed senses remain on standby. When new information becomes urgent, we can quickly reprioritize (shift). For example, if a fire alarm went off while you were rummaging through a drawer, not only would you hear it, but additional cognitive, motor skills, and reflexes would activate.

Modal focus is crucial to building skills and performing tasks, for several reasons. It optimizes attention, effort, and integration of the most important sensory, cognitive, and motor abilities. This allows us to complete tasks more easily and effectively. It gates the other senses, to reduce interference, but allows these gates to be bypassed when necessary.

FLOW

Flow is an experience state where perception, cognition, and action coalesce into effortless performance. Despite their high activity state, a person feels calm, relaxed, and energized.

SEQUENCE

Some activities are broken up into steps that follow a particular order. For pitching a baseball, it might be observing, then windup, early cocking, late cocking, acceleration, and follow-through.[7] If the pitcher needs to switch focus from striking out the batter to tagging a base-stealing runner, it is called a shift. When a sequence is *fixed*, its steps must occur in a specific order. When it is *open*, its steps can occur in any order.

SIMULTANEITY

Instead of a sequence, some activities may be performed at the same time. Driving a car blends several tasks including watching the road, pressing the pedals, turning the steering wheels, and listening to the engine and other cars. Some of these may be performed at less conscious levels to support greater focus on whatever is top of mind.

SHIFT

We need to delegate attention across quickly changing circumstances as they unfold. A modal shift might be from visual to auditory search when someone calls for help in the woods. A multimodal shift might happen in a conversation as you shift from listening to speaking. Or even more pronounced, from having a conversation to paying the check at a restaurant. A shift might be the result of natural *progression* and ending of activity (conversation over), or it might be the result of an *interruption* (tired waiter needs to go home). A shift may also be caused by internal disruptions. Needs, like thirst, hunger, and sleepiness, remind us to take care of ourselves. A sudden thought, like an idea, insight, or emotion, can also cause a shift in our attention.

---

7   Peggy A. Houglum, Therapeutic Exercise for Musculoskeletal Injuries, Third Edition, Human Kinetics, 2010

TRANSITION

The way we experience shifts are called transitions. They can be harsh and jarring or smooth and supportive, depending on many factors. Often transitions are unplanned, as with many interruptions. Other times they can be planned and orchestrated, as when a "good night" song comes on in some stores, telling shoppers it's time to shift from browsing to buying and then leaving. Sometimes the best way to ease a transition out of one modality is by creating a reliable way back in, as when apps or devices remember what their user was doing when they stopped, and provide a "bookmark" or the same state when the user returns.

SUBSTITUTION

Substitutions use alternative senses when there is interference within a modality, like finding your wallet by feel because your eyes are on the road. We've also built tools to help substitute modalities. Can't find your phone? There are several ways to track it, but the most simple is just calling it to play a ringtone. This is shifting from visual to auditory modality and then right back again once you have a sense of where you are looking, or perhaps integrating the two modalities as you scan the room for where the sound is coming from.

TRANSLATION

Translations map information to a relevant modality, when an experience lies outside of human perception or outside of practical means to obtain physical information. A weather map, for instance, can show the intensity of a tropical storm, determined by the temperature of the clouds. Translation is a common technique for information visualization as well as for alert sounds such as smoke detectors, seatbelt reminders, and doorbells. (You could consider it the basis of written media.) Unlike visual detection, doorbells are not limited by line of sight—we can hear a doorbell through walls and doors. Translation may also make certain experiences easier or more flexible when needed.

PROFICIENCY

When we repeat certain activities, the brain's response is to hardwire the activity into our brain. We no longer need to think about the activity to do it. We do it unconsciously, with little or no awareness, resulting in a cognitive state known as flow. In many cases, the less we concentrate while we are executing one of our expert abilities, the better we perform at it. Some activities simply require repetition to develop proficiency. Others required more specialized training or practice. Someone who is proficient at an activity may have an increased ability to perceive things that are relevant, called *perceptual expertise*.[8]

Common Categories of Multimodalities

While modalities are described by their focal sense, multimodalities can be more easily classified by their associated purpose or activity. These are not precise, exclusive, or comprehensive categories, and there is a lot of overlap and integration between them. They are helpful for understanding the shared intents, contexts, and sensory considerations across the behaviors:

Basic abilities

> These are core human activities that are often incorporated into other types of activities. They are essential to daily life. They include activities like sitting, standing, walking, and speech. These multimodal behaviors are usually developed very early in our lives. They become a part of the activities of which we have the least awareness and are easily integrated into multitasking activities.

Orientation and scanning

> Because vision is such a dominant sense, there are many multimodalities that prioritize visual stimuli. This category encompasses activities in which vision and, to a lesser extent, proprioceptive capabilities are used together. We use vision to navigate our surroundings and to recognize, locate, or measure specific objects in our environment. It includes some of our browsing behaviors, as we seek out specific choices, and make comparative decisions around them. It also includes pathfinding activities, where we develop spatial models of our environments. While there may be supporting modalities, they focus on enabling the absorption or analysis of visual information. Our visual ability to analyze large sets of items and attributes is unparalleled by the other senses in both speed and detail.

---

8   Michael Harré, Terry Bossomaier, and Allan Snyder, The Perceptual Cues that Reshape Expert Reasoning, Nature 2012. *https://www.nature.com/articles/srep00502.*

Hand–eye coordination (visuo-haptic integration)

This is an important category for interaction designers, because haptic tools and interfaces are by far and away the most common. Blending proprioceptive, tactile, and visual modalities, and often supported by auditory modalities, it allows us a wide range of physical interactions with objects and environments. Curiously, the term also applies to foot–eye coordination, like using pedals or kickstands. Activities can be differentiated by whether they require more precision or strength, like lifting a bag of groceries versus performing brain surgery. They can further be differentiated by whether they are manual, tool-based, or interface-based. Manual activities require direct manipulation by the hands, such as picking up a French fry. Tool-based activities employ a tool or other form of equipment that can be manipulated, such as scissors, pencils, or a guitar. Interfaces employ abstracted control systems for mechanical or computational equipment and devices.

Social interaction

Social interaction is a major component of human behavior, and we have developed sophisticated tools, norms, and expectations around it. Human linguistic ability is so strong that we have multiple modalities for communication. This includes speech, writing, and body language. We can use them in tandem or alone. The relationship between individuals plays a strong role in shaping communication and is also expressed across several multimodal behaviors such as physical proximity, contact, prosody, and even linguistic formality.

Performance and athletics

Our proprioceptive and haptic abilities are supported by other sensory abilities when activities require both strength and precision. Very often these behaviors require repetition or practice to commit skills to implicit memory, reduce response times, or increase speed, strength, or accuracy. Enabling a flow state is often a crucial component of these experiences. These activities include playing sports, acting, dancing, and specialized manual labor.

Some activities require a high level of sensory or cognitive focus. They emphasize the resolution and quality of the sensory stimuli of the experience, like listening to music or complex analysis like solving a physics problem. In these cases, maintaining focus is the priority of the experience. Some people will find external stimuli distracting to more internalized sensory or cognitive processes. Some require external tools or models to aid them. These are often subjective personal preferences. A high level of flexibility and individual control or agency can be required.

Applying Multimodality to Design

As we create products for an ever-broader set of circumstances, there are a few guidelines that are useful. Understanding the ways that our minds and senses work together, and what they need to do so effectively, offers a good set of fundamental considerations.

MAINTAINING FOCUS

Focus is to experience as understanding is to information. It's a result of the mind being successfully engaged and able to comprehend a coherent thread through the experience. Focus and flow are some of the more important considerations for designers working with multimodalities. That doesn't mean every interaction has to be achieved in a state of extreme, brow-furrowed concentration. Or that modalities must play out in seamless preordained patterns. Far from it. Focus is simply the state of mind that results from things going smoothly. It's a critical state of mind on the path to successfully achieving an aim.

When we talk about focus, we mean a few things. One is the level of awareness that we have for a particular sensation. Are we able to tune in to something using our senses and extract salient information from it? Is doing so a common practice, familiar to most people (and likely users)? What do we need to maintain this concentration, and how important is it that we do so?

RESPECTING COGNITIVE LOAD

We may be multimodal all the time, but the combination is limited by our brain's ability to process multiple inputs. Exceeding these limits carries the potential for danger, so we must protect ourselves from the results of losing focus, as psychologist Daniel Kahneman writes:

Everyone has some awareness of the limited capacity of attention, and our social behavior makes allowances for these limitations. When the driver of a car is overtaking a truck on a narrow road, for example, adult passengers quite sensibly stop talking. They know that distracting the driver is not a good idea, and they also suspect that he is temporarily deaf and will not hear what they say.[9]

Like those careful passengers, device designers must also be aware of their ability to interfere with, as well as augment, an experience. We believe that transitioning people between modalities is better than simply creating more and more activities that interrupt each other

Cognitive load varies across modalities. For instance, when reading, we use vision to absorb dense information, that requires significant cognitive processing. Libraries, designed to support reading, have rules about maintaining quiet in order to reduce interruptions and distractions that can break focus. Devices can follow suit.

OVERCOMING BARRIERS WITH SUBSTITUTIONS AND TRANSLATIONS

Sometimes the normal way of doing things turns out not to work. If you're driving, maybe your usual road is closed. So you take another. This also happens to our senses almost every day. What happens when one of your sense modalities doesn't work? Because we are complex, adaptive beings, our sensory modalities also have options, and some work better than others.

When a barrier to a preferred modality exists, or an experience lies outside of human perception, *substitutions* and *translations* can offer alternative modalities to fill in the gaps. If you lose sight of your friend in a crowd, you might call out their name, which is an example of substitution. We effortlessly substitute modalities all the time. If there's not a practical way to physically receive information, a translation may make use of a different sensory channel. A light on a dark ceramic stove top, for instance, is designed to tell you that it's hot. Finding out too late by touch is dangerous. Sometimes information simply lies outside of human abilities to perceive, such as high levels of air pollution. Normally we rely on seeing and listening to move around without

---

9   Kahneman, p.23.

danger. But airborne particulates are difficult to detect until they have already done damage. Maps and pollution alerts help people understand which areas call for protective measures or avoidance.

SHIFTS, INTERRUPTIONS, AND FLOW

When we experience cognitive fatigue and can no longer absorb or dismiss new information, or another activity takes priority, an interruption occurs. How serious this interruption is depends on the activity. Someone else talking might make you forget what you were going to say, or it might cause you to miss the fact that the traffic light has changed. We have a host of social norms around interruptions, especially ones we generally want, like phone calls, text alerts, alarms of all sorts, and the bells or music used by ice cream trucks.

The point is, interruptions happen, and in some cases are desirable. No matter how focused we are, how intent on remaining single-minded, we naturally shift. Whether that's experienced as a momentary digression or a more disruptive break depends on the circumstances. Being aware of likely shifts and possible interruptions, or even orchestrating them as needed, is important. Making a safe path out and a clear path in should be high in designers' minds.

Here are some techniques for managing attention effectively and respectfully:

Maintaining focus

Reinforce

> Deliver information using more than one sense for high-priority information or learning experiences.

Pace

> Don't overtax a user's cognition, but deliver just-in-time information, especially in experiences that require more focused effort attention or that span multiple modalities.

Block

> Shifting between different modalities or different types of sensory information within a single modality can be challenging. Try to organize similar forms of sensory information together or maintain a modality or multimodal set consistently through an experience.

Dealing with interruptions

Safety exits

This is the experiential equivalent of "degrading gracefully": a realization that interruptions will happen, so make sure that the way out of a modality is safe whenever possible.

Ease of re-entry

Provide threads that are easy to pick back up again to avoid that "what was I doing?" moment of hesitation.

Off-switch

Allow users the ability to decline interruptions, either for a period, or permanently.

Allowing shifts

Social or ecosystem norms

It's important to make high priority interruptions quickly and easily identifiable. Meeting user expectations around these kinds of cues can be helpful, but when overused become ignored. It's also important to consider the impact of an interruptive cue within a social setting, for instance.

Priming

Well-designed interruptions can help users transition their attention more effectively. Certain kinds of interruptions tap into the startle response, like alarms and sirens, prompting people to immediate action. Lower priority interruptions, however, can be calmer and more gradual, allowing people the choice to shift their attention or ignore the cue. Some audio alerts slowly fade in. Some alerts have a "pre-alert" to prepare users for more noticeable stimuli that follows. This can also give people more response time, allowing them to more fully comprehend these interruptions and respond more effectively.

FEEDBACK AND VALIDATION

Our senses are pretty invisible to us, disappearing behind all the information they provide. That's why it helps to have multiple sources that confirm each other—for example, when a sound comes from a moving object, that sound helps us to locate it and predict where it might be next, allowing us to both see and hear it better. We cross-reference between current sensory stimuli and previous stimuli to validate knowledge and train our senses to better filter information.

BODY LANGUAGE AND PHYSICAL ENGAGEMENT

There is a large body of work around *kinesics,* a term coined by Ray Birdwhistell that describes the use of gesture, posture, and movement to communicate—basically, what's known as "body language." Gestural outputs, whether conscious or unconscious, got a big boost when Apple started using accelerometers to integrate gestural interfaces on the iPhone. The XBox Kinect added a camera for similar purpose.

We have become accustomed to using a keyboard and mouse or on-screen keyboard and touchscreen together. Skills around other less common interfaces can be less developed. Familiarity is a double-edged sword. Tapping into existing mental models can make new interfaces easy to learn. They cal also get in the way of adopting interfaces that are different but might work better. There is no such thing as an intuitive interface. There are only interfaces that tap into pre-existing knowledge and skills—implicit memory in particular—developed through other activities or means. If it feels intuitive to you, challenge yourself to think about how you developed this pre-existing knowledge or skill and consider whether your users have had the same opportunity.

Metaphors have been put to good use in screen-based design, because we are good at reusing our existing behaviors and applying them to new ones. Understanding what skills people already have is key to developing new types of physical interfaces. Using a steering wheel, or using drawing tools like a pencil—these are good sources of inspiration. Physical interfaces might not require metaphor, but may reuse some of that same physical knowledge. Be cautious assuming that people know how to apply their existing physical skills to new kinds of interactions. *Test, measure, learn, and iterate* is a good approach for developing new interface modes. As with all new things, you may find a few key hacks and variations that no one saw coming.

Summary

Modalities are patterns of perception, cognition, and action that enable our behaviors. They allow us to focus on important sensations, filter out those that are less important, and adjust our senses to understand what is happening. Multimodalities combine two or more modalities to enable more complex behaviors. When barriers exist to one modality, we make use of substitutions and translations. There are important rules of thumb for designers working with multimodalities. Those include principles such as respecting cognitive load, supporting focus, maintaining flow, and dealing with interruptions.

[7]

The Opportunity: Transforming Existing Products and Developing New Ones

PROCESSORS THAT USED TO be the size of a football field are now the size of a shirt button. Batteries are portable, small, and now they're flexible. Technology has reached a tipping point in power, size, and cost to enable the next wave of computing: the Internet of Things. Like the Cambrian explosion, the IoT will bring a diversification of products designed in different shapes and sizes to suit all kinds of environments.

Nature created many different forms of locomotion: wings for flying, legs for walking, flippers and tails for swimming. Similarly, the wings of an airplane, the wheels of cars, and the turbines of boats and submarines emerged during the mechanical age. There can be many different solutions to the same problem: birds have feathers but bees have exoskeleton wings. We have helicopter blades, jet engines, and hot air balloons. As computing expands beyond screen-based devices, there will be waves of morphological divergence and convergence across hardware products—not by evolution, but by design. We will be able to blend these new and existing technologies with our natural environments like never before.

Just look at the IPV6 protocol internet addressing scheme, a plan to accommodate the tremendous number of connected devices expected to come online within the next 20 years. It creates over a trillion internet addresses for every person on the planet. One of the well-known slogans for IoT is "Anything, anywhere, at any time." "Anything" is a pretty big word all by itself. Even so, it keeps expanding. The category of wearables has branched out to include "hearables," "ingestibles," and "embeddables." New verticals are emerging, and they are evolving rapidly. Existing products are being updated with new computing abilities. The range of possible products and the ways to interact with them can make it hard to know where to begin.

Luckily, existing design practices and deliverables for product development can be adapted to develop multimodal experiences. During early-stage product definition, multimodality introduces an expanded set of user considerations. Product and business capabilities are leveraged against user needs in new ways. This chapter helps identify the unique challenges and opportunities that multimodal design introduces.

Key Applications of IoT: Monitor, Analyze and Decide, Control and Respond

It's not a coincidence that the key IoT applications are inspired by human abilities. What is valuable about the IoT is that it partially mirrors human adaptability and intelligence: devices can go wherever we can go, and like us, they can directly interact with the environment. These devices have sensors, like we have senses, though they lack our robust multisensory integration. They have new analytical and decision-making capabilities through technologies like big data and AI. This gives them deep but narrow capabilities to understand and decide. Advanced mechatronics and robotics give them the ability to take action within highly structured or focused contexts. The technologies can be used to complement a wide range of human behaviors and interactions. Products that already exist can be optimized for human use.

While it might seem like giving devices capabilities similar to human perception, cognition, and action would put them on a collision course with human evolution, it's the differences that make the IoT powerful. Ingestible technologies like nanobots blend chemical and thermoreceptive capabilities to conduct automated biopsies. It's like combining the sense of smell and touch into a single sheet of material the size of a pinhead. Driverless technologies use a navigation system called lidar, an order of magnitude more powerful than radar, sonar, and even our own hearing and vision. They have to: transportation speeds will not be bounded by the limitations of human reflexes for much longer (see Figure 7-1). These are transformative technologies, and in many cases, products will have powerful new behaviors and capabilities of their own.

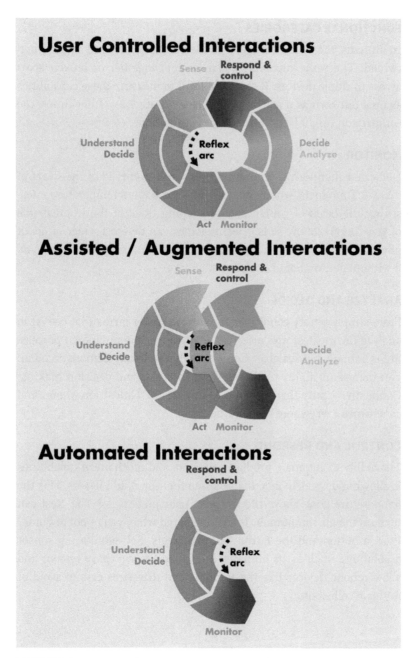

User Controlled Interactions

Sense · Respond & control

Understand Decide · Reflex arc · Decide Analyze

Act Monitor

Assisted / Augmented Interactions

Sense · Respond & control

Understand Decide · Reflex arc · Decide Analyze

Act Monitor

Automated Interactions

Respond & control

Understand Decide · Reflex arc

Monitor

FIGURE 7-1.

With augmentation or automation, the responsibility for parts of the experience shift from user to device. Rather than complementing a human modality, they run parallel with our experiences, or take over certain aspects altogether.

FUNCTIONAL CATEGORIES

In humans, the abilities to sense, understand, decide, and act are intertwined. The same capabilities can be kept together or broken apart across multiple devices. It can be helpful to measure these capabilities against our own as a starting point (see Figure 7-2). Other times, the comparison might be an unnecessary limitation.

MONITOR

Dedicated monitoring of environments and events is at the heart of many IoT products, whether it's taking your home's temperature, measuring the beats of your heart, or keeping track of the whereabouts of your puppy. Many sensor technologies can detect a wider range of physical stimuli with greater precision than humans. They can also do it without getting bored or sleepy.

ANALYZE AND DECIDE

From simply binary conditions to massive server farms that use AI to analyze the greatest mysteries of the universe, computational processing is remarkably scalable. Computers have already demonstrated an ever-increasing ability to augment data analysis and decision making. Connectivity puts that power into any device almost anywhere, and sometimes everywhere at the same time.

CONTROL AND RESPOND

The ability to automate product behaviors and mechanical capabilities is allowing devices to take matters into their own, uh, flexors. Has the temperature gone above the range of user preference? The Nest can turn on the air conditioner. Is the dog bored when you're not at home? Push a button and the Furbo will toss treats. Self-monitoring sensor capabilities, such as in humans, are called *proprioceptive systems* and allow robotic devices like the Roomba and driverless cars to avoid or mitigate collisions.

Building Blocks of Interfaces

Monitor (Input)

Devices have a wide range of abilities of gathering information about the environment, a specific task, or about the people interacting with them. Sensors like keyboards, microphones, and cameras are used in human-computer interfaces to detect both designated and inferred intents from a user. Devices that provide more autonomous or assistive functionality gather information directly from the environment, monitor their own activity, and can be networked for functionality performed at a larger scale or within shared social contexts.

Analyze

The speed, scale, accuracy and endurance of computer processing allow devices to make decisions and take action, or to do so on our behalf. This includes many methods for verifying, manipulating, and applying information. These methods, including all of their rules, are still designed by people, and therefore subject to the same errors, biases, and unintended consequences of comparable human efforts.

Decide

Once information is gathered and analyzed, it can be used to identify options. Devices then support human decision-making, decide on our behalf, or share decision-making cooperatively. Failsafes, like confirmations and overrides ensure that users accept these decisions. The rising use of AI and machine learning can blend multiple models of information analysis and decision-making together. Many of these models are based on theories about how human intelligence works.

Respond & Control (Output)

Devices also have wide range of capabilities in communicating or applying information. Screens, haptic motors, and speakers can display information, create vibrations, or play sounds or simulate speech in various user interfaces. In automated or assistive functionality, they can provide a wide range of communication or mechanical activity on our behalf.

FIGURE 7-2.

The building blocks of interface are present whenever device activity replaces that of humans

Existing Device Modes

Existing modes in both mechanical and digital products have set user expectations for new multimodal interfaces. *Ears free,* or *silent mode,* has become a nearly default setting for most mobile phone users, at least in urban and office settings. While funny ringtones or quirky alerts add distinction and levity, the joke stops being funny after the second meeting interruption. Designing silent alerts has become a standard challenge for mobile designers.

Hands-free describes voice interfaces that allow people to use devices while permitting manual tasks. This was embraced early on by car makers though it has received increasing criticism, because talking drivers are still distracted. The promise of heightened productivity and performance is seductive, and hyperstimulated users can mistake dull or repetitive tasks as easy. It is up to product teams to prioritize and respect safety, cognitive load, physical performance, and focus, despite users' overly optimistic self-estimations.

Eyes-free describes interfaces that use voice, sound, or haptic interfaces without visual engagement. Inspired by manual tools, haptic interfaces rely on shape and layout that users can memorize, such as game controllers, keyboards, mice, and remote controls. However, these interfaces require practice to use optimally. Many alarms, like smoke detectors and security systems, are designed to be interruptive and to demand focus. Assistive technologies, like turn-by-turn navigation, are less intrusive, and rely on timing, context, and brevity to deliver functionality with minimal cognitive load.

"Disruptive" Technologies

Early IoT products focused on making existing products "smart"— the phone, the watch, the home, and the car. The term described adding computing functionality that ranged from improved interfaces to complete automation. The term "connected" is now being used to describe the addition of an internet connection, using WiFi, Bluetooth, and other technologies. These transformations give products valuable new features, but sometimes their negative impact is less understood. They can challenge social norms, result in government regulation, and the longterm impact to users, especially children, is under increasing scrutiny.

The user experience of new products can be trial by fire. These technologies can disrupt existing industries and markets, but they can be pretty disruptive to user experience as well. Both design flaws and impossible to predict real-world situations contribute to this, so a public product launch becomes a living phase of user research.

REMOVING SOUND—AND PUTTING IT BACK

As mobile phone use grew in the mid-1990s, the need for another way to alert users to incoming calls without disturbing the peace in social contexts led to the Motorola SmartTac being given a silent mode that could be switched to haptic vibrations (see Figure 7-3). This has become standard across all smartphones.

FIGURE 7-3.
A Motorola StarTac phone could be muted by the user, otherwise known as being put into silent mode (Source: ProhibitOnions, Creative Commons Share Alike)

The opposite of the noisy phone intrusion occurred with electric cars. The silence of the Toyota Prius in all-electric mode proved dangerous to nearby pedestrians—who, in a twist of fate, were probably distracted by their smartphones (see Figure 7-4). In 2010, Toyota found that its electric car had caused that type of danger, and responded. They created an onboard sound generator that mimics the sound of an electric motor. According to Toyota's news release at the time, "the sound—aimed to alert but not annoy—rises and falls in pitch relative to the vehicle's speed, thus helping indicate the vehicle's proximity and movement."[1]

FIGURE 7-4.
The Toyota Prius added sound to accommodate social (and safety) norms

Studies of electric vehicles confirmed the difficulties caused by the removal of a key sensory input, in some surprising ways. In the United States, the National Highway and Traffic Administration found that "pedestrian and bicyclist crashes involving both HEVs (hybrid electric vehicles) and ICE (internal combustion engine) vehicles commonly occurred on roadways, in zones with low speed limits, during daytime and in clear weather, with higher incidence rates for HEVs when compared to ICE vehicles."[2] Interestingly, it was in the moments of least predictability, like slow driving, or backing up, that the lack of sound increased collision. If the cars were going in a predictable straight line, having sound made no difference. In moments of uncertainty, sound has an important function as an alert, one that has been

1   Christopher Jensen, "Toyota Prius to Get Sound to Alert Pedestrians," New York Times, August 2010, *https://wheels.blogs.nytimes.com/2010/08/25/toyota-prius-to-get-sound-to-alert-pedestrians/*.

2   U.S. Dept of Transportation, Incidence of Pedestrian and Bicyclist Crashes by Hybrid Electric Passenger Vehicles, *https://crashstats.nhtsa.dot.gov/Api/Public/ViewPublication/811204*.

taken advantage of historically. It must be adjusted periodically as contexts and needs change. A car moving around is a legitimate reason for all nearby people to receive an alert. On the other hand, a bus passenger getting a phone call or message isn't quite as material to personal safety. Violations of social norms or etiquette should be identified early in user research. Safety issues have significant impact, but may be harder to identify and measure, and more complex to resolve. Product teams should be vigilant about unintended impact when introducing or modifying interface modalities—especially in broader social usage contexts.

MAPPING APPS KNOW WHO IS IN THE DRIVER'S SEAT

A thoughtful approach to user needs and active modalities can make or break the success, safety, and adoption of new products. Mobile mapping applications are extremely popular, with usage of Google Maps and Apple Maps in the tens of billions of requests per week. When human safety is at stake, multimodal human–machine interaction must be taken seriously.

Hands-free and eyes-free operation are important modes, as they prioritize the driver's sensory, cognitive, and physical activities, while the device serves a supporting role. While knowing where you are going is pretty important, the safe operation of a two-ton vehicle at highway speeds can be life or death. To enable adequate response time, the just-in-time verbal directions vary based on speed and driving conditions. The directions can be easily ignored and reroute fairly quickly to accommodate both user choice or error.

Beginning Inquiry

When is a multimodal design approach valuable? The answer is all the time. Most personal computing devices are multimodal already and are very often connected to additional devices that enable even more modes. It's simply becoming a standard user expectation and experience. Mobility and specialization of devices means that they are also increasingly used across a wider range of contexts and user behaviors. If someone is unable to look at a screen, they increasingly expect a sound or vibration to help or alert them. On the other hand, voice assistants are now "always on"—they have a special wake up command word, because voice is often used when the device itself is not within arm's reach. Voice, by itself, allows the creation of interactions at farther range from the device—something that haptic modes cannot provide. Blending multiple modes isn't just mashing a whole bunch of screens and sensors together into a minimal glass and metal case. To be effective, it requires a tailored approach that accounts for shifting user expectations and device capabilities, and anticipates the cognitive state of the user and their physical context.

Developing multimodal products can also have many different starting points. It can mean developing a completely new product from scratch within a product category that does not yet exist. It can also mean adding multimodal capabilities to a mature product ecosystem with an international user base and a network of complex platform and partnerships. From either extreme and in between, product teams should start from the same place: the users.

WORKFLOW TO IDENTIFY OPPORTUNITIES

Multimodal design addresses the way people experience physical information and how they begin to apply it back to their own decisions and actions. There are many aspects of a user's needs, behaviors, and contexts to consider. Empathy exercises begin by asking designers to step into the shoes of their users. Multimodal design asks you to step into their eyes, their ears, and their skin. What kind of physical information is available within an experience? How will people need to use it to accomplish their goals? What kinds of previous experiences will shape their expectations and aptitudes? Will they need to develop any specific skills? Develop hypotheses about these aspects of the experience and explore how individual or integrated modalities enable different user responses. Because multimodal design is about products that fit across the shifting contexts of people's lives, much thought and imagination should be centered around focus. Take inspiration from other work. Think experientially. Think conversationally. Think cinematically.

During these initial stages of product development, there are several areas of the user experience to explore for multimodal design considerations. The user, their context, and existing product modalities in the product you intend to replace, or a comparative example, are all good places to start.

Assessing user needs

Does the context of use raise the likelihood of interference? Or could the user be experiencing *situational or permanent disability*? Interference can include the temporary disruption to the user's sensory or physical abilities. Stress, emergency, and even simple daily inconveniences can introduce situational disabilities, both physical and psychological. Noisy environments, like a crowded work or public place, bar, market, or public transportation, can make ringtones difficult to hear. Carrying groceries can make typing a challenge.

Interference can be overcome by amplifying the primary mode, like raising the volume or making letters bigger and brighter. It may also call for the introduction of a secondary *substitute* mode, like enabling haptic vibrations when ringtones are inaudible.

Would users benefit from having optional modes in certain contexts? The ability to switch from ring to vibrate, or shut off alerts with the "Do Not Disturb" setting, makes sense for the way people use smartphones, especially newer features that can detect when someone is driving. They are now always with us, within arm's reach, even as we sleep. Other features like color-shifting screens take cues from our body's natural reactions to daylight, darkness, and sleep. The choice of multiple modes can allow people to use products in ways that are more responsive to their context. Products that support additional modalities within the same focal sense, like both visual scanning and close-up examination, not only strengthen perception but aid in fluid completion of a task.

Would it feel more natural to users to involve another sense or modality? Some existing product technologies have now been surpassed. For a long time, lightweight, portable paper was the optimal material for cartography. Then we figured out lamination, and people could trace their planned routes with erasable markers. Now, digital maps can show the entire world and pretty much read algorithmically tailored routes to us. This enables the interdependencies between navigation and driving to be more seamless.

Do users need to create or maintain focus within another modality? Because people constantly use their hands throughout the day, the hands-free modes of home assistants like the Amazon Echo and Google Home are a natural complement to home activities. Shopping lists can be created while looking through the fridge, or just as you spread the last pat of butter. The addition of another mode can also be used as a reassurance when users need to maintain a flow state in a related activity. The red light on a microphone or tape recorder is meant to be seen peripherally as a sign that it's on and recording. It's an ongoing equipment check that helps users feel confident that they will not miss a thing.

Would the support of an additional modality strengthen perception, deepen understanding, or aid learning and retention? Multimodality can play an important role in activities that require a high level of sensory resolution or where sensory information can be unreliable. People cross-match between modalities to more finely attune their sensory, cognitive, and physical abilities. This is very common in manual tools like drawing or musical instruments and surgical tools that require a high level of hand–eye coordination. Tools like data visualization and physical modeling can powerfully advance our understanding of phenomena like mathematics or chemistry, which exist outside our powers of direct observation. By embodying this information within our sensory modalities, they become more approachable and more likely to be grasped and remembered.

Are there human limitations where technology would be helpful? Thermometers allow us to tell the temperature of things that would burn us. Visual interfaces for sound editing make some auditory properties much more understandable. Infrared cameras are often used at night for security, where human vision fails. The human umvelt is a pretty narrow slice of reality. There is a whole bunch of universe out there.

Are there variations in personal preference for modalities? When checking a melon for ripeness, some people check its color. Some thump it like a drum. Others swear by pressing on the navel, while others go by smell. All of these melon interactions are used to help predict the one sensory characteristic that matters the most: its taste. Some preferences in task modality are straightforward, but there's always more than one way to make a bed. Modalities are living structures within human experience, and while products can be designed to support existing modalities, we are also modifying them or creating new ones throughout our lives.

Would adding novelty to usage be interesting and appropriate?
Sometimes an interesting detail, or even surprise, creates excitement, delight, and appeal. Play, leisure, and rest are crucial to our well being. Play, in particular, is too often overlooked or underestimated. All intelligent animals play; it is important for developing cognitive abilities, not just for children but throughout our lives. The Wii's gesture-based controllers are an easier interface to learn for casual gamers. When launched, it was a surprising breakthrough that convinced many non-gamers of all ages to try it out. It may be tempting to eschew originality in some areas, particularly where playfulness can harm credibility, but it may be surprisingly compelling and beneficial.

Is there an easier, better way for a user to understand and do things?
Sometimes you just have a better idea for how to accomplish a task or convey information. Whether through research, observation, or intuition, ideas happen. This list is not exhaustive, and maybe you don't even know the answers to any of these questions yet, but you simply have a hunch that it might be useful to explore additional senses or modalities. Sometimes just noodling around and plain old trial and error can reveal new design solutions. Because human modality is such an embodied experience, physical prototypes, and open-ended ideation and exploration can reveal a great deal.

Hardware as a Service

Consider hardware as a service. Given the connectivity and the infrastructure that lies behind much hardware, a device itself is simply the tip of the iceberg. What lies underneath? Understanding the broad service goals and opportunities should inform the direction of design.

Alexa is a wonderfully functioning speaker and microphone, and an interesting example of conversational user interface. But beyond that, it is a gateway to Amazon, a vast commercial enterprise of varied offerings. As if that wasn't big enough, through "skills" it is also a gateway to a much greater network of commerce and information. Playing music, telling jokes, keeping a shopping list, hearing the news, calling a ride, and ordering a Domino's pizza all happen through the same voice interface on the same device. But be careful. Learn the lesson of the ill-fated Juicero.

It may also be that the iceberg has many tips. That is, the value of a service, or information is surfaced in many different ways, on different devices. This requires considering all of the different tips in relation to each other. Do you need to build them so that users consider them all parts of the same thing, or is there a need to keep them separate, either because of complexity or distinctiveness? For instance, you may want a dedicated music device with little additional functionality. Or you may hope to sell concert tickets so surfacing artists with upcoming local performances would be valuable.

Combining multimodal and service design can be integral to an overall experience strategy, where a user can develop a brand relationship over several devices, locations, and channels.

Assessing user context

Developing an understanding of product context is critical. What are potential users accustomed to experiencing in specific moments, what are they accustomed to doing, and how do they typically decide to do it? Is there a current object whose role your product will replace? An activity that it will subsume? These are important questions, and because they are so fundamental, there are many design research methods that are used to answer them, usually based on some combination of interview, observation, and empathy.

Context of use analysis and *contextual inquiry* are broad terms for this type of assessment that also includes *context mapping*. These can be expanded upon to include multimodal considerations. *Scenario planning* and *use cases* can also be extended in this way. These can blend concept testing with research that aligns with key modalities. As with any effort that aggregates observation, inquiry, imagination, and empathy, the quality of all the inputs is important. Of course, the time, money, and effort required to have top research will vary greatly between types of work, so developing the approaches that best fit the project scope and resources is necessary.

As we see with the Prius example, it can be important to not only account for product users, but for non-users who share the environment. Not enough people had thought about the noise of an engine as an interaction between driver and pedestrian, but for all these years it functioned as one, playing a definitive role in pedestrian modalities and behaviors. And while it may not matter much to the driver of a car that an electric motor doesn't project the noise of an engine, it sure matters to the pedestrians who need to avoid a moving hunk of metal. Products can have broad and unexpected impact on social relationships and public contexts, and vice versa.

Assessing changes to existing product modes

A quick assessment of multimodal impact can start with asking which of a few types of changes you will be making: adding a new mode to existing product, augmenting existing product modes, replacing a mode in an existing product, or innovating a new type of multimodal product.

Adding a new mode to an existing product is probably the easiest change to grasp. The new device doesn't just blink—now it also beeps! This can be done for a number of reasons. Additional modes can extend the types of response loops and interactions available to a user. They can extend the range or resolution of an interaction to increase the quality or richness of an experience. Substitution modes provide accommodation around situational or permanent disability or support modality preferences.

Augmenting an existing mode in a product can require some comparison between human modalities. Cognitive load, learning periods, and response times can change significantly. For instance, when street crossing signs went from simply Walk/Don't Walk to offering a countdown timer, they granted extra information to pedestrians and drivers (see Figure 7-5). However, this little bit of information introduced more complex decision making for everyone as well, which may not have been a net benefit. A simple "yes" or "no" decision—"Should I keep going?"—became one that required pedestrians and drivers to calculate their speed and trajectory, increasing sensory and cognitive load. It's still yet to be decided conclusively whether this one addition has made for safer crosswalks, as test results vary from city to city.

FIGURE 7-5.
The information in a
countdown timer at
a crosswalk informs
decision making but
adds cognitive load

Replacing a mode completely can be a dramatic shift. Because of the time and effort invested in creating existing skills and how effortless they feel as they become more non-aware behaviors, replacement modalities need to offer immediate value or at least clear potential. They may even need to be "insanely great," depending on how invested people are in their preceding experiences. These shifts may not require a great deal of product development effort. However, it's user effort in behavioral change and learning that can be the decisive factor.

New modes can be developed for a number of reasons, but they can be powerful drivers of innovation. The GUI introduced a new type of haptic mode to users and unlocked the personal computing revolution. The touchscreen introduced gesture-based haptics and enabled the mobile wave of computing. Human modalities shape our ability to adopt new technologies. Harnessing their power has played a major role in how quickly new technologies become a part of our lives.

Adding and Augmenting Modes within the Same Product

Adding and augmenting modes strongly improved the experience with the Nest Protect (see Figure 7-6). The typical low battery "chirp" was replaced with a changing colored light that indicated the power level without being as disruptive to sleep. A spoken alert replaced the usual startling blare, significantly improving the experience and providing users with the additional detail of where the smoke was detected.

FIGURE 7-6.
The Nest Protect added and augmented modes to provide greater actionable context to users

Summary

The pace of technological development means that identifying new opportunities and deciding which are worth pursuing can be dizzying. Starting with an assessment of user needs, user contexts, and current product modes presents a reliable way of finding opportunities to develop or update products. Similar to the ways humans function, many new IoT technologies can be categorized by abilities to monitor, analyze and decide, and control and respond. Conceptually matching technologies with human functioning helps us assess their new possibilities in the probable context of human use and make good design assessments.

[8]

The Elements of Multimodal Design

In Osaka, the subway system, like any other, connects a number of stations all around the city (see Figure 8-1). What is unique is that a different song plays at each stop. Each station has its own melody, allowing people to hear when and where they are getting off. This is especially important in a city where many people catnap during their commute. The station arrival songs double as a kind of spatial alarm clock—for arrival at a place, not a specific time. The world is an easier place when one's location in it is thoughtfully but memorably communicated.

FIGURE 8-1.
Subways in Osaka, Japan, play a different tune for each stop, subtly alerting zoned out or sleeping passengers that their station is near (Source: Tennen-Gas, Creative Commons Share Alike)

The physical world is pretty self-evident to us. We can sense the ocean is nearby from the smell of salt and the sound of waves. We know that coffee is almost ready by the smell wafting from the kitchen. When we start to shiver and feel uncomfortable, we put on a sweater. We do a reasonably good job of figuring out what is going on around us. There are many different kinds of sensory information, and we use them in many different ways.

Using Physical Information

There are many different ways to tell when someone is attracted to you. Their pupils may dilate, making their eyes appear darker or more deeply colored. They may stand up taller or blink more often. They may stand up taller or blink more often. They may stand closer to you, or touch you (refer back to Figure 1-18, back in Chapter 1). They may touch their hair, smooth down their clothes, or other preening activities. Whether they like you or not, people recognize faces by the proportions between features. We can tell milk is sour by smell—we don't even have to taste it.

Each of these bits of sensory information is a *cue*. When we are trying to find out a specific aspect about what is going on around us, we use different kinds of cues. For depth perception, we use several types of cues. *Occlusion*, or whether one object blocks our ability to see other objects, is one type of distance cue (see Figure 8-2). Some studies suggest that the vestibular system—providing our sense of movement and balance—is also critical to depth perception. Our ability to feel gravity may affect our visual perception of distance.[1]

---

1 Ágoston Török , Elisa Raffaella Ferrè , Elena Kokkinara, Valéria Csépe, David Swapp, and Patrick Haggard, "Up, Down, Near, Far: An Online Vestibular Contribution to Distance Judgement," PLoS ONE, January 2017, *https://doi.org/10.1371/journal.pone.0169990.*

FIGURE 8-2.
Occlusion informs the perception of distance

Graphic designers have intuited this for decades, but it has been confirmed in perceptual psychology studies: we use the breaks between letters and words to pace our eye movements while reading. While the glyphs themselves contain linguistic information, the whitespace between them enables our reading modality; we use it to establish the rhythm of reading (see Figure 8-3). This is not just a matter of personal taste or aesthetic. It's how we turn on and off visual processing during eye movement to prevent motion sickness in our close-focus visual activities.

FIGURE 8-3.
Whitespace, even when it's gray, helps establish the rhythm necessary for reading

Similarly, in spoken language, the stressors—an element of prosody characterized by emphasis through volume, enunciation, or rhythm—help listeners break apart strings of sounds into individual words.[2] Poets and dramatists knew this and used poetic meter to improve the flow of spoken poems or theatrical dialogue. It's now a part of the markup language for designing speech interactions too. We use outlines to recognize familiar shapes and objects, which iconographers and illustrators understand very well to create simple graphics that are still recognizable. Across all of our senses and modalities there are cues that apply to specific activities and behaviors. This means that certain types of sensory cues are more important than others, depending on modality and the user's purpose. When creating *icons*, *earcons*, and *hapticons*—and any design element for that matter—there are certain sensory details that people really seek out and need to successfully sense and analyze information.

Across many of our senses and modalities, time is an important piece of information. Within vision, time helps us understand movement. In hearing, the difference between when each ear receives a sound helps position its source. In touch and proprioception, it helps us guide our own movements and our position relative to objects around us. It's often an overlooked design detail, but one that traverses all of our experiences in critical ways.

Constructing Knowledge, Interactions, and Narratives

Like with Legos, we use different types of sensory stimuli to construct our experience of reality. The scent of freshly cut grass, a warm breeze, and the dazzlingly bright sunshine tell us that it's going to be a beautiful summer day. We grab our swimsuits and head to the beach. The smell of smoke wafting from the oven, the blare of the smoke detector, and the rumble in our bellies may tell us it's time to order takeout for dinner—and fast. We hear the alarm clock, feel a little disoriented, but

---

2   Keith Rayner and Charles Clifton, Jr., "Language Processing in Reading and Speech Perception is Fast and Incremental: Implications for Event Related Potential Research," Biological Psychology, January 2009.

the bed is so warm and the pillow is so fluffy. So we hit the snooze button. Each moment of our lives, we are taking a cross-sample across all of our senses to figure out what is going on and what to do next.

But these sensory stimuli are always relative to what we have experienced already and what we are trying to accomplish. For one person the smell of freshly cut grass might mean that it's time to take allergy medicine. In another context, a smoking dinner might mean barbeque. How we use the information defines its value, and there are several different ways to use it (see Figure 8-4).

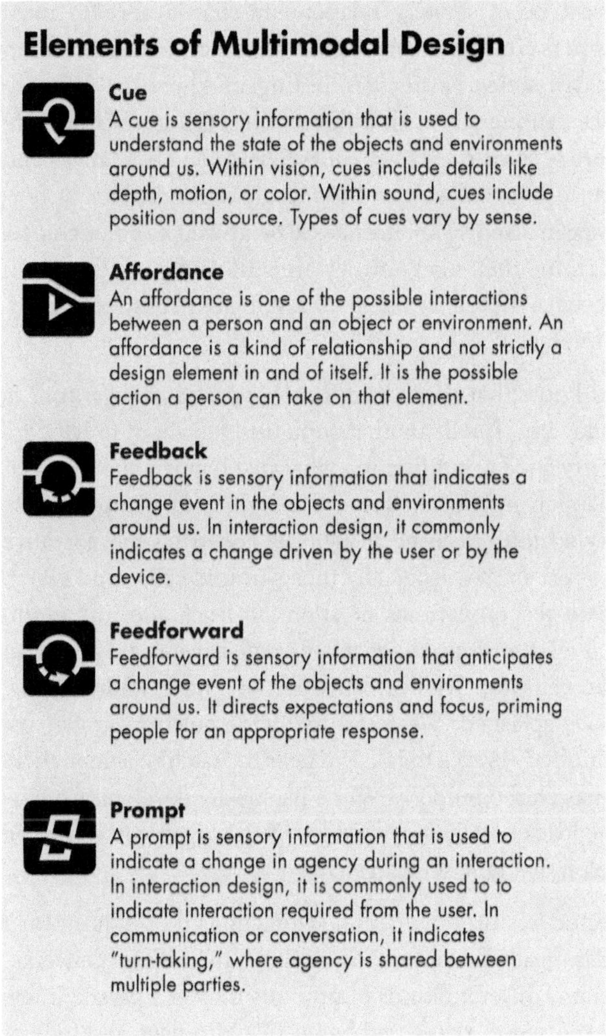

Elements of Multimodal Design

Cue
A cue is sensory information that is used to understand the state of the objects and environments around us. Within vision, cues include details like depth, motion, or color. Within sound, cues include position and source. Types of cues vary by sense.

Affordance
An affordance is one of the possible interactions between a person and an object or environment. An affordance is a kind of relationship and not strictly a design element in and of itself. It is the possible action a person can take on that element.

Feedback
Feedback is sensory information that indicates a change event in the objects and environments around us. In interaction design, it commonly indicates a change driven by the user or by the device.

Feedforward
Feedforward is sensory information that anticipates a change event of the objects and environments around us. It directs expectations and focus, priming people for an appropriate response.

Prompt
A prompt is sensory information that is used to indicate a change in agency during an interaction. In interaction design, it is commonly used to to indicate interaction required from the user. In communication or conversation, it indicates "turn-taking," where agency is shared between multiple parties.

FIGURE 8-4.
The elements of multimodal design are used to inform, guide, and reinforce how users sense, understand, decide, and act

Cues are a type of sensory relationship that help us understand what is happening around us and to recognize objects and environments. We can look at a house plant and see that it is a bit droopy. It probably needs some water. We can look at dog, and by its size, coat, and shape, we can tell it's a Yorkshire Terrier and not a Great Dane. We can listen to water and tell the difference between rainfall, waterfall, and ocean waves. Through repeated experiences, we learn to use sensory information in different ways. We use cues to recognize our car from similar cars. They help us to construct new knowledge and understanding, and to remember that knowledge when we repeat an experience.

Affordances are a type of sensory relationship that is perhaps most familiar to designers. Introduced by Donald Norman to design, affordances are *perceived action possibilities*, letting us know the different ways in which we can interact with different objects and environmental features. There is some overlap of course, between affordances and cues. If we want to know if we can lift a dog, we might look at how large it is. But we can also use an animal's size, as well as other characteristics, to determine their age—if they are still young or full grown (which is then a cue). Affordances help us develop our abilities by guiding the way we interact.

Feedback lets us know that something has happened. *Feedforward* is real life foreshadowing. It tells us that something is about to happen. Humans are pretty good at confirming what just happened or predicting what will happen next when given the right information. These kinds of sensory stimuli are used to help us construct the narrative aspects of our experiences—especially those around cause and effect. In activities where response times or attention levels are important, the sequence and relationships between connected events are powerful drivers of human behavior. We hear the crash of a wave, and we know we are about to be splashed. We feel a foot slide out from under us, and the rest of our body braces to fall. We hear the latch of a door click, and we know it has closed properly. When people are developing a new physical skill, feedback and feedforward can play a big role in ensuring that people develop that new skill correctly.

Prompts are specific to shifts in agency, interactions that require turn taking in communication, control, or activity. In human conversations there are many different kinds of prompts that let a person know when they are expected to speak and listen. We also have all kinds of nonverbal language to manage how to hand objects to each other, lift sofas together, and pass each other the ball during a game of hoops. Because humans are social creatures, we have a wide vocabulary of prompts around these kinds of exchanges. These are beginning to become more important in the design of assistive or automated products or interfaces like voice where turn taking is required.

Summary

Designers use different types of sensory stimuli to help users to understand, decide, and act. These elements can be categorized as cues, affordances, feedback, feedforward, and prompts. Thoughtful use of them is the basis of good multimodal design.

[9]

Modeling Modalities and Mapping User Experiences

"Don't design things. Design behaviors."
NAOTO FUKASAWA

How is it that one person may thrive by doing several things simultaneously and then barely stay awake doing only one? How can people struggle to stay in their seat during a meeting, but be glued to their sofa during a Netflix binge? Paying attention can be effortless or exhausting. Some activities require deep focus on one thing, while some require distributing attention across a few. Some activities heighten the senses, while some dull or confuse them. Focus is critical to difficult activities like brain surgery, rocket science, or driving with kids and dogs in the backseat. Distraction can be dangerous, and interruption is becoming a growing issue with the quality of experiences and life in general.

Multimodal product design emphasizes focus, behavior, and context to enable users to accomplish their goals. Product experiences should enable the right level of focus, provide the right functionality or information to support user activity, or simply get out of the way, depending on the situation. Understanding how perception and cognition contribute to those experiences is an important step in the process.

Multimodal experiences have many intangible layers, like user behaviors, contextual factors, and cross-modal transitions. These aspects of product design are perhaps not as concrete or as easily valued as that slick new locking hinge mechanism that uses supermagnets. They are all the more necessary to understand because they can be so elusive, nuanced, and complex. The design of multimodal interactions is a form of systems design, which tends to be used in a more open-ended and flexible way. There are generally also a lot more moving parts to the experience.

These kinds of interactions are responsive to ever-changing dynamics across context, user need, and real-time events. To design for them requires a shift, similar to that described by Donella H. Meadows and Diana Wright in their introduction to systems thinking: "Dynamic systems studies usually are not designed to predict what will happen. Rather, they're designed to explore what would happen, if a number of driving factors unfold in a range of different ways."[1] To be able to provide the range of interactions, it's important for designers to be able to identify the driving factors and how they will converge during an experience. Multimodal designers do so much more than simply decide whether people hear, see, or touch a user interface. They need to think about what experiences are most likely and why, and then determine which modes will be most appropriate across several possible use cases.

Behaviors Shared Between Users and Devices

With assistant-style applications, automated functionality, and the conversational nature of speech recognition and other modalities, our devices behave more responsively. To design responsiveness, rules must be established and documented. And like many other things, rules are designed. They aren't just procedural triggers for interactions; they can express empathy to the user and earn trust for a device. It's kind of like setting up a good working relationship or service.

The expanding physical presence of connected devices also means that environmental and physical factors, such as those typically addressed in industrial design or architecture, must also be considered for interaction design. At a high level, well-integrated behavioral and context models help identify, integrate, and prioritize these factors with UI considerations and apply them to solutions.

The dynamics between modalities, contexts, device activities, and user goals are key to creating multimodal experiences that work. Models and diagrams illustrate these kinds of dynamics and systemic considerations and can play a larger role in specifying multimodal experiences than other forms of interaction design. They help teams identify design considerations, ask the right questions, establish priorities, and structure experiences.

---

1 Donella H. Meadows and Diana Wright, *Thinking in Systems: A Primer*, p. 46.

Because too many details can sometimes defeat the purpose of clear team communication, different types of diagrams focus on particular aspects of the experience. Sequential activities are often shown with journey or experience maps, while focus and input/output diagrams can help make human and device factors easier to understand and to keep top of mind.

Demanding Contexts and Complex Interactions Call for Alignment

Take the GoPro. The tiny, sturdy camera has been taken on a space jump, a Formula 1 race, and to the top of Mt. Everest. Its designers build simple, rugged interfaces that can even be used with gloves. These unpredictable contexts require the same level of industrial design that allowed, say, the Hasselblad camera to take pictures on the moon during the Apollo missions. Space is an unforgiving environment to design for, but extreme sports enthusiasts can be pretty tough on their gear, too.

Other examples abound. The greater connectivity offered these days means that a multimodal interaction can take place across several devices working together. For example, smart locks and the location-based protocol, iBeacon, work together with a user's smartphone to determine their proximity, and then respond appropriately based on a number of different factors and the availability of certain kinds of customer data. Depending on settings and conditions, a smart lock may prompt someone for a code to unlock the door or simply open by itself when it senses the homeowner. The iBeacon does things like sending you location-based marketing messages when you're near the right store in the mall.

Interactions may be between devices that all belong to a single user, among several users, or between users and a multichannel brand or service. The interface of a shared device must accommodate multiple users, or multiple devices must work together. Social interactions require a nuanced understanding of fluid social relationships, dynamics, and communication, and often entail systems designing around permissions, privacy, roles, and turn taking. Mapping the sharing, networking, users, and systems to each other requires planning and coordination that can be difficult to do at the interface level.

Payment technologies enabled with near-field communication (NFC) sometimes allow a specific physical gesture to replace a heavily secured multistep authentication and financial transaction. While there has yet to be one common default gesture, explorations of "bumping" or waving to pay have been used.

It's easy to see how teams working on products like these need ways to keep all that interactivity straight. Done right, the process of mapping draws teams together to share insight and vision, as well as align on common goals. This book supplements common design models with additional factors based on the needs of multimodal product design and introduces a few new ones.

Experience Maps and Models for Multimodality

It's a good idea to enter the mapping or modeling process with a clear, shared objective in mind, at least for what you're hoping to address. How much of the user experience, device activity, or extended network resources are you hoping to capture in the map?

DIFFERENT MAPS COVER DIFFERENT SCOPES AND DETAILS

The difference between types of maps is often a question of story, scope, and fidelity. What is the experience you're describing, how much detail is helpful, and which variables are most important to the experience? The following are common ways to map user experiences that are also used in multimodal design, with a few variations. Multimodality calls for a few additional facets to be incorporated, kind of like additional pins or layers on a Google map.

Some design maps and models don't change very much and should be familiar. The following can be used for multimodal interactions in the same way they would normally be used, with the addition of some multimodal considerations. Multimodal design adds a few others that aren't as commonly used (see Table 9-1).

FAMILIAR MODELS		
TYPES	PURPOSE	MULTIMODAL CONSIDERATIONS
Scenarios, treatments and user stories ("happy" and "exception" paths are sometimes broken out individually)	Vignettes to identify user needs, and to explore opportunities for a product to help fulfill them	User goals, requirements, and behaviors, as well as environmental contexts and conditions, with attention to multimodality.
Storyboards	Image-based flows that show the story of product use, illustrating contexts, goals, and meaningful moments.	Narrative structure and event quality from the user's point of view **Focus requirements:** focal, peripheral, interruptive, and filtered modalities, etc. **Modality characteristics:** sequence; continuity; interruptions or distractions, etc. **Multimodal user behaviors:** sensing, understanding, deciding, acting **Multimodal product behaviors:** monitor, analyze, decide, respond and control
Experience map (also journey map)	Understand a user's experience over time to identify relevant goals, hurdles, decisions, and attitudes.	Align product and user behavior to reach goals, from a bird's eye view **Focus requirements:** focal, peripheral, interruptive, and filtered modalities **Modality characteristics:** sequence; continuity; interruptions or distractions, etc. **Multimodal user behaviors:** sensing, understanding, deciding, acting **Multimodal product behaviors:** monitor, analyze, decide, respond, and control

TYPES	PURPOSE	MULTIMODAL CONSIDERATIONS
Ecosystem maps	Maps interdependencies between device, information, social, physical, and other systems that are relevant to the experience. Used to inform technology, device, platform, information, service, and other architectures.	Contextual considerations, including environments, infrastructures, norms, user segmentation, and other shared resources, standards, or characteristics
Decision trees	Capture all meaningful possibilities and paths to ensure comprehensive designs. Mainly used as reference, not for communicating vision or user empathy.	Shifts in agency, contextual interaction triggers, how transitions and interruptions are managed

MULTIMODAL-SPECIFIC MODELS

TYPES	PURPOSE
Context map	Understand physical, social and institutional, and device and information contexts. May be about one or all of these, or other type of context when deemed important.
Keyframes or animatics	Show significant moments and transitions within an experience to understand a flow, without having to yet fill in all the dots. Include user building blocks: sensing, understanding, deciding, acting, and device building blocks: monitor, analyze, decide, respond and control.
Focus model	Assess where a user's concentration lies and depth of engagement, throughout an experience and how it needs to be supported. Prioritize focal, peripheral, substitute, interruptive, and filtered stimuli.
Input/output map	Asses all input and output modalities, noting focal, peripheral, substitute, interruptive, and filtered stimuli.

Key Considerations of Multimodal Design

Modeling product experiences with a multimodal approach will usually contain several important differences, mostly rooted in the senses and how we use them. The following are some of the design factors that may need to be understood when constructing a model or map of a multimodal user experience.

MODALITIES AND SENSES

What are the modalities of an experience or activity and which are dominant at any given point? Knowing this can tell you a lot about user expectations, habits, as well as what is needed to support the experience. We can start to think about the category of activity, like whether it is orientative, social, athletic, expressive, or analytical. Those are non-exclusive categories, and you may go much further in your definitions of them, but starting high level and then digging deeper is often a good way to proceed.

FOCUS

What is the most important sense or cognitive activity occurring? How do you manage the amount of information, choice, or activity possible? What are the consequences of minor or major disruptions? If a typist loses track of what they were typing, they might lose an elusive thought; but if a driver loses track of the road and cars around them, they might just lose their life. Whether the interface itself should be the focal point of an experience becomes one of the most important questions a designer should ask. It's a profound shift from designing for engagement or "stickiness."

Despite designing some of the most iconic objects of the 20th century, Dieter Rams believed that, "Space does not exist for objects, space exists for people." We can apply the same humanist principle to preserving mental space.

LEVEL OF FOCUS AND ENGAGEMENT DEPTH

Every type of product requires varied depths of engagement. At the dead simple end, it's just on and off, engaged or disengaged. On the more complex end of the spectrum, there are always-on devices, ready to subtly adjust their contribution and accommodate varied user engagement. Their useful presence may shift from ambient to deeply engaging, depending on the moment's needs.

Even the dead simple end has a twist: when someone is using a product for the first time, and learning how to use it. Take a hammer. Most people get that you hold it from the light end and whack things with the heavy end. It still takes a little time to figure out the right swing. For more complex products, the learning curve can be steeper and require even more consideration. It might be worth modeling this learning curve as a way of understanding and possibly reducing the initial complexity.

Where will the high and low points for your product engagement occur? What kind of attention does each state call for from the user, and in which modalities will they occur? Are there points where the user will be have difficulty keeping focus, and is this caused by internal or external factors? What are the demands on a user's attention at the deep end? Will they need to stop whatever else they are doing? Will the engagement require focus throughout product use, or can it become a more routine and effortless habit over time? This is often the case with tasks like setting preferences, initiating activities like phone calls, or deciding which music to play. Hence the popularity of default settings, stored phone numbers, and playlists or automatic music stations: they ease some of that cognitive load, and thus the strain of engagement depth.

CONTINUITY

A sense of continuity, that sequential events are tied together, is essential to most experiences. It helps us feel in control and allows us to focus within our thoughts and activities. Causality, an understanding of why and how events unfold, contributes to continuity by assembling information into events and events into narratives. When experience counters expectation, we may feel surprised or disoriented and have difficulty responding appropriately. Repeated disruptions to continuity can cause a person to abandon an experience.

SEQUENCE

As we've seen, a baseball pitcher executing a standard pitch follows a sequence of windup, early cocking, late cocking, acceleration, and follow-through. As with a pitch, the sequence of activities in many multimodal experiences is important. One step leads to the other, especially in that realm between mental and physical, where habits and non-aware activities ("muscle memory") reside. In these kinds of procedural activities, later steps depend on those that came before them to make sense or work effectively.

SHIFTS

When circumstances call for changes in focus, it's known as a shift. Providing ways to mentally or physically shift out of a sequence, and back in, can reduce friction enormously. Even though shifts occur naturally, and more frequently in our era of connected distractions, it's not ideal. Attention switching has costs. "A state of continual partial attention is basically a state of reduced cognitive activity, and that has a large cognitive cost," notes professor of computer science and author Cal Newport, whose work has focused recently on "deep thinking" and how to overcome distractions.

FLOW AND HABITS

Flow is the state of being immersed and focused on an activity. Habits are how people approach an activity in repeatable ways so that doing them becomes nearly automatic. How much does your device support an activity that is likely to be best experienced as a flow? One main determinant is how expert the user already is or will become. If they are already expert, or have strongly developed habits, it may be important to consider how willing and able a person might be to change existing behaviors. It's true what they say: old habits die hard.

INTERRUPTIONS

Sequences may be disrupted beyond the user's ability to shift smoothly in and out of them. Required sensory input may be impeded, or events requiring attention may pop up. The user might remember something suddenly or simply become tired and unable to maintain a flow state. Whether from external factors or from the internal state of the user, unexpected breaks in a product experience call for smooth recovery, exit, and re-entry. In some cases of surprise or danger, this smoothness is not just a buffer for the quality of the experience. It can help reduce certain kinds of startle response, allowing users to respond to sudden change in a calmer and more rational way.

SUBSTITUTIONS

There are many cases where the most common way to interact in an experience may not be available. Situational, temporary, and permanent disabilities are experienced in one form or another by everyone fairly regularly. A person's hands are filled with groceries. The majority of people have some form of vision loss. We all need alternative methods of doing things when we hit up against our own limitations or when contextual factors are working against us. Anticipating these kinds of experience blockages, designers can create options to provide flexibility and avoid complete disruption. Many devices handle this by creating redundancy of information: flashing alerts and buzzers; a vibration, screen message, and alert sound. (That last triple threat can sometimes be an interruption more than a substitution.)

In many cases, a well-developed substitution strategy can address both variations in preferences and situational, temporary, and permanent disability. This hybrid approach is especially useful for products with large and diverse user groups. Closed captioning works great whether you can't hear your favorite show because the upstairs neighbors started tap dancing, or because your ears have been damaged from too much rock 'n roll, or because of permanent hearing loss. The discoverability of alternative modalities can prove challenging, depending on how often it is needed by varying user groups.

SPECIALIZED INTEGRATION

There are special combinations of multiple modalities that are well understood and are deeply innate to human behaviors. There are also specific categories of activity that call for unique modality combinations. In these combinations, like audiovisual, or haptic tool use, the way that sensory information, decision making, and action are so tightly interwoven means they need to be considered together. Take the example of language—some people mouth words while they are reading or writing, which enhances comprehension. Taste and smell combine to create our experience of flavor. Our sense of touch extends into tools when we use them frequently.

This integration can often occur on a non-aware level—especially around highly developed skills, which can also be difficult for people to describe, separate, or even remember correctly. This can require user research techniques that learn more heavily on observatoin than on self-assessment, like surveys or interviews.

KNOWLEDGE AND SKILL

Is there any special knowledge or skill necessary to perform a task in the experience? Is the device designed to accommodate all level of expertise, or does it bias toward a certain range? Are there different products altogether for the novice and expert? Does it reward improvement or reflect growing expertise by unlocking additional possibilities or removing some guidance? If it was made for users who are already experts, what are their habits, preferences, unique skills, and expectations?

KEY CONTEXTS IN MULTIMODAL EXPERIENCES

Context is a broad concept, and it's up to designers and their teams to understand which part of any situation is relevant to a product experience. It can be helpful to think about context as layers of an experience. Designers often need to consider physical and environmental contexts, social and institutional ones, and device and information ones.

Physical and environmental context

Put simply, the senses exist as a way to know where we are and what's happening in and around us. Supporting them in that capacity, as well as considering how any change in contexts might affect how they function, is important.

A voice-based interface is designed much differently for indoor and mobile usage. Indoors is relatively quiet and power is readily available, supporting the always on, always listening mode. If it is portable and intended to be used outside in crowded places, always on would drain the battery, and the noise might cause mistaken commands and interruptions.

Social and institutional context

We are social beings, and our technologies are also—and they are becoming more so. Designing products encodes a host of assumptions, expectations, and behaviors that are shaped by, and in turn affect, social norms. When a product is released and put into use, we often see very quickly if it has risen to the occasion or not, so spending time to get that right beforehand is useful. Pundits may debate why Google Glass seemed to fail, but it's no surprise that a hidden camera focused straight on you in any context would be at least a little awkward. The SnapChat Spectacles, on the other hand, were less visibly high-tech and more playful and toy-like in their design.

Settings like households, offices, and public spaces all have different social structures and expectations. Outside of personal zones, more social interactions happen, intended or not, and that's an important consideration for safety and privacy. In addition, those people around the experience, with no direct interaction, may also be impacted.

How much privacy should any participant in a particular setting expect, and does the device affect that? There are laws and practices that address these questions in different settings. Are you an employer making a recording of employees? Video might be legal, but sound recording probably isn't. Interactivity often carries norms and regulations, software encodes them, and devices physically embody them. Knowing the expectations for any setting is a good practice.

Device and information context

Which other devices, information, and processing resources are a part of the experience? While still somewhat choppy because of permissions, network reliability, and the explosive proliferation of devices and their smart apps, interaction between devices is becoming more common, and user expectations of a smooth experience are higher than ever. We want our wireless speaker system to sync with our smartphone, our television, and even our shopping list. The chain of connectivity and dependencies is steadily growing longer.

Mapping diagrams are unlikely to illustrate all of the information in an experience, but they should highlight the important ones, as well as drawing out key user or device needs, based on time, context, and coordination. The point is to get those important factors in mind for thinking and discussion. If the experience might unfold in more complex ways based on multiple factors, other documents like business rules can describe that complexity in detail.

Events and Experience Models

Most of us use the word *event* pretty loosely, but some recent work by psychologists brings together psychology and neuroscience to establish some precision around the term, as well as the mechanisms that establish how events are perceived and processed by our brains. "Events," write Gabriel A. Radvansky and Jeffrey M. Zacks "are one of the most important classes of entities in our everyday psychology. They are the 'things' of experience just as much as objects, sounds, and people." Referring to internal models that our minds create to understand events, Radvansky and Zacks use the term *experience model* to describe "event models derived from live, interactive experience. Experience models are representations of events derived from perceptual-motor experience, such as our own interaction with the world, television, film, and virtual reality technologies."This work can help us see just how users understand what's happening throughout an experience and how they might develop familiarity and aptitude with new products. It also helps place human understanding of sense-based experiences in context with other types. By understanding the way people tend to organize clusters of experiences in time, it becomes easier to identify the natural beginnings, endings, and segues. It's also possible to establish design patterns using the rhythm—an important aspect of the way we experience time—to establish priority, continuity, and certain forms of engagement momentum and focus within an experience.

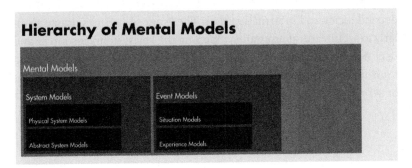

Hierarchy of Mental Models

Mental Models

System Models

Physical System Models

Abstract System Models

Event Models

Situation Models

Experience Models

FIGURE 9-1.
Radvansky and Zacks' hierarchy of mental models, with event models split between situation and experience models. Situation models are events based on language and in their view probably share most of the properties of experience models. System models represent the understanding of how a functional system works, divided between physical systems like devices, or abstractions like math theories.

Example Maps and Models

Because the range of experiences and interactions covered by multimodal design is so broad, the diagrams a design team requires will vary. We've included some broad types and examples here.

EXPERIENCE MAP: TRANSITIONAL FLOW

When there is are transitions between modalities, a diagram of those transitions is helpful. This is a time-based, sequential map. Task modalities can appear as swim lanes, with the main types of sensory data feeding them as the user moves through the experience. Your device may or may not be in all the swim lanes; it might be the star at any moment, or it might not, as it might play different roles at different times, allowing people to focus on aspects of the task they perform alone and those which are supported by the device. A tighter variation on this is an internal map, which describes a user's decision points. This could also be a starting point from which a more comprehensive map is built that also reflects external factors (see Figure 9-2).

ECOSYSTEM MAP

When it's important to get a sense of the information, processing, devices, and other kinds of resources utilized in the experience, an ecosystem map can help make those very clear (see Figure 9-3). The important goal is to illustrate a functional symbiosis, in this case drawing out dependencies and information flow. These are sometimes drawn similarly to architectural programs, mapping the key systems resources and user needs and behaviors to each other. These focus less on designing multimodal experience, but are used to help inform device, platform, or service architectures of multimodal experiences.

CONTEXT MAP

A context map is a way of visualizing and resolving the dynamic external factors in which your product may operate (see Figure 9-4). At the start of this chapter we listed some key contexts, including physical, social and institutional, and device and information contexts. Depending on what you're hoping to illustrate, you might include one or more of these. One might play a stronger more prominent role than another in shaping the experience. For instance, resources needed and their availability spans both device and physical contexts. Does your device require a regular recharge? How will that work? Are you making a device that includes voice commands? How will that work in different physical contexts? Will people feel awkward engaging that function with others around them? Will those others around them feel put upon?

FOCUS MODEL

Where is a person's attention within an experience, and what are the details of the senses they are using to achieve that focus? The dimensionality, range, and resolution of the senses, as described in Chapter 2, are important points to consider for the practicalities of a focused sense experience. It is equally important to document the points of focus necessary to achieve the overall goals of an experience, even when they don't align exactly with your product. In other words, if it's crucial for a user to stay focused on a separate task, either fully or intermittently, then charting just what they need to focus on will help you best understand your device's part of the experience and its restraints (see Figure 9-5). Early makers of mobile apps were probably not considering what happens when someone wanted to use their app while driving. But as they grew in popularity, it became clear that they were likely to be used by drivers.

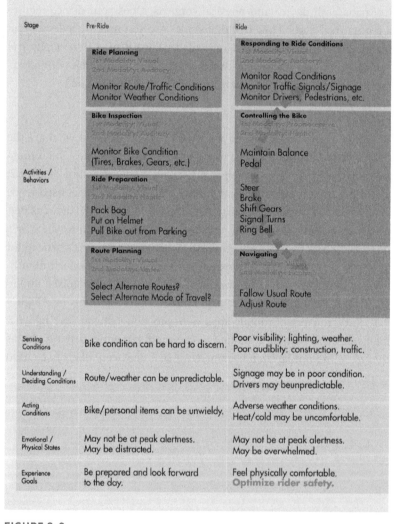

Biking to Work

Stage	Pre-Ride		Ride	
	Ride Planning 1st Modality: Visual 2nd Modality: Auditory Monitor Route/Traffic Conditions Monitor Weather Conditions		**Responding to Ride Conditions** 1st Modality: Visual 2nd Modality: Auditory Monitor Road Conditions Monitor Traffic Signals/Signage Monitor Drivers, Pedestrians, etc.	
Activities / Behaviors	**Bike Inspection** 1st Modality: Visual 2nd Modality: Auditory Monitor Bike Condition (Tires, Brakes, Gears, etc.)		**Controlling the Bike** 1st Modality: Proprioceptive 2nd Modality: Haptic Maintain Balance Pedal	
	Ride Preparation 1st Modality: Visual 2nd Modality: Haptic Pack Bag Put on Helmet Pull Bike out from Parking		Steer Brake Shift Gears Signal Turns Ring Bell	
	Route Planning 1st Modality: Visual 2nd Modality: Verbal Select Alternate Routes? Select Alternate Mode of Travel?		**Navigating** 1st Modality: Visual 2nd Modality: Verbal Follow Usual Route Adjust Route	
Sensing Conditions	Bike condition can be hard to discern.		Poor visibility: lighting, weather. Poor audiblity: construction, traffic.	
Understanding / Deciding Conditions	Route/weather can be unpredictable.		Signage may be in poor condition. Drivers may beunpredictable.	
Acting Conditions	Bike/personal items can be unwieldy.		Adverse weather conditions. Heat/cold may be uncomfortable.	
Emotional / Physical States	May not be at peak alertness. May be distracted.		May not be at peak alertness. May be overwhelmed.	
Experience Goals	Be prepared and look forward to the day.		Feel physically comfortable. Optimize rider safety.	

FIGURE 9-2.

Experience map

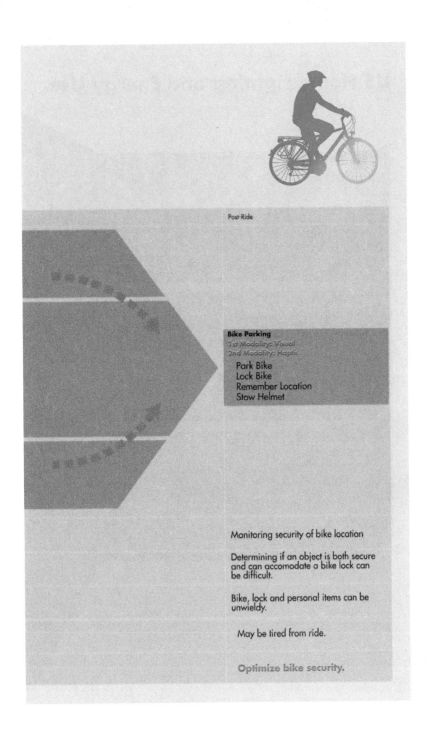

Post-Ride

Bike Parking
1st Modality: Visual
2nd Modality: Haptic

Park Bike
Lock Bike
Remember Location
Stow Helmet

Monitoring security of bike location

Determining if an object is both secure and can accomodate a bike lock can be difficult.

Bike, lock and personal items can be unwieldy.

May be tired from ride.

Optimize bike security.

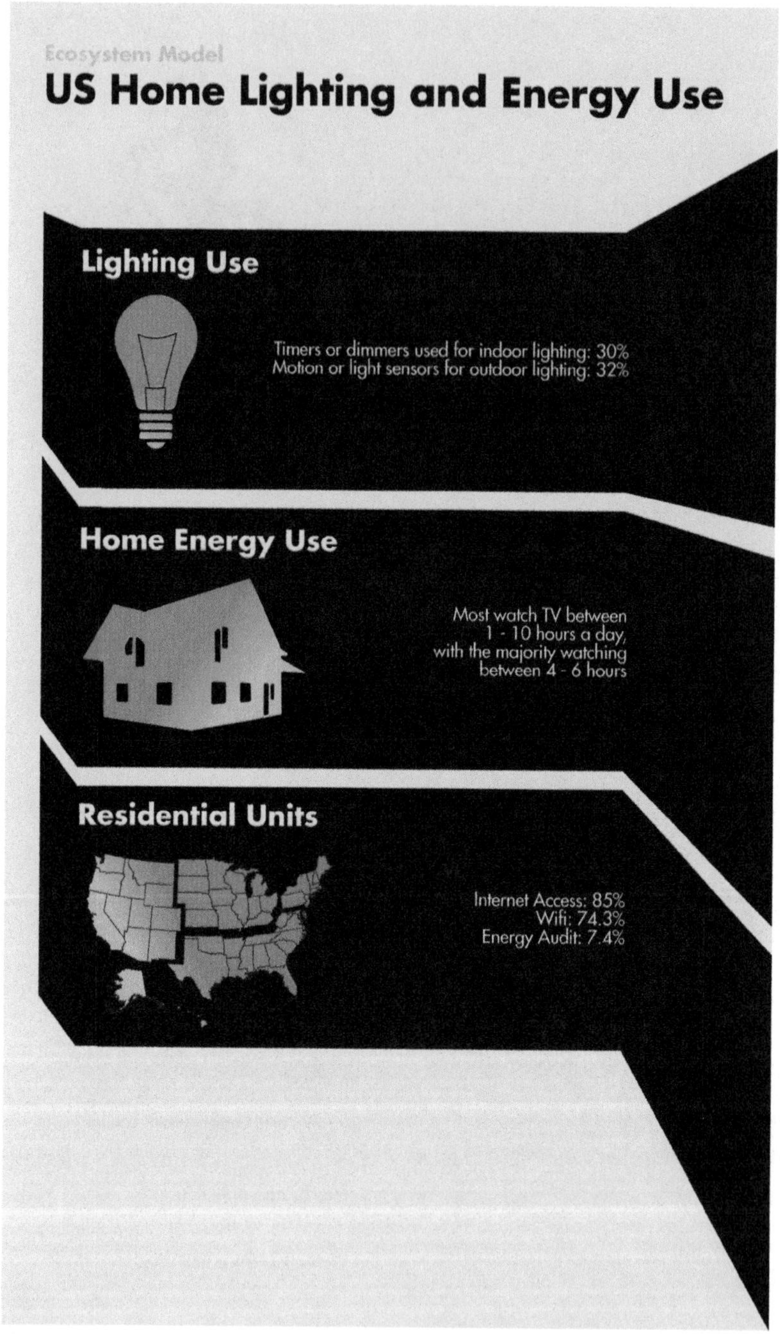

FIGURE 9-3.
Ecosystem map

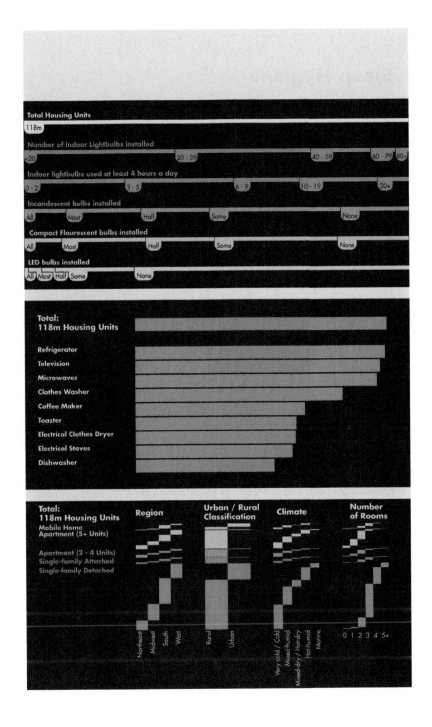

Sleep Hygiene

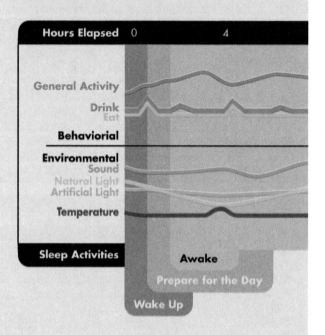

Prepare
Create a dark, cool, quiet environment for falling asleep
Create light, warmth, and sound for waking up
Create consistent wake up and bedtime routines

Avoid
Noise and light before bedtime
Physical or mental stimulation before bedtime
Worrying about the time when having trouble falling asleep
Late day naps close to bedtime
Drinking fluids before bedtime to prevent waking during the night
Heavy meals later in the day

FIGURE 9-4.

Context map

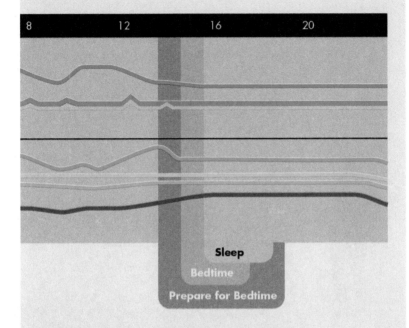

Activities
Exercise when waking up boosts energy for the rest of the day
Exercise well before bed time improves sleep quality and duration
Enjoy relaxing activities that induce sleepiness before bedtime

Eat
Eat meals well before bedtime
Sometimes a small snack before bedtime can be helpful

Drink
Drink regularly throughout the day, but well before bedtime

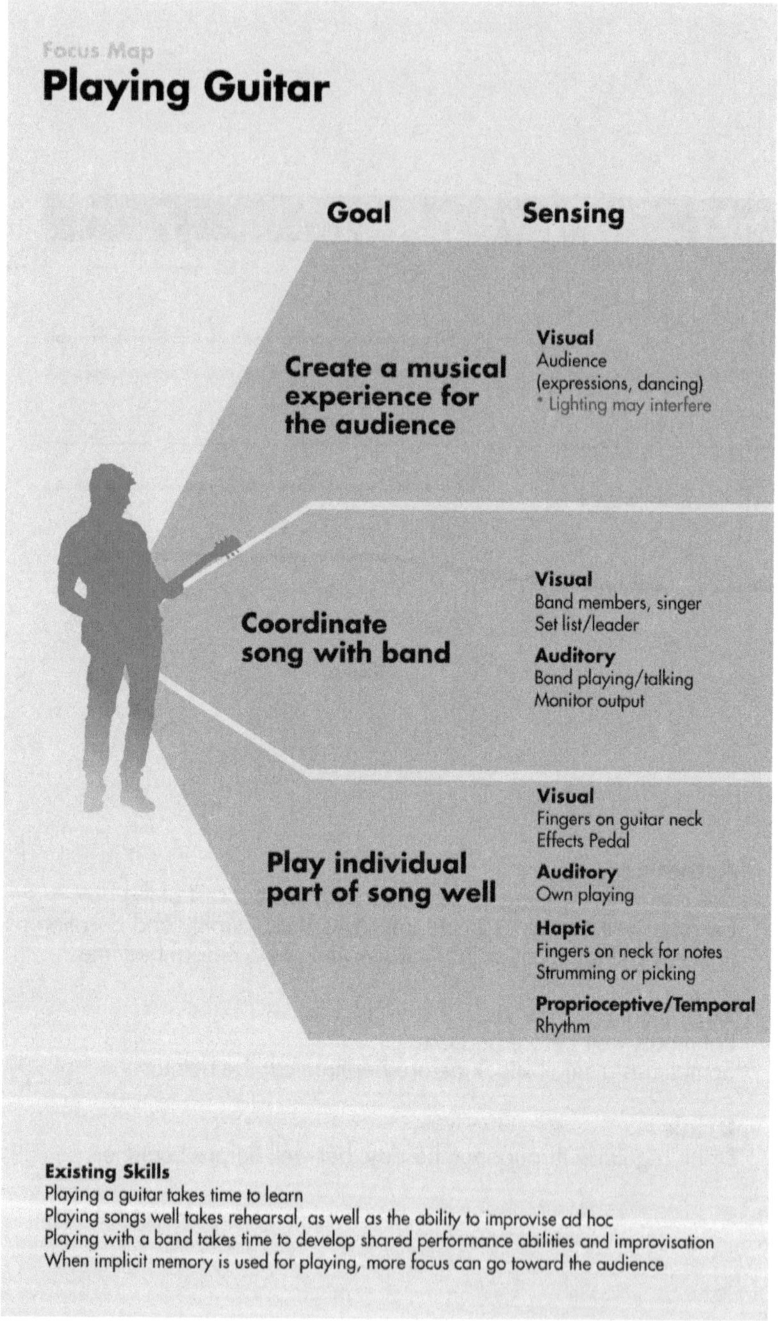

Playing Guitar

Goal **Sensing**

Create a musical experience for the audience

Visual
Audience
(expressions, dancing)
* Lighting may interfere

Coordinate song with band

Visual
Band members, singer
Set list/leader

Auditory
Band playing/talking
Monitor output

Play individual part of song well

Visual
Fingers on guitar neck
Effects Pedal

Auditory
Own playing

Haptic
Fingers on neck for notes
Strumming or picking

Proprioceptive/Temporal
Rhythm

Existing Skills
Playing a guitar takes time to learn
Playing songs well takes rehearsal, as well as the ability to improvise ad hoc
Playing with a band takes time to develop shared performance abilities and improvisation
When implicit memory is used for playing, more focus can go toward the audience

FIGURE 9-5.
Focus model

Understanding	**Deciding**	**Acting**
Are they getting into it? Is this an audience fave? Can they sing along?	Change up the song order. Improvise on a favorite. Let the audience sing.	Play different song. Stay on a favrotie song. Accompany the audience.
What song is next? Are we playing this right? Is someone's solo coming up? Break or chorus coming up?	Check set list/look at leader. Speed up/slow down. Pull back on stage. Move more.	Check set list/look at leader. Speed up/slow down. Pull back on stage. Move more.
How does this song go? Am I in tune? Volume good? Pedals/settings correct? Is my solo coming up?	Guitar is sharp/flat. Volume/effect is off. Different pedal effect. Try a new improvisation.	Tune guitar. Tweak amp settings. Change pedal settings. Wail.

Shifting and substitution between goal-level and multimodal focus

All of the activities are highly multimodal, and require rapid shifts between activities. Playing an instrument emphasizes a strong audio/haptic multimodality, while body language and vision play a stronger role in interpersonal communication, because it is blocked by the volume of the music played and the audience cheering.

STORYBOARDS AND KEYFRAMING

Used during the process of creating films, storyboarding gained popularity as interactions became more complex and were expected to maintain a fluidity that matches real life. It's even been adapted by software designers using Agile methodology as a way of capturing interaction nuance that user stories don't allow. It's basically like a comic, and it can be as detailed or sketchy as required. Ideally it is image-based, but it may start out with some words. The way that stories are told has a strong relationship with the way that we perceive meaningful events; storyboards can help "block" the pieces of your experience appropriately and really help develop the user's point of view and sometimes even the device's itself.

What we're talking about isn't filmmaking; you won't have dialogue between superheroes and villains in bubble quotes. For multimodal design, storyboard annotations include technical details as well as the sensory and interaction dependencies that underpin each part of the story. The idea is to bring your vision of an experience to life in a way that communicates both the user's intention and the thought behind the product's affordances. Noting the user's modality and focus—as well as why, when, and how those shift—is important.

Cognitive scientist and comic author Neil Cohn blends cognitive event models with visual storytelling techniques, which we have adapted for design storyboarding:

Orienter

Provides setting information, like location and time

Establisher

Sets up the users and their relationships

Initial

Introduces the conditions and needs of the user that drive the interaction

Prolongation

Focuses on a moment within the interaction to more fully explore it. This may include emotional states of the user, like a sense of anticipation, excitement, hesitation, or concern; reactions to interruptions or changes in contextual conditions; shifts or transitions in modality and how it changes a user's engagement. These allow a "beat" to create empathy for the user.

Peak

Delineates the interaction, demonstrating the behaviors required of the user and product

Release

Illustrates the effects of the interaction, demonstrating how it fulfills the user's need, and addresses the contextual and conditional requirements

Cohn's work suggests that like speaking and writing, visual language has a grammar that is structured similarly to the way our minds understand events. This approach to storyboarding, using the elements that Cohn identifies helps designers ensure that the interaction both fulfills user needs and follows an event model that users can recognize, easily learn, and remember.

Keyframes focus on describing important events to quickly get a larger story across, and to identify phases rather than individual events. They often include several interdependent interactions, rather than focusing on just one (see Figure 9-6). These accented moments give a sense of the important moments of a flow, but without having to connect all the dots. It's a lot like outlining a story or essay: it lets you make sure you're getting the point across and pulling the users along for the ride. This kind of document also emerged from filmmaking, to show key moments of character development or plot. They are used to inventory and sequence multiple interactions or events. Once the order and number of keyframe events is right, they can be fleshed out into storyboards, which provide more detail about each interaction and the details that will make them effective.

Fire Evacuation in an Apartment

FIRE ALARM is activated

HEAR the alarm or SEE the flashing light

ALERT those who require assistance and provide help

FIGURE 9-6.

Keyframes

Proceed carefully to fire exits and provide calm directions for those requiring help.

Close doors as you leave to prevent the spread of fire.

Move a safe distance from the building or assemble at a planned meeting place.

UPDATE AS NEEDED

The artifacts of the design process should always be looked at as provisional. This is especially true at the beginning of the process: the activity of diagramming expected uses, and possibly working with others on the team to workshop, enhance, and align will undoubtedly spur more and better thinking, as will testing your assumptions through prototyping activities. Never be so impressed with your map that you become precious with it: remember it's just a tool.

Summary

Creating models of user experiences allows designers to use understanding, empathy, and imagination to better understand how design will come together. Different types of models can be created, depending on product functionality and user needs. Those models include customer journeys, decision trees, ecosystem maps, focus models, and storyboards. The user factors of sensing, deciding, understanding, and acting are important to keep track of in most models, since they are so fundamental to multimodal experience, and because they are each so intertwined.

[10]

Form Factors and Configurations

To PROTECT SPACE TRAVELERS from the 500-degree temperature swing, radiation, and the unforgiving void of space, the original astronaut suits went through countless concepts and prototypes. What many people might not know is *who* made the handmade suits worn by Neil Armstrong and Buzz Aldrin when they first stepped on the surface of the moon. The company Playtex, at the time most well known for creating women's undergarments like girdles and bras, lent its expertise and seamstresses to that groundbreaking mission.

Each of the 21 layers of the suit served a specific purpose, from managing pressurization to wicking body moisture and sweat. The suit itself was modular, which ensured the integrity of the suit and its life support systems. This also allowed the astronauts to put it on, take it off, and maintain it. In an open competition to design the suit, the unlikely team from ILC (originally International Latex Corporation) won against engineering teams who already worked often with the space program at the time. The comfort and physical dexterity of the soft suit (combined with its ability to fulfill the environmental requirements of extravehicular activity) gave it the edge against submissions from two other manufacturing competitors who had done a great deal of work already with the space program.[1]

While outer space is a much harsher context than the average personal device is designed for, the same principles apply. *Form factors*, or the physical specifications of devices and their components, allow a device to withstand its usage environment as well as provide usability and delight. The *configurations*, on the other hand, are the types of

---

1   Nicholas de Monchaux, Spacesuit: Fashioning Apollo, MIT Press 2012.

components and software used to enable of functionalities that meet performance requirements. Together, these two sets of specifications drive the physical experience and interface modes of a device.

Creating Multimodal Properties

Form factors and configurations have a great impact on each other. Form factors determine the overall physical design of the product, which influences how much space is available for the componentry inside. Configurations determine what kinds of physical capabilities are available. Buttons have to be reachable; speakers and microphones have to be positioned correctly. Overall, components like processors create heat, and batteries add weight, which must all be accounted for in the user experience. Physical requirements (like water resistance and scratch proofing) have technical attributes, and they also contribute to the overall style and impression of quality of the device.

Over the course of humanity's history, we have figured out quite a bit about the physical phenomena of the senses, and we use them as inspiration. Acoustic guitars use hollow bodies the way the hollow of our chest and lungs amplify the sound from our vocal chords. Reed instruments emulate the way our vocal chords vibrate when air is passed over them. Old ear trumpets magnified the cup-shape of our ears to concentrate sound to a single focal point—our ear canal (see Figure 10-1). Similar inspiration exists for more complex devices. Mercury tilt switches are a sensor component that use the movement of mercury against electrical contacts. This works much like the vestibular system within the inner ear, responsible for balance and the ability to detect our own physical rotation. These capabilities are termed *biomimetic*, because they mimic solutions found in biology.

FIGURE 10-1.

A Victorian-era ear trumpet and a modern guitar: both emulate the properties of human bodies and how they enhance hearing (Source of top image: Wellcome Images)

In some cases, technologies reverse the ability to sense as a way to create new sensations. Speakers can be the reverse of an eardrum, causing the vibration of a membrane to emit sounds rather than gathering them. RGB pixels work similarly to how our eyes detect light: the cones in our eyes are usually differentiated by sensitivity to long, medium, and short light waves, which *do* roughly correspond to red, green, and blue. This phenomenon is known as *trichromatic vision*. Technologies simply developed along similar lines as human ability (see Figure 10-2).

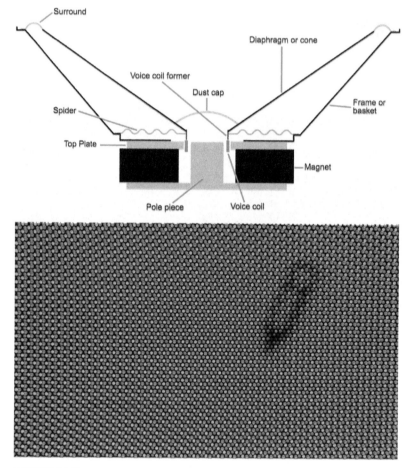

FIGURE 10-2.

Speakers reverse the way ears work, and screen pixels roughly follow the ways the eye responds to light (Source speaker diagram: Iain; pixel: Prateek Karandikar. Both Creative Commons Share Alike)

Visual arts can physically simulate surface textures and shapes that reflect or refract light into our eyes in the same way that real physical objects do. Film aspect ratios, like CinemaScope, were meant to capture the full range of visual field in order to create the most visually immersive experience possible. There were just different schools of thought on what should be included in the definition of the visual field, which accounts for much of that variation.

Other interface properties are simulated mathematically via software visual or audio effects, like global lighting in 3D animation and rendering, or echo and reverberation within sound. These kinds of effects take advantage of the physics and mathematics of the stimulus, familiar environments, and the abilities and limitations of our senses. Binaural sound recording physically re-creates the dampening of sound by the presence of our head between our ears, and how it affects the behavior of a sound wave traveling through and around it. Dolby Atmos re-creates this mathematically. Convolution reverb uses audio samples taken from one location and then applies that same reverberation to other audio. Now more than ever, interfaces can harness incredibly convincing simulations of physical experience (see Figure 10-3).

FIGURE 10-3.
Digital interfaces now closely approximate the physical properties of experiences and tools (Source: Digital images created with Wetbrush by artist Daniela Flamm Jackson; painting detail by Fritz Welch)

Many product interfaces are now completely within the realm of physical simulation but still draw from real physical controllers of the mechanical age. Tap is similar to the spring-loaded buttons. Slider and rocker switch elements are common to most interactive form design. Our onscreen keyboards are reproductions of mechanical typewriters (see Figure 10-4). The technology within many devices has been profoundly transformed. Our senses, minds, and bodies develop in the physical world and shape our internal logic and understanding of interaction. It's not a surprise then that interfaces stay rooted in the physical world along with us.

FIGURE 10-4.
Following our existing understanding of how things work means that interfaces continue interaction paradigms from earlier products (Source, Ericcson phone: Alexandre Dulaunoy)

Multimodal product design focuses less on any one of the traditional design disciplines like industrial, graphic, and interaction design. Instead, an interface is the sum of the physical, mechanical, and computational interaction elements and how they work together. There are also more ways to directly integrate digital technology into existing physical interfaces and environments. Blurring the lines between physical and digital experiences opens up many new doors within the realm of interaction design.

Configuring Interface Modes

There are three important experience factors when selecting the technologies for creating multimodal interfaces. The first two are the building blocks that are required for the mode, and the dimensions and resolution required for each of those building blocks. Different technologies vary by characteristics including mode, resolution, power consumption, input/output capabilities. The last, but definitely not least of the experience, is the level of focus that is comfortable and safe for the user within the experience. This is often comprised of several factors, such as learning curve, balancing between the level of attention needed, the urgency and complexity of the information, as well as the context of the user experience.

For example, televisions allow us to watch shows and films. At a very high level, the viewing experience is deeply immersive, and the quality of the images and sound are really important to creating that immersion. Most televisions now have a remote control, with some form of on-screen and audio feedback during usage. In this case, the input is primarily a low-resolution/low-dimension haptic mode (buttons). Two of the most important forms of image and sound processing are buffering and rendering. Buffering is the ability to store enough immediate video and audio information to ensure smooth playback, and rendering is deciding which video or audio information to play at any moment (as well as how to display any additional interfaces with it). These require memory for storing large files and a moderate amount of processing for rendering the UI and video together. The output for using the remote control and for watching films and shows is a high-resolution/low-dimension audiovisual mode (screen and speakers). Within the context of watching television or movies, there are generally few additional needs to support other modalities or focus within the experience. The screen is designed to dominate the visual field and home speaker systems can be custom configured to the size and layout of the room.

The controls and dashboard of a car have similar modes to watching television: the input is primarily haptic with supporting visual and audio modes, and the output is also audio-visual modes. The big difference is the context of experience. The driver of a car must maintain a high degree of visual, auditory, and haptic focus on their driving. In this case, driving a car is a low resolution/high dimension visuo-haptic mode (steering wheels, pedals, gearshift, signals, and various mechanical knobs and sliders for music and environmental controls) with supporting audio modes (various gauges, warning lights/alerts, as well as certain external cues). The information has been highly prioritized and simplified to minimize distraction from the primary visual focus—allowing the driver to keep their eyes on the road. The position of the instrumentation panel is right below the field of vision, requiring only a small shift in visual direction to read, minimizing the amount of time a driver's eyes are not on the road. The field of vision is dominated by the windshield and viewing mirrors, allowing for maximum visibility of the driving context.

When creating interfaces, several technology characteristics tie back to supporting individual human modalities. In many cases, these technologies—especially hardware components—can serve multiple functions and sometimes even modalities within the same device. Of course there is a range within each type of technology. For example, both OLED and e-ink screens are used for visual modes, but the slow refresh rate of e-ink screens does not allow it to support motion graphics very well. Speakers can range in capability from the tinny beeps of a portable alarm clock to those configured to deliver Dolby Atmos spatialized sound in a movie theater, with sub-woofers so powerful that moviegoers can both feel and hear the rumble.

The following tables are common technologies used to create interface modes. While visual and audio technologies are highly developed, there is a wide array of haptic input technologies. Despite this, output remains limited compared to the human tactile and proprioceptive capabilities. Additional technologies can be used to create interactions when physical information lies outside the range of human sensibility.

TABLE 10-1. Visual mode technologies

MONITOR (INPUT)	
	Cameras *Varying resolutions, low dimenion* A blend of optical sensor arrays and lens technologies, for single images or image sequences **Types of cameras:** • **Stereoscopic cameras** create two streams of images or videos (this can also be simulated digitally). • **Photography and video cameras** capture images or film for human viewing. • **Infrared (IR)** cameras have unique properties, like showing human bruises that might be invisible on the skin surface. • **Laser** cameras are used for 3D imaging and can often do cool things like "see" around corners.
	Optical/Electromagnetic Sensors *Low resolution, low dimension* Used to detect a specific range of the electromagnetic spectrum, they can be customized across a wide array of applications, like optical heart rate sensors, telescopes, microscopes, and radiation detectors.

ANALYZE	
	Optical character recognition (OCR) *Medium resolution, low dimension* Converting scanned images of typed or handwritten text into text files that can be edited, serached, or analyzed.
	Machine vision *High resolution, low dimension* Services like Microsoft Computer Vision, Google Cloud Vision, IBM Vision Recognition, Cloud Sight, and Clarifai are used to automate object recognition and tagging.
	3D Scanning *High resolution, low dimension* Used to create spatial models of physical objects and environments.

Motion tracking

Varying resolution, low dimension

Used to track physical movement, there are a number of different technologies depending on the level of resolution required.

Lidar

High resolution and dimensions

Uses pulsed lasers and sensors to measure distance in 3D mapping for a variety of uses including autonomous vehicle navigation systems.

DECIDE

Image recognition/tagging

High resolution, low dimensions

Automated object, content, and location information, often an extension of machine vision.

Autonomous navigation

High resolution and dimensions

Often blending multiple modes to allow autonomous movement of vehicles, robots, and drones.

RESPOND AND CONTROL (OUTPUT)

Screens

Varying resolutions and dimensions

Screens convert electrical measurements into pixels, and there are many different kinds.

Types of screens:

- **Liquid Crystal Display (LCD)** screens are perhaps the most common type of screen across many different types of devices.

- **Organic Light Emitting Diodes (OLED)** work without the backlight required by LCDs, are more energy efficient, produce deeper blacks, and can be bendable.

- **E Ink** is the name for a range of screens that emulate the look of paper, so frequently used for e-readers like Kindle, but also watches and public signage. They consume very little power compared to other types of screens. Though lower resolution, and with a slower refresh rate, they look better in sunlight and cause less eyestrain.

Types of screens, continued:

- **Virtual Reality (VR) or Augmented Reality (AR) goggles** such as the Oculus Rift and HTC Vive use bicameral screens that must render two video streams—one per eye—at higher than HD resolution to creat the 3D field of vision of a person.

Lights

Low resolution and dimension

An LED simply emits a specific color and brightness of light. Adding the restful breathing pattern of brightening and dimming poetically indicates the sleep mode of Macbook. The Nike Fuelband used an array of LEDs to playfully create a sports inspired scoreboard style text display, instead of using a pixel-based screen. The Amazon Echo uses its ring of LEDs to create directionality—it almost seems to look at the person speaking. Traffic lights use three different colors to control the flow of traffic.

TABLE 10-2. Audio mode technologies

MONITOR (INPUT)

Microphones

Varying resolutions, low dimension

Microphones convert the mechanical waveforms into electrical measurements.

Types of microphones:

- **Stereophonic microphones** create two streams of sound (this can also be simulated digitally).

- **Binaural microphones** match the acoustic properties of head positioning and separation, to simulate human hearing.

- **Microphone arrays** are used to track positioning or to create spatialization effects.

- **Micro-electro-mechanical systems (MEMS) microphones** have a very small form factor, allowing them to be used for noise cancellation, hearing aids, and beam forming.

Natural language processing and speech synthesis

High resolution, low dimension

Two technologies often paired to understand and recreate human speech.

Real-time translation

High resolution, low dimension

Increasingly used to allow human speech to be translated across languages.

Speech-to-text

High resolution, low dimension

Allows speech to be captured to text files.

Spatialization

Varying resolutions and dimensions

Processes audio stream from multiple microphones to triangulate location, which can be cross-referenced with GPS. It can also be used to position playback of sounds across an array of speakers, like in movie theatres.

DECIDE

Noise reduction/cancellation

Varying resolutions and dimensions

Often a precursor to audio analysis, filtering unnecessary sound during analysis or playback.

RESPOND AND CONTROL (OUTPUT)

Speakers

Varying resolutions and dimensions

Speakers convert electrical measurements into mechanical wave-forms. Different kinds of speakers, like tweeters, woofers, and sub-woofers are used to create different ranges of sound wave-lengths. Parabolic speakers can focus sound to a specific location in space.

TABLE 10-3. Haptic mode technologies

MONITOR (INPUT)	
	Motion/location tracking *Varying resolutions, low dimension* A blend of sensors including accelerometers, gyroscopes, GPS, and barometeres (for altitude) used singly, together, or in arrays, used to detect the movement and/or location of devices and their users.
	Multitouch *Low resolution and dimensions* A combination of a touch-sensitive screen and force sensitive resistors—both technologies use arrays of sensors and cross reference them against each other to measure the position, direction, movement, speed, and pressure of contact with a screen, usually with fingers or a stylus.
	Force Touch *High resolution and dimensions* This Apple technology extended multitouch technology by combining a touch-sensitive screen with force-sensitive resistors.
	Temperature *Low resolution and dimensions* Used to detect the temperature of objects or environments.
	Fingerprints *High resolution, varying dimensions* Can be sensed using optical, ultrasonic, and capacitance sensors. The last method is generally deemed more secure and used on phone by Apple, Galaxy, HTC, LG, and others.
ANALYZE	
	AR and VR *High resolution and dimensions* Use specialized hardware and software services to map and render 3D environments, tracking our field of vision, gaze, and head movement.

Activity recognition

Low resolution, low dimension

Used with motion tracking to determine the activity of a user, like when fitness trackers can detect walking, running, and biking, or a smartphone can detect driving.

Location recognition

Low resolution and dimensions

Cross references motion tracking with geographic informations systems (GIS) to determine the specific location of a device or user.

RESPOND AND CONTROL (OUTPUT)

Haptic motors

Varying resolution, low dimension

A form of actuator, used to create more precise vibrations, and are useful when a user needs more information, like smartphones, game controllers, and power steering.

Speakers

Low resolution and dimension

Can sometimes be used to create tactile vibrations such as alerts on pagers and GPS devices.

Actuators

Varying resolution and dimensions

PP

Encompass a range of technologies like motors, muscle wire, and materials that demonstrate mechanical properties when exposed to energy. These are often used to create autonomous movement for driverless cars, robots, and functional prosthetics.

Mapping Modal Behaviors to Modal Technologies

While these technical variations are important in creating products that deliver multimodal experiences, it also means that there are endless ways to merge digital and physical experiences together. With that said, having a voice interface on a lawnmower is probably a really terrible idea—well, at least until we can make their motors quieter and their blades safer. Product modes should be selected to support the preferred human modalities within the activity.

Some human behaviors are thought of as unimodal, meaning that one sensory modality is sufficient for that specific activity. For example, reading is considered unimodal with vision, though it can be enhanced when blended with other visual behaviors, like spatial mapping, and other modalities. This is why reading a physical book allows for better comprehension and retention than reading from a screen. We use the physical layout of the book itself to help us reinforce the narrative and sequential structure of what we are reading. Listening to music is also considered unimodal, but our sense rhythm almost magically syncs what we hear to our other modalities. Some musicians can feel how a song is sung in their throats or how it is played on an instrument with their fingers while listening to it. People very commonly tap out the beat with their feet. On the other hand, spatial orientation is very obviously multimodal. For most, it isn't possible to figure out where you are in a specific location without both vision and proprioception. If a room goes completely dark, a person almost immediately freezes, because they cannot see where they are going.

There are many different ways to categorize form factors and configurations for multimodal experiences, but there isn't really a neat and tidy system. Products can vary across wide range of form factors and technology configurations, even when they fulfill the same purpose. Our modalities are equally flexible. For example, when searching for an item in the pantry, we may use vision to see which bottle we are trying to grab. But for shelves that are above eye level, we may rely more on touch to recognize that item by shape, weight, or the material of the bottle. We shift modalities in an instant, without thinking about it, or remembering that we did so later. Comparative case studies highlight the effect of different multimodal combinations on a product's capabilities and overall experience.

VISION DOMINANT ACTIVITIES

Because vision is our dominant sense—even within multimodalities—we have developed a great deal of technology for it. The most fundamental technologies are of course our written languages and image-based technologies, including visual and film-based media. We have been writing and drawing for millennia—by definition, all of recorded human history. It is somewhat unique, because with stereoscopic vision, we can use it for sensing both 2D and 3D forms. Along with hearing and smell, it is one of our abilities that we rely on for perception across distance. This is why the technology used to create visual experience runs a very wide gamut, across multiple types of engineering and design. In addition, our eyes, heads, and bodies move, allowing us to focus on specific visual depth ranges or objects within our visual field, to track objects moving across it, or to steady what we see when we are moving ourselves. We can change our view, perspective, and proximity to objects and environments.

Many of the modalities within vision provide sufficient information to support understanding and motor skills. This is why they can also become building blocks of multimodal behaviors. Many experiences that we cannot directly experience are mapped to visual technologies, using learnable visual languages and systems or specialized ones requiring a legend or key for the user. Vision can often be a decision-making factor for how we apply sensory abilities as well. The sight of a vibrant red apple increases our desire to taste it. Seeing and hearing water boil in a pot warns us not to touch it. Seeing a big pile of garbage spilled across the street perhaps convinces us to hold our breath while we walk past it.

IMMERSIVE ACTIVITIES: SCREEN-BASED EXPERIENCES AND VR

Screen-based activities are among the most visually immersive experiences available, requiring that we focus our attention away from the physical world around us and to the events and images on the other side of a piece of glass. When we are looking at them, we focus and fill our visual field and may not spend a lot of time perceiving visual stimuli outside that frame of focus. We are most often reading, observing, or examining the visual information in front us. When we are watching a film, the experience is largely passive. We are simply observing a story unfold before us. Filmmaking has a great many techniques for maintaining visual focus, and for drawing the eye into the frame, where the movements of a camera simulate the way we ourselves would look at an event unfolding. Combined with sound and in some cases, haptic vibration through subwoofers, we are immersed in a story. We are empathizing with the emotions and decisions of the characters in front of us. In this case, a screen need only be the sufficient size, distance, and resolution to engage our visual field and focus.

Experiencing the story for ourselves takes the experience to a deeper level of physical embodiment, engaging our proprioceptive and in some cases, our haptic modalities in the experience. Like many advanced interactive technologies, VR was developed largely for gaming, though other applications are being rapidly explored. Gaming itself extends the techniques in filmmaking in terms of world building and creating characters that the user can easily step into and embody, becoming an actor in what we see. (It would be a bit more challenging to step into the body of a Pegasus with four legs, and learn how to flap our wings, though perhaps really fun!) The goggles use small stereoscopic screens a short distance from our eyes, making it easier to fill our visual field and provide 3D vision. They block out visual stimulus external to that screen experience, forcing us to rely on the screens for our visual reality. Proprioception and vision validate each other for spatial orientation and balance. When they do not align—because of timing or because they are sensing two incompatible experiences, people can suffer from motion sickness or dizziness. Even in just 2D film, unsteady camera movement can also cause motion sickness. This is aggravated when, for example, a screen is showing that we are moving, and our bodies are seated. When playing a video game, the stationary edges of the screen anchor our spatial reality, to offset that physical reaction. In VR, that spatial anchor is deliberately suppressed, and so a great deal of technology is used to anchor spatial reality to the virtual environment.

The speed and tracking of user movement is essential to VR experiences. The Oculus Rift uses a great deal of mathematical computation to build 3D virtual worlds. However, it takes a great deal of computational effort to keep our bodies from rejecting it. To prevent motion sickness and to accurately sync user movement to 3D rendering, the Oculus team turned to motion capture techniques more commonly used in the visual effects realm of filmmaking. The Constellation motion tracking system uses the position of infrared LEDs on the headset to map the movements of our heads quickly to its 3D world building, stabilizing the movement of the images in front of us.

AUGMENTED OR AUXILIARY ACTIVITIES: VISUAL INDICATORS FOR PERIPHERAL INFORMATION

We already "augment" our physical realities with graphics and text that don't require head-worn gear. LEDs, printed labels and icons, and small are very common in physical devices. They are often used as an indicator for power level or for other factors, like connectivity in a router, or letting you know which elevator in a bank has arrived. Lately, the usage of LEDs has become very sophisticated, especially with the type of housing and material used around it. A common technique is called counterboring, where small depressions are molded or drilled into the back of the housing material. This allows the light to be seen and focused when it is on, but the surface of the housing remains visually uninterrupted when it is off. This is related to punch-cut screens, which only allowed light to pass through certain areas, using predetermined shapes to spell out numbers, letters, or special characters, like old digital clocks and cross walk signs. Some examples of this include indicators on Apple laptops, and the Areaware wooden clock. Jawbone created custom shaped icons for their counterbores, and used color, indicating states for specific functionality.

In addition, color and animation play a strong role in creating visual systems or codes. "On" or "off" is a binary, usually mapped to "yes" or "no" of some state. Colors can mean a few different things, if people learn them. This idea has been around since stop lights, with red, yellow, and green. Increasingly, some of the technologies that are applicable to LED usage can be applied to other light sources, using "smart" technologies. One example of this is the Phillips Hue, which can be used to emulate sunlight as a kind of wake-up alarm clock. Home lighting has always been an indicator of sorts. When a fuse blows, or there is a blackout, it's always reassuring to see the lights come back on, which lets you know that the power is running again. It also lets others know that someone is home.

AUGMENTED REALITY VERSUS AUGMENTED PRODUCTS: VISUAL ARRAYS OF CONTROL AND CHOICE

For a long time, control panels and dashboards have been a very important part of our interactions. We use dashboards in cars, planes, and other forms of transport, but they are not just for heavy equipment. Artists use their palette to review the colors they have available for drawing an image—both with physical paint and in software such as Photoshop. We have signage to help us determine where in the grocery store we would find a can of peas, or where to find a book in a library. In these cases, we are given an array of information that we can use to inform our focal action, whether it's driving, drawing, or shopping. These kinds of visual arrays are most commonly used for activities that require a high level of focus or decision making. But the most important experience attribute of dashboards is really *not* how much information we can cram into them. It's the fact that we can look away or ignore them, and then easily remember where to focus our eyes for a specific bit of information or control. It is on a need-to-know basis, over which we develop effortless control, after much repetition. On a car dashboard, all the radio controls are in one place. All the heating and cooling systems are in another. After a time, we can use them without looking, because the spatial position and haptic information is sufficient.

With augmented reality technology, particularly for vision, that ability to look away is not as effortless, and there isn't always a learning period. It can be difficult to apply the technology to complex activities correctly.

It may be better to use sensory substitution or to add extra steps to the focal experience, to prevent distraction. Splitting cognitive focus has limits, and may not be quickly repeatable or easily sustainable over long periods of time. This is why *hands-free* technologies are receiving increasing scrutiny. When we divide our attention across two activities, it's not split 50/50. Our performance in both activities degrades significantly. The more activities we add or the more focus and cognition one activity requires, the more rapidly our performance on any of them deteriorates. People seem to know this to some extent. You wouldn't try to explain a complex mathematical equation to someone who was driving, and expect them to understand or remember later—especially in difficult driving conditions.

Over time, however, the gap between 2D and 3D screen-based media will be bridged, allowing a more contiguous experience between traditional screen-based UIs, AR, VR, and the physical world.

AUTOMATED VISUAL CAPABILITIES

One of the more interesting aspects of recent technology is re-creating vision through machine learning. People can do a great deal of visual analysis, drawing many important ideas and information with sight. We can recognize who a person is, how they are feeling, and if they are paying attention to us or if they are distracted. We can estimate how fast a car is moving toward us, how many people are in that car, and most importantly, whether we need to get out of the way. We can do all of them at the same time to a certain extent.

This ability to analyze what we see, and to parse it into meaningful information is a bit more challenging for technology. There isn't one specific technology that can encompass all of human visual ability. Instead, it's broken across several technologies and applications, and different companies have different capabilities within them. Driverless cars have special emphasis on avoiding obstacles: determining the speed and position of other cars and objects that will enter the projected path of the car. Facial recognition however, focuses on the geometry of our face, and cross referencing it against existing catalogs of faces to make a positive ID. Image tagging focuses on recognizing objects, colors, and other visual attributes within a specific image. In the Google Vision API, there are algorithms that will even try to recognize the breed of dog, if it recognizes one in an image.

The Google driverless car uses a blend of sonar, stereo cameras, lasers, and radar for obstacle detection. "The lidar system bolted to the top of Google's self-driving car is crucially important for several reasons. First, it's highly accurate up to a range of 100 meters. There are a few detection technologies on the car that work at greater distances, but not with the kind of accuracy you get from a laser. It simply bounces a beam off surfaces and measures the reflection to determine distance. The device used by Google—a Velodyne 64-beam laser—can also rotate 360-degrees and take up to 1.3 million readings per second, making it the most versatile sensor on the car. Mounting it on top of the car ensures its view isn't obstructed."[2]

Facial recognition requires cameras facing the person, usually at eye level, and in some cases infrared, to determine the contours of the face, and where to focus, as in autofocus cameras. Image tagging requires scanning of image files that are already data files, and so does not require particularly specialized hardware at all.

CREATING FOCAL EXPERIENCES WITH AUDIO AND SPEECH

Creating auditory and speech experiences entails a stronger emphasis on social experiences. Talking is something we do with other people, and so the social aspects of voice interactions will always play a

---

2   Ryan Whitwam, "How Google's self-driving cars detect and avoid obstacles," Extreme Tech, September 2014, *http://www.extremetech.com/extreme/189486-how-googles-self-driving-cars-detect-and-avoid-obstacles.*

strong role in their design. While several people in a room can choose to look at a screen or not, sound vibrations carry through the air in all directions—at sufficient volume, everyone can hear them. They also travel through liquies and solids, which makes possible warning sirens, sonar, and sadly, annoying neighbors. Hearing through solids, however, generally requires direct physical contact. Solids can conduct lower tones better than air, so our voices sound lower to us than they are, because we are hearing them through our jawbones and skulls. Our sense of hearing depends largely on the frequency or pitch and the volume of the sound. This is relative to the distance between the listener and sound source, because soundwaves have physical properties like decay (they lose energy as they travel), echo (they bounce off solid objects), and the Doppler Effect (they can get compressed or stretched out depending on movement), which all impact the sound quality. Those qualities also help us to roughly position the source of a sound in space. Like all of our other senses, we can detect patterns in sounds, especially in time and frequency, resulting in our experience of rhythm, harmony, and melody.

PERSONAL SOUND EXPERIENCES

Typically, the larger the speaker, the lower the pitch and louder the sound it can create. Lower pitched sound waves are physically larger and therefore require more physical volume. That is why headphones can sound tinny (it's difficult for them to create low frequencies at sufficient volume), and why subwoofers are usually so big. This can be a physical challenge for sound-based devices. Headphones and earbuds are designed to keep sound personal. They may cover our ears, trapping sound against the side of our heads. Earbuds are funnel shaped to fit securely into our ears and take advantage of the little bump in our ear, called the *tragus*, to hold them snugly in place, trapping both the buds themselves and their sound inside our ear canals. There may be externally facing speakers to detect environmental sound, used for sound cancellation, where the peak and trough of the detected sound wave are inverted in a second sound wave, thus neutralizing the first sound wave. Increasingly, the directionality of sound is being explored.

The downside to all of this innovation, however, can appear when we are actually having a phone call or other conversation. We can look like we are talking to ourselves, or seem like we are addressing someone when we aren't, creating awkward situations. For now, the social stigma of talking to yourself is still pretty strong. As the technology for auditory experiences advances, many related services are being integrated into the earbud (see Figure 10-5) or headphone form factor.

FIGURE 10-5.
Google Pixel Buds integrate services like translation and assistance

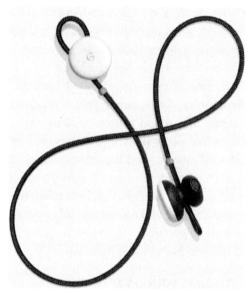

Parametric speakers, on the other hand, take advantage of the ultrasound—mechanical waves that rise above our threshold of hearing. These waves can force audible sound waves to travel along a specific path and distance—in effect targeting where an audible sound can be heard. This is still a somewhat experimental technology.

SOCIAL EXPERIENCES: BROADCAST

Ancient Greek and Roman auditoriums were designed for both hearing and speaking. Their name literally means "a place for hearing." They were shaped in the same way sound travels from our mouths: facing from one direction with a small starting point that radiated outward and grew larger. Seats were arranged to fall within that radiating shape, so that those sounds could be heard. They were smaller than those we have now because the human voice alone can only travel so far.

Modern technology allows us to amplify sound to be heard over longer distances, but some of the fundamentals still apply for social auditory experiences. In some cases, many small speakers can be used to replace one large speaker. They sound the same within a specific spatial range, but can be more directionalized, preventing sounds from carrying too far. This can be helpful for public spaces like stadiums, or museums with multiple auditory displays in close proximity to each other. The Amazon Echo is cylinder-shaped to allow for a 360° microphone array and speaker configuration to be able to "hear" and "speak" to anywhere in a room from any place in the room.

CONVERSATION EXPERIENCES: SPEECH

On the flip side of social auditory experiences is conversation. The often-quoted number of how 75% of communication is nonverbal is correct in spirit, though perhaps not mathematically accurate. Conversation is a multimodal experience, and we use many visual, auditory, gestural, and spatial cues when we are speaking to one another. We are very good at predicting when it is our turn to speak or listen or what a person is about to say, and use many different behaviors to communicate emotion, attention, and other aspects of dialog and empathy. We are so good at conversation, in fact, that our turntaking response time in conversation is unbelievably fast. The pause between turns can be as little as 200 milliseconds, literally faster than the blink of an eye. This can make creating speech interfaces a bit challenging, as longer than that breaks expectations of dialog. We can also process large quantities of verbal communication. We can listen to a person speak for hours at a clip. Alexa, on the other hand, can handle up to ninety seconds of sound file, and its response time varies on a number of factors, including the speed of your household internet. Despite these technical limitations, its interaction design took cues from how people really converse. A ring of LEDs on the device responds as quickly as a human does in conversation, but it tries to point at the direction of the person speaking, like it's "looking" at you. This makes the delay feel like thoughtful listening and consideration of response, rather than latency.

The multimodal cues around conversational speech are translated into experiences that may not have the same physical experience of chatting with someone, but echo the timing, conversational cues, and other social qualities of conversation. Other perceptual attributes of conversation may help increase the acceptability of the experience for users.

CREATING HAPTIC EXPERIENCES

Our sense of touch is the most multidimensional, detecting mechanical, electromagnetic, and chemical stimulus. It is our most direct sensory ability, requiring physical contact with objects and environments. It's also tied to some of our most non-aware and our most engaged activities. We feel the smooth, cool cotton of a shirt when we put it on in the morning, but then stop noticing it touching our body almost immediately. We can feel the shape and cushioning of a chair, but quickly forget when we are watching a really great movie. When we do notice, we get tremendous pleasure from touch-based experiences: the fluffiness of down pillows on our faces, the satisfying crunch when biting into a crisp crust of bread, the funny jiggle when poking Jell-O, a warm bath after a long day. We laugh when we are tickled, and we recoil with horror if something fast with a lot of legs touches our feet unexpectedly. Touch can be our most experiential sense—the one that most quickly and effectively immerses our bodies into being in the physical world.

While the cosmetic design of a device may have tactile material characteristics when being handled, it's quite another thing to simulate them using hardware componentry. All of our other senses have physical focal points: the eyes, ears, nose, and tongue. We have touch receptors all over our bodies, and deep in our muscles, bones, and organs—even in the previously mentioned eyes, ears, nose, and tongue. There are sensors that can detect moisture, but there is no technology that can re-create the feeling of wet without the immediate presence of liquid. Just think about what it feels like to be in a jacuzzi: warm jets of bubbles and water all over our skin, steam and splash hitting our faces. Because of the range and degree of sensitivity in our haptic experiences and how deeply tied they are to our bodies, they are difficult to re-create with digital technology. For now, a full haptic body suit seems a bit farther off into the future.

There is, however, a wide array of sensors that can detect the same kinds of information we can through touch. Sensors can detect many of the physical stimulus we can, like wind speed, temperature, and the presence of moisture. This helps us avoid direct exposure to unpleasant weather conditions, like tsunamis, tornadoes, and raindrops falling on our heads. On sunny days with a cool breeze, birds singing, and flowers blooming, the weather report can be a tease if you are cooped up inside. It is about as experiential as reading the list of ingredients on a chocolate wrapper versus actually tasting one.

Common haptic technologies fall within four dimensions: our ability to detect force, contact, movement, with surface texture sometimes playing a supporting role. They focus more on sensing what we are doing, and are limited in creating a meaningful range of haptic stimulus for us to sense. Helmets can detect force of impact during football, and determine whether the force was significant enough to cause a head injury. Fitness trackers can differentiate between fitness activities like biking, running, walking, and swimming. Between sensors and cameras, game consoles can create 3D avatars of our bodies and approximate many different kinds of interactions, from your golf swing to shaking up a bottle of champagne. Touchscreens can tell a great deal about the way we touch our screens, and used with peripheral devices like styluses, they can simulate many different types of hand tools and instruments, from pencils and paintbrushes, to pianos and steering wheels. Because hand-eye coordination and tool use are so fundamental to human interaction, there is still probably a great deal more we can still do with haptic interfaces.

Summary

The form of a device and its configurations are interdependent and designing for them can quickly become a complex puzzle balancing heat, weight, physical properties, product capabilities, and stylistic considerations. Multimodal products really are greater than the sum of their properties, and the weakest element can quickly drag down the whole. In the same way that many design innovations of the past looked to biological properties for inspiration and elegant solutions, multimodal design can also look to the way that the senses work, and how the mind processes them. This grounds designs in the user's reality.

[11]

Ecosystems

SMARTPHONES NOW SERVE AS the front door for many devices. Standards like Bluetooth used in tandem with development frameworks like HomeKit enable a diverse range of products in the smart home. IPV6 integration offers a network infrastructure that will scale to the trillions of anticipated IoT products. These are all examples of ecosystems, interconnected networks of resources. New products may draw from existing platforms or services, or have to fit in with them, despite the fact that these infrastructures may be competing with each other.

Multimodal devices will connect and blend different layers of ecosystems in new ways. They should, because these devices will become a part of our daily activities while taking advantage of devices that people already have and use. By understanding the facets of ecosystems that are brought together, designers can create more seamless multimodal experiences and take full advantage of the contextual resources available.

In your grade-school ecology class, you might have followed the journey of a raindrop through clouds, groundwater, river, reservoir, and into your drinking glass. In the same way, the handful of bits that appear on a screen or that play through a speaker went through quite a journey to get to you. Stored somewhere on a server, those bits traveled through miles of cable, maybe bounced through the atmosphere between a few satellites or cell towers and through to your antenna, and then zipped around the device a little to end up under your fingertips and gaze. With the rise of the cloud, the elements of a user's experience pass through several ecosystems before coming together in their hands and may have a few more steps even after that to complete the journey. Each ecosystem brings with it additional considerations to designing multimodal experiences.

Physical use cases and environments now play a larger role in defining the experiences of connected devices. In transportation and smart cities, the geographic position and resources of a connected experience matters more than ever. In a smart home, the constellation of personal devices for individuals are set for a pretty spectacular collision course with devices meant for shared multimodal experiences. It will be possible for personal and shared devices to be more deeply interconnected, to support multiple users, and to switch between different users through various identification technologies. The questions that arise from "Who is holding the remote" become a bit more complicated when the answer is "Everyone."

It's useful to think about our connected devices as nodes or touchpoints across a greater ecosystem. And as the number of ways to interact with multiple devices increases, so does the number of intersecting ecosystems. These intersections allow product design teams to tap into rich networks of existing resources—but beware their complexity and varied states of maintenance. For example, many public transportation systems cross-reference both the schedule information and sensors throughout the subway tunnels to display the arrival of the next train. Using a smartwatch to control your phone while running is a really fluid experience. With increasing access to the same product or service across multiple devices, experiences will be more about which modality is convenient to the user's immediate circumstances, rather than any one device being a single access point or interaction type.

Ecosystems fall into a few high-level categories, including device, information, physical, social, and specialized ecosytems. These systems tap into different forms of infrastructure, expectations, and resources for a product or service. There are of course overlaps between each of these categories. An example would be a medical information system, which carries patient identification, health records, medication history, and treatment plans. Different facets of this information are used differently by doctors, nurses, laboratories, and patients themselves. In addition, the access and storage of this information is heavily regulated in the US under HIPAA (Health Insurance Portability and Accountability Act of 1996) legislation to protect privacy concerns and to prevent biased treatment. It's very important to know how a product is using information and whether new information created by the product is protected under HIPAA and requires compliance. Another example would be device ecosystems. When creating new devices it is important to understand what people already have. Around the world almost everyone who could have a mobile phone does have one. However, cellular service can be unreliable and WiFi may be less available. For creating connected products, it's important to match connectivity requirements with both the availability and capacity likely to be accessible by the devices. Each of the types of ecosystems that impact a product introduce these kind of considerations (see Figure 11-1).

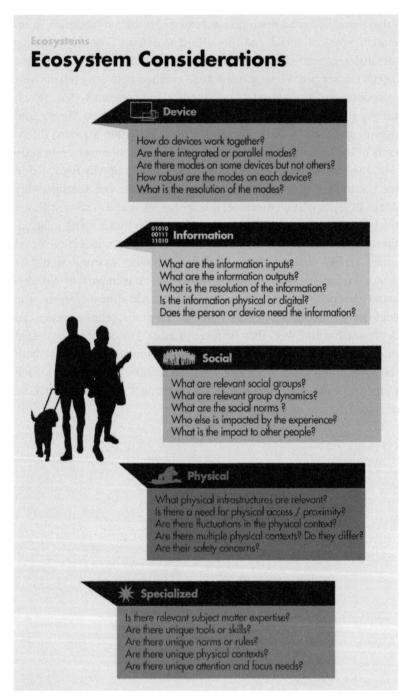

Ecosystem Considerations

Device

How do devices work together?
Are there integrated or parallel modes?
Are there modes on some devices but not others?
How robust are the modes on each device?
What is the resolution of the modes?

Information

What are the information inputs?
What are the information outputs?
What is the resolution of the information?
Is the information physical or digital?
Does the person or device need the information?

Social

What are relevant social groups?
What are relevant group dynamics?
What are the social norms ?
Who else is impacted by the experience?
What is the impact to other people?

Physical

What physical infrastructures are relevant?
Is there a need for physical access / proximity?
Are there fluctuations in the physical context?
Are there multiple physical contexts? Do they differ?
Are their safety concerns?

Specialized

Is there relevant subject matter expertise?
Are there unique tools or skills?
Are there unique norms or rules?
Are there unique physical contexts?
Are there unique attention and focus needs?

FIGURE 11-1.
There are many types of ecosystems that can affect a product's experience

Device Ecosystems

Device ecosystems allow individual devices to work with each other. Think of your laptop, tablet, and phone, and perhaps a smartwatch. It is really convenient to be able to pick up where you left off reading on your tablet last night when continuing to read on your phone during your morning commute. Ecosystems encompass devices that communicate to each other directly, or across a network, like streaming music to the speaker in whichever room you like. Certain subsets of devices work especially well together, like a phone with a smartwatch or a tablet with a television or home assistant. Core infrastructure shared by multiple devices come into play as well. Amber alerts to phones work by sending a signal to a specifically targeted area of cell towers; all the phones that are receiving their signal from them get the alert (see Figure 11-2). In multimodal experiences, the hardware, software, and data needed for multimodal experiences can be distributed across the many layers of technology we use everyday.

FIGURE 11-2.
Overlapping information and device ecosystems allow Amber Alerts to target and reach a wide, relevant audience (Source: Bob Bobster, and Zanaq, Creative Commons)

Information Ecosystems

Information ecosystems allow sets of data and data processing services to be used together. For example, Siri started out as the integration of the speech recognition service created by Nuance and the natural language query service provided by Wolfram Alpha. New assistant programs like x.ai integrate AI with natural language processing, your contacts, and your calendar. Smart grid technologies cross-reference between general power usage trends, and your own household usage. The rise of information and cloud-based services like AlexaKit, HealthKit, and Watson are especially designed to allow development teams to very quickly integrate enterprise grade functionality into new products very quickly and easily (see Figure 11-3). For multimodal experiences, information ecosystems help parse sensor information, inform decisions in physical experiences, and interpret the intentions of users' behaviors and interactions. GPS services cross-reference between several satellites as well as referencing GIS, or Geographic Information Services, to not only tell you where you are, but to fill in information like street names, restaurants, and points of interest nearby.

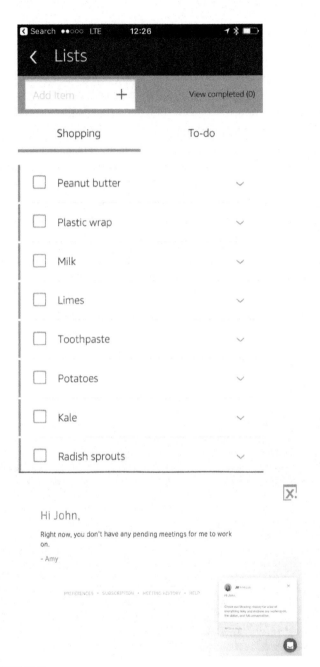

FIGURE 11-3.

Connecting device ecosystems with services lets consumers voice their shopping lists and then refine them (Alexa); integrating calendar and contacts with natural language processing lets AI assistants manage meetings (x.ai)

Physical Ecosystems

Physical ecosystems are becoming a more prominent part of the Internet of Things. Announced in late 2017, Google's Sidewalk Labs has partnered with the city of Toronto on a project called, "Quayside," a 12-acre testbed of new urban technologies. Projects like this take into consideration the physical environment, including roads, streets, and buildings in transportation or smart city uses. These tests envision how technology can change cities, literally from the ground up (see Figure 11-4). The home and the systems within the home are important for smart home and smart building technologies. Public and outdoor spaces in particular can introduce some more complex considerations. For example, certain environments are noisier than others. Public spaces can be crowded and busy, whether dazzlingly exciting or simply overwhelming. It can be hard to know where to look and to process what you are looking at when you are simply trying to find your way through a jostling crowd. Because multimodal experiences are increasingly used to augment reality—in the very broadest definition of the term—the reality that is being augmented is a crucial aspect of the experience.

FIGURE 11-4.
As part of its Amsterdam Smart City initiative, the city council can control streetlights based on pedestrian usage; the city builds on the ecosystem by soliciting and acting on suggestions from city residents (Source: Massimo Catarinella, Creative Commons Share Alike)

Social Ecosystems

Social ecosystems offer other important considerations that too often get overlooked. These include whether a device is shared, is used in shared social spaces, and the behavioral and other norms of the usage context. One of the most visible examples of this was that of the Google Glass phenomenon, where people were uncomfortable with the idea that someone could photograph them without their knowledge. They were also out of touch with fashion trends at the moment. Though the technical functionality of Google Glass was highly anticipated, the social acceptability made the product difficult to adopt—not necessarily by the users themselves—but by the people around the user. It felt threatening to their privacy.

Within the home, there may be multiple members of the household sharing a single device, like a home assistant, television, refrigerator. A parent may not want their child to have access to R-rated movies, or to the "Confirm Order" button inside a shopping app. People have different permissions or roles within a social ecosystem but shared access to functionality—for example, children might add toys to a shopping list, though purchase is reserved for parents. In retail, hospitality, or healthcare, there are specialized relationships between those receiving a service and those providing it. These roles shape the way in which a device can be used. And these attributes of social relationships—role definition, social acceptability, connection, and trust between users in a shared social structure—will become more prominent in user experiences, especially as connected products become woven into the fabric of shared resources, environments, and institutions (see Figure 11-5).

FIGURE 11-5.
Privacy expectations in many settings, such as locker rooms and libraries
are easily disrupted by technologies that extend the senses (and might allow
whatever they sense to be collected or distributed)

Specialized Ecosystems

Specialized ecosystems have considerations outside of typical usage behaviors and technology requirements. For example, certain types of hospital equipment need to be sterilizable. Medications have many different and long names, and the schedule, dosage, and whether or not a patient has received them or is showing dangerous side effects have to be exactly right. There is zero tolerance for error. Driverless cars need to follow local driving laws and speed limits. Workplaces may require specialized forms of equipment like safety glasses or gloves, or long-term exposure regulations that can make some interactions challenging.

Cloud Architectures: Distributing Resources Through Connectivity

It's common for multimodal products to have several different devices or connected resources working together to deliver a single experience. For example, the round black tower sitting on a tabletop is the just the tip of the iceberg of an Amazon Echo. The device itself is basically a speaker and microphone cleverly optimized for natural language processing and for collecting sound information and distributing it in the open space of your home. The information gathered is sent via your WiFi router and ISP modem to Alexa, the cloud-based voice service sitting in a data center—probably not so close to where you are. Your voice, and the commands you issue, go through several layers of processing. A greatly simplified flow is something like this: first, the sound is gathered and any external noise is removed. Next, the part that is going to be processed is sent to the cloud. In the cloud, the words are processed, and an appropriate response and action are selected. The verbal and visual response may be routed back to the Echo, but the action may go on through several other steps. A song might be queued up, ready to be streamed following the verbal response. A ticket may appear in front of the person who will begin to start to make your pizza. An item may be added to your shopping cart and be updated across all of your Alexa apps, or to your Amazon account. This item then has to make its way into a box with a silly amount of packing material, and then maybe hitch a ride on a few planes and trucks.

Cloud architectures are used to describe the way technology resources are made available across a network. There are a few basic categories of cloud architectures that are described by how information is used and processed within that system. They can greatly shape the way a multimodal product or service delivers an experience. It turns out that it's also very handy way to think about product architectures for multimodal design as well. The primary architectures are cloud, edge, fog, sensor network, mesh network, and tag/reader networks.

Cloud architectures are products or services that have a very thin layer of client-side access to resources that are centralized within and distributed across the cloud. Siri offers another example of a cloud-based service. Most of Siri lives in the cloud, with basically the home button, microphone, and speaker on your phone, and some screen interface. It would be pretty impractical to have the natural language processing and training happen on each individual mobile device—that would basically kill your battery and require a great deal of memory. Using a cloud architecture also makes it possible to distribute Siri across many devices but maintain it across all of them, sharing the training from all of its users to improve the service.

Edge architectures are products or services that keep most of the resources in context, like on the device itself, with minimal resources distributed through the network. An example of this might be the Oculus Rift. The visual rendering, motion processing, and interaction happen primarily on the computer connected to the Rift itself. Because visual graphics and motion processing are very processor and information intensive, and need to be delivered in real-time to make the experience more realistic, the experience is optimized around speed. This means that processing visuals or movements on a data center or even across WiFi just isn't practical—the lag it would introduce would create a critical failure of the experience.

Fog architectures are products or services that distribute resources more evenly throughout a network. An example of this might be a Nest thermometer. The thermometer itself controls the heating elements in your home directly. But account access, remote usage, integration with other Nest devices, and some of the data analysis and processing occur through cloud-based resources.

Sensor networks take advantage of how little power sensors require and distribute them across a wide area. They send their data back to a more central node—which might be a local hub or one on the cloud—where it is processed and analyzed. The sensors provide little to no functionality within context—they just collect data. Sensor networks have broad applications for transportation, smart cities, industry, and agriculture.

For example, moisture and light sensors across a farm can detect the health of crops during growing season. One slightly more robust example would be the CalTrans camera system that monitors critical points on the California highway system. In the Sierra Nevadas, it helps CalTrans and drivers monitor road conditions remotely to determine if snow chains or additional plowing is required, and perhaps how early you start driving up to Tahoe for your snowboarding weekend (see Figure 11-6). One of the most notable aspects of sensor networks is the scale: dozens, hundreds, and thousands of sensors may be very cheaply connected to a central hub.

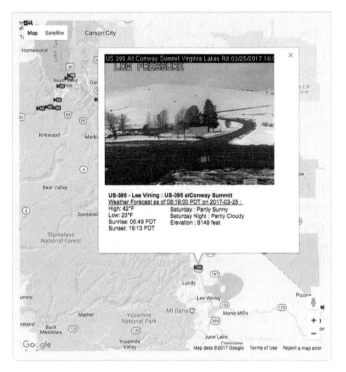

FIGURE 11-6.

A state network of traffic cameras and a website lets Californians observe road conditions for themselves before they head anywhere

Mesh networks are similar to the fog architectures of sensors, but provide both sensor data and relay data transmission together. The laptops in the One Laptop Per Child program take advantage of this technology to allow students to share files with each other and use the internet.[1]

Tag/reader networks are products or services that use a system of tags and readers. In this case, the tags themselves may not necessarily be connected in the normal sense of the word. RFID tags are powered by their readers and simply send an identification number to the reader, which can then process the data. Optical readers like barcode scanners use a visual code that can be processed by a reader. More complex systems like Apple Pay and iBeacon use the NFC chip on a phone or Apple Watch and can be tied into cloud-based payment services or to retail environments that respond to physical proximity. One of the notable things about tag/reader networks is that a single reader can read thousands of RFID tags simultaneously. Proximity-based reader networks get multiple readings of the same tag in a physical space and then triangulate position, similar to GPS.

Ecosystem and Architecture: Applying Ecosystem Resources to Multimodal Design

Networks of resources provide the informational and physical qualities of our daily experiences. Houses are a network of resources like space, sunlight, and kitchen appliances, but also utilities like gas, water, and electricity. Cities are a network of public infrastructures like transportation networks, public utilities, access to people who play different roles in our lives, and various zones of social activity, like commercial, residential, and recreational areas. Most aspects of our daily lives don't exist in isolation, but are part of a greater context.

Sensory experiences also don't exist in a vacuum. Not only do we have many different senses, we can use many different kinds of sensory information to understand the same thing. For example, we can tell that we spilled coffee by hearing the cup fall over, seeing a puddle, or perhaps, unfortunately, feeling the liquid pour into our laps. What is interesting about how our senses work is that we didn't really think

---

1 Footnote for One Laptop per Child: One Laptop per Child, "Connecting," Accessed February 25, 2018, *http://laptop.org/7.1.0/gettingstarted/connecting.shtml.*

much about how wet coffee was while it was in the cup or whether it stains. Or how dry the table was before we spilled anything onto it. We sense many things and don't pay attention until we need to notice. Then we switch gears, often very rapidly. We jump into action, quickly sweeping our phone out of the way of the encroaching puddle. Our own senses are a network that we can use very flexibly in different situations, or from one moment to the next. For example, we can use the crosswalk sign, the slowing down of cars approaching an intersection, or the movement of the pedestrians around us to decide whether or not it is safe to cross the street. It depends on whether we are paying attention to our surroundings or doing something else at the same time.

These variations determine the types of resources needed to provide one or several multimodalities within the same experience. An interesting way to understand these ecosystem configurations is to look at a few comparative examples together. Not only do they provide different benefits and constraints, they also tend to prioritize one aspect of the experience over another, depending on the design goals and approach. Comparative case studies can highlight the different types of multimodal experiences possible for specific use cases.

Sensing Experiences: Answering the Door—A Doorbell, Ring, and the August Lock

There is something elegant about an old-fashioned doorbell: a metal bell hung by the front door, with a rope or chain pull attached to a clapper. It can really only do one thing: ring. A visitor can pull the pull, which rings the bell. Perhaps a friend would have their own special way of ringing the bell, giving a hint at who the visitor might be. A visitor on urgent business could ring the bell very loudly or for a long time. But then again, so could a prankster. A peephole through the door could allow visual confirmation of the identity of the visitor, but is limited if they face away or are not directly in front of it. The resident could also ask, "Who is it?" The full activity of answering the door takes many more sensory channels than just the sound of ringing, and many smaller activities are tied to it: opening, closing, and locking the door, lending someone a key, asking who is there, and greeting them as they enter. The simplicity of the doorbell functionality was very much offset by the social etiquette and activity around it.

These different kinds of multimodal interactions around the front door of the home has made it an early focus of smart home devices. The Ring smart doorbell allows for all these interactions but emphasizes remote access and security. The primary functionality is knowing who is at the front door, when they are there. It has an HD video camera, speakers, and microphone to allow residents to see and speak with their visitors, as well as an infrared motion sensor to detect the movement of heat, allowing it to work with or without daylight. When motion is detected, the Ring sends a notification to a users' phone. When the button is pressed, a video feed is sent via WiFi to the resident's phone. This allows a user to check on the movement, whether at home or away using the video camera.

The August Lock, a competitor, focuses instead on the experience of locking and unlocking the door, relying on the door that already exists in your home, as well as a really common locking mechanism: the deadbolt. The primary functionality is whether or not the door is locked. The Lock mechanically turns the existing deadbolt of a door from the inside, when prompted by users via Bluetooth and a mobile app. With the addition of peripherals such as the WiFi bridge and video doorbell, it can also support remote answering and unlocking. It also allows the creation of guest keys for those who have been sent an invite and who download the app.

Understanding and Deciding Experiences: Determining Distance—a Pedometer, Apple Watch, and Lyft App

The original pedometers were simple mechanical devices. A small, weighted pendulum would swing as a person took a step, turning a gear that advanced the counter one step. People would have to cross-reference the information with their watch, perhaps a map, and perhaps a written log to keep track of how far they had actually traveled by foot.

The Apple Watch, on the other hand, uses gyroscopes, accelerometers, and GPS. (The first generation tapped into the GPS capabilities of a paired phone, the following generations have it built in.) It has a lot of other sensors, but these are the set used for detecting distance. In running Activity mode, the Apple Watch allows users to focus their activity on calories burned, elapsed time, distance, or open mode with no goal at all. A useful feature is the haptic notification at the halfway point of a specific goal—this allows the user to decide whether or not they want to turn around and return the way they came or to continue their run along a different path. Once the goal is achieved, another haptic notification lets the user decide if they want to keep going or stop. There is no need to keep track of any information about the run at all; the user can simply run and stay focused on their surroundings or their pace. It provides additional information like calories burned, heartrate, and other details about the runner's physical state as they are running.

While the first two examples can be used to roughly measure distance traveled, ridesharing apps focus on the distance between two points, namely a driver and a new passenger. Using GPS in both users' and drivers' smartphones, apps like Lyft and Uber are focused less on the distance and more on the amount of time it will take for the driver to arrive. Like the feature in Google Maps that tries to calculate the time of arrival of a specific route, these apps use information like current driving conditions, distance, and past driving times and traffic conditions of the route to calculate the time of arrival. This information is used to determine which driver should be assigned to a passenger, and by the passenger to decide if they want to keep or cancel the ride.

Acting Experiences: Writing and Drawing—A Pencil, a Tablet, and the Apple Pencil

The urban legend about the space race between the United States and the Soviet Union comes down to crossing your t's and dotting your i's—literally. The Americans supposedly spent millions of dollars developing a zero-gravity pen, while the Russians simply switched to using pencils. The truth is that the AG7 Anti-Gravity space pen was developed independently by the Fisher Pen Company, and offered to NASA after it had already been developed in 1965. The Russians, on the other hand, didn't just use pencils, they used grease pencils to eliminate the shavings and dust from sharpening. However, after also being offered the AG7, the Russians adopted it as well.[2]

2   Ciara Curtin, "Fact or Fiction?", Scientific American, December 2006, https://www. scientificamerican.com/article/fact-or-fiction-nasa-spen/.

From the very beginning of our education, we are taught to use writing instruments. It takes years for children to puzzle together the skills of the written language, from the big, blocky letters, we are first taught to recognize their shapes, sounds, and meanings, to cursive and perhaps even calligraphy. Whether in the chubby hands of a kindergartener or an astronaut on the Mir Space Station, we are taught a special grip for our writing instruments and use them for writing, math, and drawing. They are a very immediate tool—mightier than the sword, some might say—their trails of ink or graphite appearing instantly as their tips move across paper. They become a part of our legal identity, as our signatures form the acceptance of contracts and other official documents. Writing is one of our most highly developed and complex multimodal activities. It takes years for people to develop fine motor control, blending hand–eye coordination with linguistic cognition. Most develop the skill so highly that it becomes a flow state, where ideas, words, and their graphical representations on the page become fused together. Writers and artists can develop very personal creative styles. Activities like dictation and geometry blend other modalities and cognitive processes into the mix.

A common grip is a pinch between thumb and forefinger, with the shaft of the pencil resting somewhere along the arch between them. We can write without looking, because most of us have memorized the movements—allowing them to recede into implicit memory, but that might not always result in the most legible handwriting. The feedback of using a pencil is self-evident—the trail of graphite left behind, perhaps the sound of the friction between the paper and pencil. Flip the pencil over, and the eraser helps to remove mistakes. Your hand can easily detect the amount of pressure being applied to the tip and can detect the minute vibrations caused by the variations in surface texture. Writing takes advantage of all of our finest resolution senses together: the minute details of pressure and texture haptics, and the proprioception as we move our hands and fingers, using visual acuity to confirm and guide it all.

For decades, graphics tablets have been used by graphic artists and designers for writing and drawing. These tablets use a variety of technologies and come in a variety of form factors, including something shaped like a hockey puck. Depending on the technology, there are sensors in both the drawing surface and the stylus, or in the tablet only. The experience is basically drawing on a pad with a stylus, with the drawing appearing on a computer screen. It is similar to using a pencil, though the visual feedback is not as immediate or connected to the drawing or writing motion, breaking the strong coordination between visual and proprioceptive modalities that people have developed. The most challenging aspect of using these types of tablets is placement: it's difficult to precisely place a new stroke once the stylus is lifted from the tablet surface.

The Apple Pencil works with the iPad Pros, using a number of sensors and connecting technologies, including a spring-loaded dual tilt-sensor tip and Bluetooth as well as the capacitive touch screen. These sensors scan the position and angle of the tip 240 times a second. The key advantage to this is that both the tip of the Pencil and the surface of the iPad are pressure sensitive, allowing a variety of drawing details. The direct visual feedback of drawing is immediate, allowing users to draw in ways that are highly comparable to drawing with real pencils, pens, and other drawing tools. The additional palm rejection technology allows users to rest their hand against the surface of the iPad without accidentally drawing with it. People often steady their hand for fine details by resting it directly against the drawing surface. These details create a very realistic drawing experience that matches the existing skills that people have developed using regular writing tools. It actually takes a great deal of sensor technology to emulate the precision that humans can create with drawing tools—because our own senses for using them are so acute. But of course, what we really want to know is, can the Apple pencil draw in space, or does grease pencil still win?

Summary

Because multimodal experiences often mean multidimensional sensory inputs and physical outputs, it's not surprising that multidevice or other types of ecosystems play a strong role in their design. Smart locks tap into the shared aspect of doors by allowing multiple smartphones to access a single device or by tapping into existing attributes of the home like the front door, or the electrical wires for existing doorbells. The Apple Pencil uses multiple sets of sensors in tandem between the iPad and the pencil itself to approach the sensory acuity that people already have for writing and drawing. Ridesharing services cross-reference existing geo-information with GPS information from multiple drivers and riders to determine the most efficient routes. All of these examples intersect across several different ecosystems to provide multimodal experiences. In some cases, like the Apple Watch, they take over some modalities on behalf of the user in order to allow users to more deeply focus on just one part of a multimodal experience: like looking where they are running. Drawing from different types of ecosystem resources allows users to do more or to focus better within their experiences.

Specifying Modalities: States, Flows, Systems, and Prototypes

Introduction: A Prototype Is a Custom Measuring Tool

IN THE CHARLES AND Ray Eames film, *Fiberglass Chairs, Something of How They Get the Way They Are,* the first scene shows a sheet of connected dowels attached to an adjustable wooden block jig (see Figure 12-1). A person sits down on the prototype, and the blocks are adjusted to fit the shape of their back. Informed by the pair's work creating molded wooden casts for the military, their furniture reflected the extended body of work they developed both in creating prototypes and with the human form.

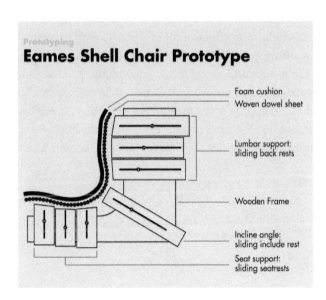

FIGURE 12-1.
The jig for the Eames fiberglass chairs had adjustable blocks throughout the form to measure and shape the seat, curve, and back of the chair.

In a workshop, a jig is a custom-made tool used to help measure, guide, and speed up the usage of existing tools. In product design, especially when using molding techniques, the jigs and final prototypes are sometimes destroyed. Other times, a jig is used as a tool in the manufacturing process itself.

In the Eameses' design process, the jig for their fiberglass chairs served multiple purposes. In earlier stages of development, it served a kind of custom ruler. They had many different people sit in it, and they adjusted the shape of the chair to fit their posture and shape. Then they documented that. The process allowed them to test hypotheses, such as "Is it more comfortable to have direct support from the chair or to have more space?" in specific contact points between the chair and the sitter. In later stages of the development process, they could use it as a working model, to find out what single shape worked best across the widest range of sitting postures and tooshie types. They could then trace that shape off to begin to create the next round of prototypes and specifications. It wasn't just an early stage design, but a custom-designed measuring tool in and of itself. It allowed the Eames to take multiple measurements, answer data-focused questions, and quickly validate or reject design hypotheses.

In the same way, multimodal design deliverables serve multiple purposes through product development: tools of research and inquiry, hypothesis proposals, guidelines, and of course production specifications and assets. It's helpful to think of all of the deliverables as prototypes—living, working models that are used flexibly to measure, shape, test, and refine solutions. Good ideas, good insights, good programming, and good products are crafted. Design deliverables can be just as often used as a stepping stone to figuring out which specifications really matter, not just the final specification numbers in pixels or inches. Don't just create prototypes. Use them. Wear them out. Then make more.

Practice Makes Perfect

The body of the Apple MacBook series has a much-touted unique manufacturing process. A custom extrusion of aluminum called a blank is cut and machined to allow the componentry to be placed inside a solid unibody form factor made of fewer parts that offer higher strength and durability. The design team doesn't just design the products. They design the manufacturing process. The same principle holds true for both hardware and software. Amazon Web Services are expressly designed to be used by other Amazon teams and third parties; core software and services are flexible and modular. This approach allowed Amazon Web Services to become a huge part of the overall company's business model. Whatever Amazon needed was probably something that another company was going to need too. Minimalism and modularity are not just an aesthetic or system rationale: they are values embodied within the design and working practices of their respective teams. In the same way a custom jig is a tool, so is the design practice itself.

The term "best practices" is something of a misnomer, because it implies that there is one superior way for everyone to do something. Figuring out the right practice, especially for new product categories, products, and interaction capabilities is a design exercise in and of itself. Multimodal design introduces a new set of human factors, integrates a blend of technologies in new ways, and addresses some new usage considerations into the solution space. A good design practice enables a team to share a clear goal or vision, provides rigor for thoughtful details and cohesive systems, and facilitates clear feedback and communication. This only becomes more important with new kinds of design solutions. A lot of design practice was really developed from screen-based experiences and products. As the type of products that design teams becomes more diversified, so will the right kind of design practice.

The Media of Multimodal Products: Information and Interactions, Understandings and Behaviors

Architects create solutions fabricated with building materials like wood, brick, glass, or steel. Fashion designers realize their solutions with fabric and finishings. Electronics industrial designers work with aluminum, titanium, sapphire glass, plastics. All of these different designers also design the behaviors of their materials: hinged doors swing, fabric drapes and folds, seat cushions give, and earbuds are inserted into the outer ear canal and mostly stay there. But how do you create with bits, and how do they behave? Some of them exist for a few fractions of a second, only to be overwritten again and again. These unruly 1s and 0s zipping through silicon chips, copper cables, optical drives, and electromagnetic waves are invisible to the naked eye, process faster than we can comprehend, and most user experiences require millions, billions, and even trillions of them. Much of what is powerful about interaction design lies beyond the range of what people are able to physically experience or comprehend. Dr. Hiroshi Ishii, who leads the Tangible Media Group at MIT, has made it his work to make these bits "tangible," focusing on how information and computation require representation. His group explores how to reintegrate physical and digital experiences. One of the key themes of exploration in his work is to better couple the sensory properties of physical media with the dynamic properties of computing. In his framework for tangible user interfaces, information and computation is represented to users across a wide range of physical media and properties.[1] He believes that the common ground between atoms and bits is not how we give bits shape, but how bits can shape human behavior. Human behavior is comprised of sensing, understanding, deciding, and acting. Important questions that product designers must answer every day include: How do bits help people perceive information? How do they affect the way we think and make choices? How do bits help us do what we want to do? Most importantly, designers must ask themselves, are we using these bits to make peoples' lives better?

---

1   Cara McGoogan, The MIT Media Lab is waging war on pixels, Wired, October 2015

The Product Development Process for Multimodal Products

Once the foundational and exploratory facets of product development are identified, there are many kinds of deliverables that can be used. Because multimodal products span multiple design media, including visual, audio, and haptic elements, they are more complex, as each mode needs to be designed individually. Physical designs call for 3D models and production specifications. Wireframes are used for screen-based experiences. Dialog scripts are used for speech. Haptic deliverables can look something like a choreography score. Designing multimodal experiences is much more like scoring a symphony (see Figure 12-2). Like instruments in an orchestra, there are individual scores for each mode of the experience, and a conductor's score that coordinates them all. However, unlike conductor's scores, multimodal design has multiple choice or choose-your-own-adventure sections. And sometimes self-playing instruments that improvise.

FIGURE 12-2.
Like an orchestral score, multimodal design syncs different technologies into a unified experience.

Another set of techniques that inform multimodal design is borrowed from theatrical, film, and animation processes. Because filmmaking is by nature multimodal, many of the techniques used in filmmaking help for multimodal design. The cameras and microphones are constantly moving between different layers of visual information, sound and dialog streams, and story arcs. The way they move prioritizes specific sensory elements: this is comparable to sensory focus within a multimodal user experience. Art critics have spent the last century debating whether film is the closest existing media to human experience. Wherever they landed on that topic, thinking like a director or a conductor is a good mindset for creating multimodal design. It is coordinating multiple sensory elements together over time into a cohesive experience.

In this book, mapping and modeling are treated separately from prototypes and specifications. This is to allow a closer look at the new kinds of human factors, design considerations, and design elements that are becoming a part of interaction design. In practice, these aspects of product development are much more fluid and ideally highly integrated and iterative. On small teams, they may be done by the same person. For new products and new product categories, a hypothesis-driven approach is used when there is little precedent for the product typology. Depending on the scale of the product and the team, many deliverables can be folded together into one deliverable or broken apart and shared to ensure alignment at different levels of the product architecture. Fair warning: if you skipped ahead to this chapter to get right to the good stuff, then you might be disappointed. There are new types of design factors (Chapters 2–5) that are included in specifications, as well as design elements (Chapter 8). Without them, it might be tough to understand this chapter.

Creating prototypes and specifications has roughly four phases that are also fluid and iterative: exploratory, generative, foundational, and elaborative (see Figure 12-3). Exploratory design identifies important design inspiration, information, and concepts that are central to creating a design solution; generative design explores possible solutions within those constraints. Often shared with user research and engineering, these help inform the starting hypotheses of what a design solution might be. Some of the deliverables designers might create during this phase are mood boards, style frames, concept or user point-of-view videos, material investigations, and formal studies. These provide inspiration and a reference library of materials, design techniques, and aesthetic qualities. During the foundational and elaborative phases of design, core user behaviors are established, and product and manufacturing specifications are developed. These may include design metaphors, interaction models, input/output maps, wireframes, sound design, colors/material/finish (CMF), and various functional and nonfunctional prototypes developed with engineering and manufacturing teams. There is a broad range of design deliverables and activities that can be used for multimodal products. Like jigs, a design team may end up needing a few custom ones.

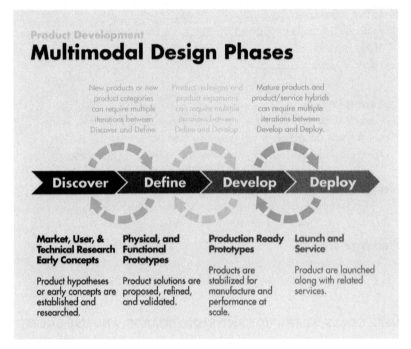

FIGURE 12-3.
Each phase of the design process provides different pieces of the solution. The number of iterations in each phase can depend on the maturity of the product.

Defining Design Requirements

Start by expressing a clear set of the user goals. There are many ways to do this, but a fun, quick way is using a first-person "fill-in-the-blanks" style template (see Figure 12-4). Be concise.

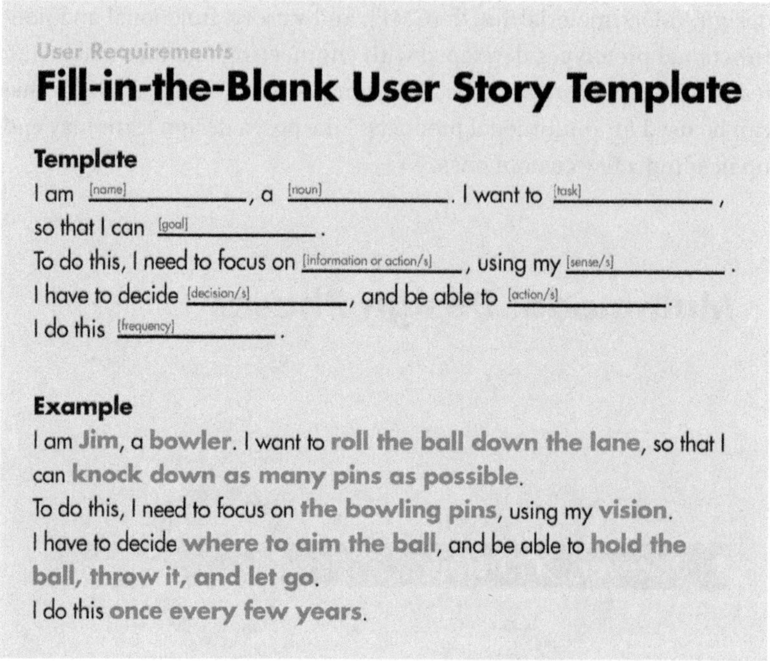

User Requirements

Fill-in-the-Blank User Story Template

Template

I am [name]_____, a [noun]_____. I want to [task]_____,
so that I can [goal]_____.
To do this, I need to focus on [information or action/s]_____, using my [sense/s]_____.
I have to decide [decision/s]_____, and be able to [action/s]_____.
I do this [frequency]_____.

Example

I am Jim, a bowler. I want to roll the ball down the lane, so that I can knock down as many pins as possible.
To do this, I need to focus on the bowling pins, using my vision.
I have to decide where to aim the ball, and be able to hold the ball, throw it, and let go.
I do this once every few years.

FIGURE 12-4.
Fill-in-the-blank user goals may not be comprehensive, but they are a good way to break the ice and get teams thinking about users and their needs

USER GOALS, SCENARIOS AND STORYBOARDS, AND USE CASES

User scenarios describe the situations in which a user might experience specific needs or try to achieve certain goals, including details of the environment, the general state of the user, and other considerations. For multimodal design, these kinds of deliverables are extended to include physical context and sensory focus (see Figure 12-5). For repetitive use cases and those that have safety requirements, it is important to explore suboptimal conditions for user experiences, to identify the types of errors or hazards that may occur as part of the experience. It is also important to explore circumstances that may require a substitution mode or a range of modes, to accommodate personal preferences.

Some topics to explore are pain points, hero moments, transitions, and social context during the interaction. These can be documented as a storyboard, photo narrative, or video. The primary goal is to drive out use cases and to ensure that the priorities of the experience are identified. Once the important events are established, the experience can be *blocked*, a technique also borrowed from theatrical and film production. Blocking ensures that each modal interaction is complete and properly integrated with the other modalities. The sequence of frames is also reviewed, to ensure that each step in the experience provides the information and functionality necessary for the next step. At this stage, the pacing of the experience can be established.

PSEUDOCODE AND SWIMLANE LOGIC FLOWS

Once all of the user experience steps have been identified (and the pathway of those steps has been established), some of the high-level technical considerations are reviewed. Pseudocode and swimlane logic flows are used to design the technical elements of the experience.

Pseudocode comes from programming, where plain language is used to describe the way a program is supposed to work. For designers, it's useful to be able to describe the conditions or triggers that invoke a certain type of interaction, and then the multiple pathways that can unfold during the experience. It can be used to describe conditional or complex use cases. Many speech design tools are variations of pseudocode. It's helpful for open-ended and nonlinear experiences, where it's possible to jump around inside an experience.

Swimlane logic flows are useful when multiple modes are being used simultaneously or there are multiple transitions or substitutions between modes (see Figure 12-6). These can be very helpful to create smooth transitions or entry and exit points within a multimodal experience. They are also useful in highly responsive experiences with high levels of automation, external triggers, or turn taking.

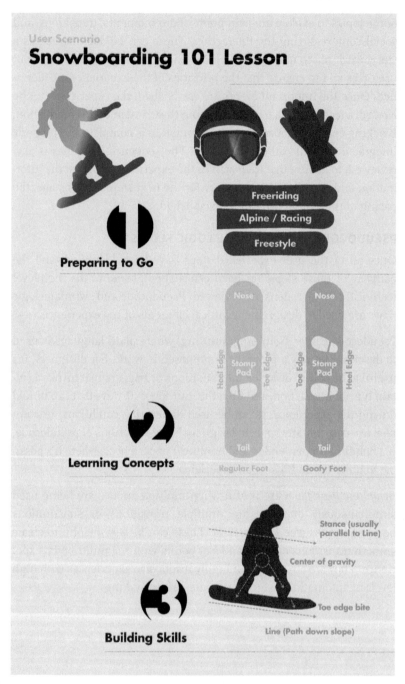

FIGURE 12-5.
The user scenario for a snowboarding lesson is more structured, to enhance learning; and more open-ended, to allow flexibility across riding styles and left- or right side dominance.

SELECTING CLOTHING

Allow Freedom of Movement
Protect from the Environment
Ensure Safety

- Fitted helmet protect the head from impact. Goggles protect the eyes from wind and glare.
- Wind and waterproof clothing. Gauntlets, gaiters, bibs, and "skirts" at the wrists, ankles, and waist keep out snow.

SETTING UP EQUIPMENT

Identify Stance
Finding Boot Type
Choosing and Fitting Bindings
Selecting A Board

- Right ("regular") or left ("goofy") dominant and foot angle towards the nose of the board.
- Bindings for different types of riding style and terrain. Both secure and responsive to movement.
- Boards vary by riding style, length, width, weight, foot dominance of rider, and other factors.

COMMON RIDING STYLES & CONDITIONS
Freeriding or Backcountry: Flexible riding for various terrains and conditions.
Freestyle: Performing tricks on both natural and manmade features or in parks.
Freecarving or Racing: Riding on groomed snow for speed and turning style (carving).

SNOWBOARD ANATOMY
Nose: The "front" of the board, with the dominant foot towards the back.
Tail: The "back" of the board, towards the dominant foot.
Edge (Heel and Toe): The "sides" of the board specified by the position of heels and toes.
Stomp Pad: Between the bindings, where a foot can rest when not in the bindings.

RIDER MOVEMENTS
Gliding: Sliding over snow, without using the edges
Turns, Carving, Slash: Changing tthe direction of the board.
Press (Front or Back): Bring weight down on the front or back foot, to allow turns or tricks.
Pop: Lifting off the ground with the snowboard.
Switch: Riding "backwards," with the opposite stance of the rider's dominant foot.

BALANCE
Center of Gravity: Feeling where the rider is holding their weight in relation to the board and riding surfaces.
Weight Distribution: Leaning weight onto the toes, heels, back, or front foot to control speed, direction, and to set up tricks.
Counterbalance: Figuring out how to combine the rider's body weight, direction, edge grip, and momentum together to increase control and speed while riding.
Bite: The contact between the edge of the board and the snow, which provides control.

RIDING
"Scooting": How to get around on flat terrain.
Falling: How to fall and how to get up from a fall.
Control: Basics of gliding, starting and stopping; speeding up and slowing down; and turning.
Lifts: How to get on and off a chair lift.

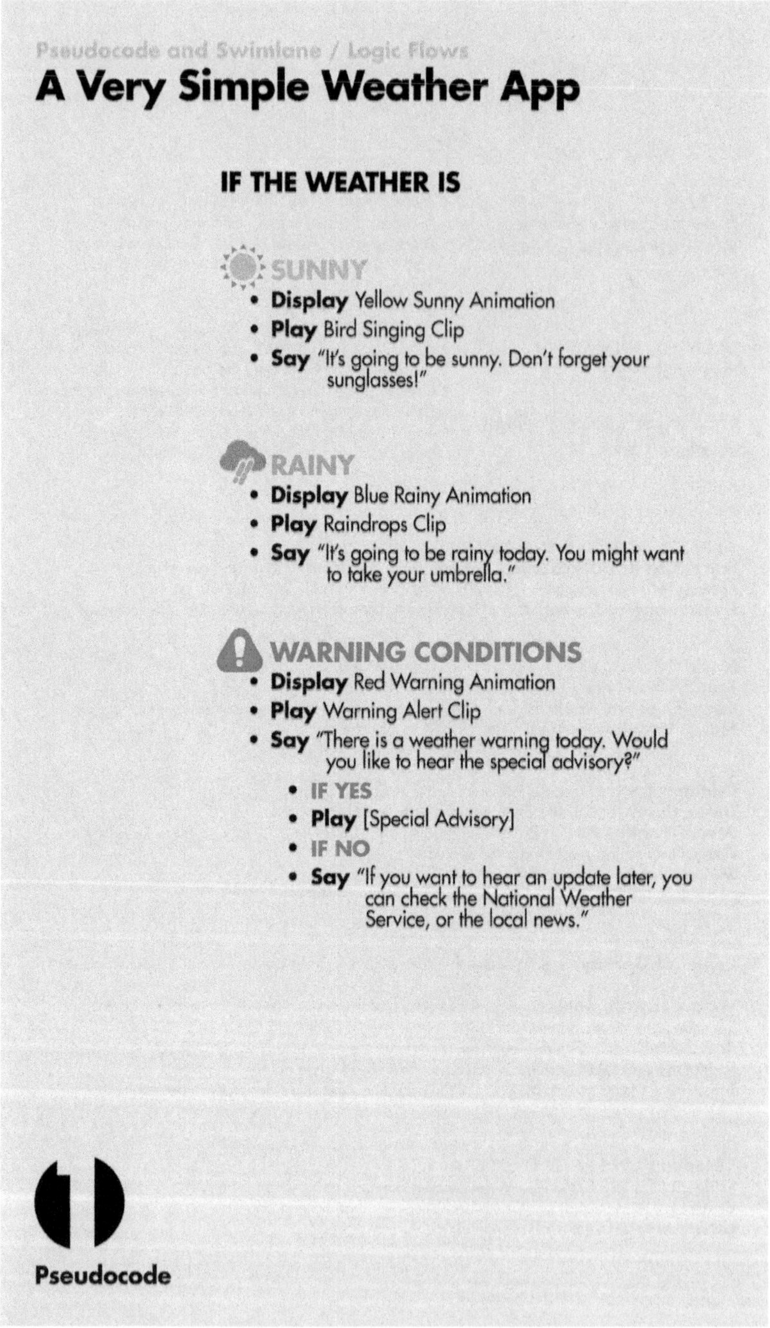
Pseudocode and Swimlane / Logic Flows
A Very Simple Weather App
IF THE WEATHER IS
SUNNY
• Display Yellow Sunny Animation
• Play Bird Singing Clip
• Say "It's going to be sunny. Don't forget your sunglasses!"
RAINY
• Display Blue Rainy Animation
• Play Raindrops Clip
• Say "It's going to be rainy today. You might want to take your umbrella."
WARNING CONDITIONS
• Display Red Warning Animation
• Play Warning Alert Clip
• Say "There is a weather warning today. Would you like to hear the special advisory?"
• IF YES
• Play [Special Advisory]
• IF NO
• Say "If you want to hear an update later, you can check the National Weather Service, or the local news."
1
Pseudocode

FIGURE 12-6.
Both pseudocode and swimlane logic flows can help create flows for multimodal experiences.

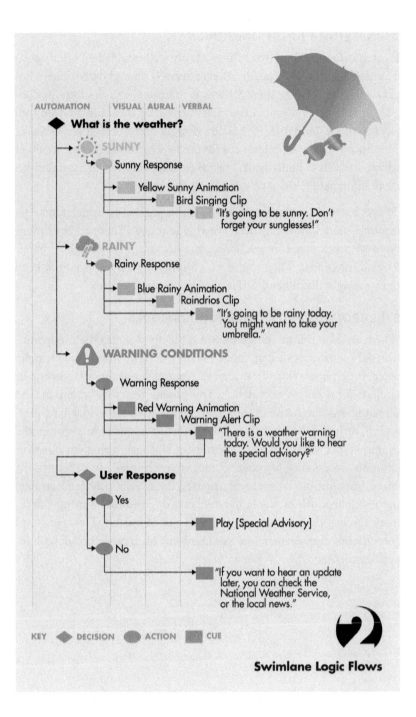

AUTOMATION | VISUAL | AURAL | VERBAL

What is the weather?

SUNNY

Sunny Response

Yellow Sunny Animation

Bird Singing Clip

"It's going to be sunny. Don't forget your sunglasses!"

RAINY

Rainy Response

Blue Rainy Animation

Raindrios Clip

"It's going to be rainy today. You might want to take your umbrella."

WARNING CONDITIONS

Warning Response

Red Warning Animation

Warning Alert Clip

"There is a weather warning today. Would you like to hear the special advisory?"

User Response

Yes

Play [Special Advisory]

No

"If you want to hear an update later, you can check the National Weather Service, or the local news."

KEY ◆ DECISION ● ACTION ■ CUE

Swimlane Logic Flows

Specifying Multimodalities

Most interface modes already have a fairly well established set of specifications. Multimodal specifications are really about how to create connective tissue between them, or how to indicate focal, auxiliary, peripheral, or substitution modalities. This book isn't meant to go deep into any one mode, but rather look at how designers can design across them. There are many great references for the less common modes, many of which are also O'Reilly books. See the Additional Reading section for more information about designing specific modes.

To specify multimodal interactions, it's important to understand why multiple modes are being used together and how. There are four main types of multimodal interactions: synchronous, asynchronous, parallel, and integrated. They sound a bit similar, so it's important to keep them straight. Each has a different experience objective.

SYNCHRONOUS AND ASYNCHRONOUS MODES

When an experience integrates multiple modes together, the multimodal elements can come together in different ways. For example, when your phone rings, the screen, ringtone, and vibration occur in tandem for a single experience. The phone gets your attention, the screen shows the name of the caller, and the vibration may be a preference, or it may be a substitution when your phone is in silent mode. In these types of multimodal experiences, the design elements are synchronous, occurring together to support each other. In other experiences, the multimodal elements are used asynchronously. For example, in the Amazon Alexa, the light ring is used to indicate waiting, and to mark the beginning, continuation, and end of speech. The visual and speech cues complement and counterpoint each other but don't happen simultaneously.

PARALLEL AND INTEGRATED MODES

Parallel and integrated modes serve a different purpose. An example of a parallel mode would be navigating the XBox using the controller, Kinect, or Cortana. Button controls, gesture, and voice commands can each do the same thing. At any point in time, a user can easily switch from one mode to another. Parallel modes allow a single user to choose their mode preferences or to allow for substitution if it is needed. Integrated modes are when multiple modes are used simultaneously, allowing different user subgroups to experience the same thing at the same time. For example, a crosswalk uses both visual and sound cues to indicate the time to cross.

In these kinds of experiences, how the different modes map to each other becomes important. In one example, text can be entered through both dictation or typing. In another example, a feature may be accessed through a keyboard shortcut or a gesture. Input/output maps can be used to ensure consistency between different modes that provide the same functionality. Parallel experiences are common for core interactions and navigation shared across different kinds of devices.

INPUT/OUTPUT MAP

An input/output map shows all of the core multimodal interactions in one place. It is used to ensure that the modes map correctly to key features or interactions. It also ensures—across parallel or integrated modes—that there is a clear rationale and consistency within and across modes.

It's important to note all interactive points of input and output, and their pertinent attributes and expectations. This can be a very useful starting point for developing prototypes and imagining the forms they might take, as the design works to accommodate the inputs and outputs of all modalities. This kind of document is especially useful if a number of different devices share a set of features and interactions across them but have variations in modes (see Figure 12-7).

A Sidescroller Game

Game Controller

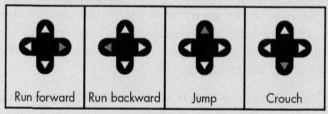

| Run forward | Run backward | Jump | Crouch |

Keyboard

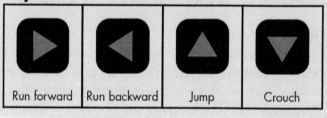

| Run forward | Run backward | Jump | Crouch |

Touchscreen

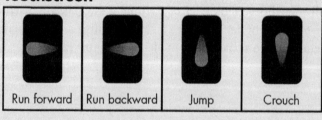

| Run forward | Run backward | Jump | Crouch |

FIGURE 12-7.

Input/output maps help keep interactions consistent but not identical across related devices and experiences.

Summary

Creating prototypes and specifications has four phases: exploratory, generative, foundational, and elaborative. Because of the interdependent nature of multimodal products, building, using, and refining prototypes is essential. Real-world product use is an integral stage of design, and using prototypes effectively can both reveal and address design considerations as they emerge. In addition to standard technical specifications, deliverables like storyboards and flows can help communicate purpose and context among the team so that everyone understands the experience goal and can apply their own expertise when needed.

[13]

Releasing Multimodal Products: Validation and Learning

AFTER DOZENS OF ITERATIONS, ruthless prioritization, countless cups of coffee, and whirlwind factory visits, your completely operational ~~Death Star~~ multimodal product is ready to meet the ~~Rebel Alliance~~ your users. It may feel like discovery was completed many phases ago, but a new kind of discovery may be just beginning.

Release methodologies like dogfooding, alpha, and beta play a larger role in hardware product releases: they give designers a great opportunity to validate real-world usage that can be difficult without both functional products and the real-life contexts of users. Running acceptance tests to validate multimodal designs can provide valuable insight that can only be found "in the field."

During full releases of multimodal products, initial user experiences reveal unexpected adoption behaviors. When Siri first came out, there were countless stories of how users tried to "stump" the service only to discover funny Easter eggs in her repertoire. Further releases broadened this playful aspect of Siri, and continue to both delight users, and also deepen their learning of the service through play.

This is one of the most rewarding parts of designing multimodal interactions. People will always manage to surprise you. As designers, we get to try to surprise and delight them back.

Release Is About Process

The industrial designer Eva Zeisel said, "As a designer, it's your job to give people gifts every day."

One of the ways to make sure that your users are able to receive those gifts is to have a product that is easy to learn and easier still to live with. Releasing products is when you get the chance to see if you're really doing that. There are many different approaches, and they are generally tailored to both the product type and organizational profile of the product teams. There are also many books, and much expert knowledge about launching products; clearly this book isn't going to substitute for that. What we hope to do is point out a few of the aspects of launching product that matter the most to multimodal design.

The release process is, well, a process. It's not a one-moment event. A common approach is to start with smaller, more familiar groups of users, and gradually scale up that group of users to better represent the target user audience. Earlier stage launches are a chance to validate the core ideas and value of products as well as identify critical defects or gaps in the product experience. Later stage launches test the appeal of the product to wider, more diverse audiences and identify stresses and defects of system integrity across contexts and scale. It might also show you whether or not people will understand and use it as intended, and possibly even surface interesting new uses.

Alpha Release

The first step is the Alpha release, which might start with the appetizing name dogfooding (coming from "eat your own dogfood"—i.e., if it's so tasty, you try it!). Not everything is polished, and not all features are complete. That's OK—this is the time to get initial feedback and observations, as well as getting your team primed for responding to those as you move forward with later releases. Generally speaking, this is where you start to ask, does the product do what you'd hoped? What do the users expect and need? Does it fail at any points?

The earliest alpha stage starts with the project team but quickly includes as many other colleagues as possible. Once a level of initial confidence is reached, the circle is expanded to friends and family. This may be a tough hurdle, but making it happen as soon as possible is valuable. This is also often the stage at which many product partners are given access, and coordinating that may be an effort in itself.

ORGANIZING ALPHA

1. *Create a list of all participant groups, including any legal agreements for each type.*

   Employees are probably covered, but there may need to be releases and non-disclosure agreements for friends and family. If you are working in a compliance-heavy field like health or finance, this legal part is especially important and likely to include other regulatory hurdles. Your team better have a robust plan to address those.

2. *Define testing goals and success metrics.*

   You should start with a list of success criteria for features overall, as well as a list of use cases. In some cases, lifestyle fit may be an important factor.

3. *Develop a set of objectives for each type of participant.*

   This is the time to test user experiences and general functionality. Since multimodality is so context-dependent, try to test in real-world conditions or as close as you can get. If there are particular features that need to be understood, it helps to create a combination of direction and education for first-time users.

4. *Create a system for soliciting and processing feedback.*

   Make sure that participants are motivated to use the product as much as possible and are given a clear path to submit feedback. Explicitly calling for particular types of feedback may help prompt users, though the fact that the feedback was prompted should be noted. See "Validation and Feedback" for more ideas.

Once the feedback starts to come in, it's important to parse and prioritize it. Interpretation is the better part of research.

LEARNING FROM ALPHA

1. *Identify critical user errors, or main weaknesses that could jeopardize product stability and viability.*

   If something sticks out as critical, make sure that it is flagged, communicated, and given the right weight. These are larger issues, at the level of product requirements and definitions.

2. *Prioritize bugs and assign them to responsible parties.*

No doubt your team has a bug tracking system in place; that's where these go. It's probably a good idea to split the issues into addressable fixes; known issues for support; and challenges for user education and support.

3. *Organize efforts with partners by addressing any needs and concerns that lie outside of bug fixes.*

You're now starting efforts that probably fall outside of your bug tracker, and dealing with partners' needs is likely to include some overlap between bugs and contractual agreements. Be aware of any pitfalls.

4. *Develop educational priorities.*

You should be learning a lot about where misunderstandings or interface difficulties occur. This is great insight for developing any support materials that you will create for later releases. You can even begin to draft and test those.

5. *Understand what users like and don't like.*

This is a great time to see if the features that your team likes and has prioritized are aligning with users. This can help with prioritizing bugs, driving any revisions, and it can also feed into marketing efforts and user communications. You probably also want to add to use cases if it turns out that people are doing things that hadn't been considered. Do you want to support these? Discourage them? A good first step is knowing about and documenting them.

Have a responsive team ready to take on what will hopefully be a nice stream of new product insight. And get ready for beta.

Beta Release

All concerns about product definition and core features should be resolved before entering beta release. This may mean that there are a few alpha iterations before you get there. Beta releases focus on functional feedback, start to inform customer service protocols, and open product usage to wider audiences and real-world conditions. Learning from this stage of release increases reliability, flexibility, and team and product responsiveness when faced with unpredictable external factors. Some product teams prefer to think of product release as "perpetual beta," because many software and now hardware development processes can support a continuous stream of testing, iteration, and refinement. This mindset is especially useful for automated or assisted products where user behaviors can provide insights or data used to improve or train product behaviors.

ORGANIZING BETA

1. *Set participants, licensing terms, and beta release agreements.*

   Some betas are open to anyone, while some are invitation only. Commonly, an invitation is requested, which can create a sense of excitement and buzz around a product launch.

2. *Decide how to announce the release.*

   Many people shun the major PR blitz kind of releases these days, especially in the realm of Lean Startup. The idea is to let the bugs work out and let the user base develop momentum before making a larger push for awareness.

3. *Excite and educate users, explain nuances.*

   Develop content that conveys the product benefits. Whether printed, on a website, video, or all of the above, you should be able to use the release announcement to get users excited to use your product, and educate them in the best ways to do so. No matter how you announce the release, you might consider ways to get the word out from trusted sources. Are people having a great experience? Find ways to amplify their sentiment through a word-of-mouth or influencer strategy.

4. *Build and engage the product community.*

   Certain kinds of products can be supported through community forums or other types of social engagement like user-generated content. Others may require higher touch forms of support or service to accompany the product. There may be a range of engagement dynamics between users, like friendly competition, different forms of support and guidance, or collaborative usage. This is a good place to take cues from the audience members themselves, and to approach the relationship with them on their terms.

5. *Refine system for soliciting feedback.*

This may include channels through the user communities, surveys or other research methods to understand user attitudes and satisfaction, direct channels within the product itself, as well as more traditional methods of customer support, such as phone or chat help.

6. *Implement real-world quality assurance strategies.*

Real users will now have their hands on the devices and in the software. If you are making physical products, there can be layers of quality assurance and calibration standards. This is especially true for medical devices, financial services, or any others that rely on more protected groups of user or forms of user data (in which case, you'll also need to manage compliance issues and standards).

LEARNING FROM BETA

Many of the approaches for an alpha release are the same here, just on a different scale, and more public facing.

1. *Identify critical user errors, or main weaknesses that could jeopardize launch.*

This is still the top priority.

2. *Prioritize bugs and assign them to responsible parties.*

Continuing this effort is ongoing.

3. *Refine educational priorities.*

Are there nuances that people are just not getting? Are there features that are so great they need to be celebrated? User education and communication should help prioritize these.

4. *Understand what users like and don't like.*

You may have shaped your product based on the input of staff, families, and friends. Get ready for a whole lot of people who are not predisposed to go along with your vision or forgive your dumb mistakes. Try to learn from them, and respond without getting discouraged even if there is negativity. Some communication channels are really lightning rods for negative feedback. It's important to discern inappropriate dissatisfaction from reasonable complaints and unvarnished feedback.

By now, your responsive team will be familiar with the ins and outs of the product and the audience, and ready for that nice stream of new product insight to become a flood. Because now it's public release time.

Public Release

For many companies, the distance between the later phases of beta release and the early stages of public release is very small. "Perpetual beta," in which a product is constantly improved, has become a key approach in the success of many of the most innovative companies like Google. While it can be harder to re-create the fluidity of software updates in physical devices, approaching releases with that same spirit can be valuable, especially when the software components are an ever-increasing part of devices. Hardware development processes are evolving to replicate this tighter, faster feedback loop between product teams and their users.

VALIDATION AND FEEDBACK

It doesn't do much good to get products in the hands of users if you are unable to learn from the experience. Feedback can take several forms: quantitative versus qualitative; and observed versus self-reported. There are benefits to each of them.

Start with the most important things to learn. You probably already have a good idea of the kinds of things that you want to validate. Depending on the design and build methodology you have used up until now, you may even have a headstart in organizing, prioritizing, and resolving them.

Important metrics

Success should be considered from both the user and business perspective. You are likely to have clear goals overall, as well as steps along the way. If you created user journeys or models, this is a good chance to validate those.

Focus has been an important theme in this book, and testing it with users should be a top priority. Validating the focus of the user's intended tasks is a good way to get at what's working and what isn't. Are users able to focus on the task at hand when using your product? If there is a learning curve, and are they able to eventually overcome it and reach a state of focus? How long did that take, and what were the main hurdles?

Time might be very easy to quantify, less easy to interpret. Time spent with a new product can indicate pleasure, interest, or confusion. It is therefore often useful to pair time with other factors, whether qualitative or quantitative to arrive at workable insight.

Frequency of use can be a big positive indicator that the product is enjoyable, especially if it is sustained.

Modalities can be tricky to assess through self-reporting, especially when they are subtle or preexist product use. The same goes for things like transitions, shifts, and other aspects of multimodality. So you probably have to work backward a little and see how well the system as a whole is working, and then dig into any problems with more detailed observation. Field research, outside of labs and more automated forms of user testing, is returning to prominence in the development of multimodal products. An informed, anthropological eye for context is invaluable.

Safety is a higher concern with many multimodal products than others, by virtue of their use beyond the desktop, out in the world. The world is a busy place, and distractions can lead to bad results. Anticipate where this might happen, but also stay alert for signs that less obvious dangers might arise.

Feedback methods

Surveys are an easy place to start. When getting at the right questions, try to get input from many people on the team, but use one editor to ensure consistency.

Video diaries can be very useful, if complicated by the fact that many of the products we're discussing are very immersive, so videos will likely be about users talking about their experiences. Videos of actual usage might be accomplished with the help of friends, but it's hard to count on that. There are several user research companies that offer apps and hosting systems for creating these kinds of diaries.

Support is a great source of insight into what works and what doesn't, as well as the steps necessary to get a user up and running. In an alpha release, you may not have a dedicated support staff yet, but if possible, set someone up as point on that, ideally someone that might help make a smooth transition to the official support staff for beta release.

The Out-of-the-Box Experience

The experience of buying, receiving, unboxing, and using a product for the first time can be clear, easy, exciting—even magical—and lead to adoption, word of mouth, perhaps even buzz. Or it can be off-putting, confusing, frustrating, and lead to abandonment or worse, product returns. As consumer sophistication and marketing finesse have both developed, expectations for all points in this experience have risen. Orchestrating this out-of-the-box experience has become a desired skill for interactive designers.

The experience is generally divided into a sequence of days:

- *Unboxing* is when the product is opened. Apple famously set the bar high with its consumer products, starting with the iPod and later the iPhone. Other companies have followed suit, with a similarly themed message: this is a special moment, when a new, somewhat alien but exciting and human-centered piece of technology is entering your life. Marketing awe aside, a clear emotional as well as experiential benefit is now expected to be a part of the packaging.

- *First-time experiences* include that moment of awe and purchase excitement, but should quickly move to getting hands on the product and understanding what it does.

- *First 9 minutes: Setting up the product* by following one of those Read Me First booklets has become the norm, but as much as possible the packaging and product itself should do the talking.

- *First 90 minutes: Trying the key feature* is the agenda, or in many cases, trying whatever happens. Hopefully that's the key feature, or an exciting Easter egg at least.

- *First 9 days: Trying all the key features* is a likely scenario, though if the first days, or even hours, fail to impress, many of today's fickle early users may abandon the cause and return or discard the product.

- *First 90 days* is when driving frequency of use becomes very important. Creating moments of use that in turn become habits is key to product adaption. Enabling or prompting ties to the product by making useful connections with other activities and platforms can create value for the user and make the device part of regular routines.

That's a lot. Managing to tie together good design, ongoing research, and responsive marketing (and to do it all on time) is impressive—and that usually takes a good balance between coordination and accommodation.

Summary

Releasing multimodal products follows the same general schedule of phases as other interactive products, moving from alpha, to beta, and then public release. Understanding that it is a process, and working to organize each part of it to communicate and learn helps to manage and make the most of each step. Learning from each phase is particularly critical given how likely it is that complexities—either from users or real-world contexts—will add unforeseen challenges and opportunities. Creating hypotheses and setting the metrics for gauging success and analysis is an important part of each phase. Leave room for your users to surprise you with new challenges, opportunities, and ideas. Multimodal design is a new lens on delivering delightful product experiences that reflect how people really experience products and the world.

Speaking of which, we'd love to hear your experiences with designing, launching, and using multimodal products. You can reach us at the following email addresses:

- *christine@designingacrosssenses.com*
- *john@designingacrosssenses.com*

[*Appendix*]

Further Reading

Diane Ackerman, *A Natural History of the Senses* (New York, Vintage Books Edition, 1990).

Blandine Calais-Germain, *Anatomy of Movement* (Seattle, Eastland Press, 1993).

Neil Cohn, *The Visual Language of Comics: Introduction to the Structure and Cognition of Sequential Images* (London: Bloomsbury, 2013), 70.

Henry Dreyfuss, *Designing for People* (New York: Allworth Press, 2003), 24.

Henry Dreyfuss, *Designing for People* (New York, Allworth Press, 1955).

David Eagleman, *Incognito: The Secret Lives of the Brain,* Reprint Edition (New York, Vintage, 2012): 56.

David Eagleman, *The Brain: The Story of You* (New York: Pantheon Books, 2015), 41.

The Eames Office, *Fiberglass Chairs, Something of how they get the way they are* (1970), *https://www.youtube.com/watch?v=PYptIkjS6zk.*

B.J. Fogg, "B.J. Fogg's Behavior Model," accessed January 20, 2018, *http://www.behaviormodel.org*

B.J Fogg, *Persuasive Technology: Using Computers to Change What We Think and Do* (Interactive Technologies) (San Francisco: Morgan Kaufman Publishers, 2003).

Jacob Fraden, *Handbook of Modern Sensors: Physics, Designs, and Applications,* 5th Edition (New York, Springer, 2016).

Alberto Gallace and Charles Spence, *In Touch with the Future: The Sense of Touch from Cognitive Neuroscience to Virtual Reality,* (Oxford, UK: Oxford University Press, 2014), 148.

Jennifer M. Groh, *Making Space: How the Brain Knows Where Things Are* (Belknap, 2014).

Edward T. Hall, *The Hidden Dimension* (New York, Anchor Books Editions, 1966).

Kenya Hara, *Haptic* (Japan, Takeo Co., Ltd., 2004).

Edward T. Hall, *The Silent Language* (New York, Anchor Books Editions, 1959).

John M. Henshaw, *A Tour of the Senses: How Your Brain Interprets the World* (Johns Hopkins, 2012), 160.

Daniel Kahneman, *Thinking, Fast and Slow* (New York: Farrar, Straus and Giroux, 2011), 20.

Jaron Lanier. *Dawn of the New Everything: Encounters with Reality and Virtual Reality* (Holt, 2018).

Peter H. Lindsay and Donald A. Norman, *Human Information Processing* (New York, Academic Press, 1977), 499.

Ellen Lupton, *Beautiful Users: Designing for People* (Princeton, Princeton University Press, 2014), 26.

Christine L. MacKenzie and Thea Iberall, *The Grasping Hand* (Amsterdam; New York: North Holland, 1994).

Donella H. Meadows and Diana Wright, *Thinking in Systems: A Primer* (White River Junction, Vermont: Chelsea Green, 2008), 46.

Nicholas de Monchaux, *Spacesuit: Fashioning Apollo* (Cambridge: MIT Press, 2012).

Donald Norman, *The Design of Everyday Things* (New York: Basic Books, 2013), 55.

Gabriel A. Radvansky and Jeffrey M. Zacks, *Event Cognition* (Oxford: Oxford University Press, 2014), 2.

David Rose. *Enchanted Objects: Design, Human Desire, and the Internet of Things* (Scribner, 2014).

KTH The Royal Institute of Technology. "Feeling small: Fingers can detect nano-scale wrinkles even on a seemingly smooth surface," *ScienceDaily*, (accessed February 3, 2018), *http://www.sciencedaily. com/releases/2013/09/130916110853.htm.*

Barry E. Stein and M. Alex Meredith, *The Merging of the Senses*, (Cambridge: MIT Press, 1993), 15.

Barry E. Stein, et al. *The New Handbook of Multisensory Processing* (MIT Press, 2012).

Glossary

Affordances

Perceived possibilities for action that inform, and are informed by, the different ways that we can interact with objects and our environment.

Cognitive load

The amount of mental effort used the intellect at any moment, according to cognitive psychologist, John Sweller, who applied the concept to using good design to the presentation of information.

Cue

Perceived qualities of objects or environments that signal other qualities such as the state of that object. We use them, and often depend on them, to help us understand what is happening around us, what we should do, and to recognize the state of objects, environments, and situations.

Dimension

Types of stimuli that a sense detects. The many dimensions of touch include warmth, texture, and pressure, whereas light is the single dimension of vision.

Haptic

The combination of the tactile, proprioceptive, and vestibular systems together. (Often thought of as primarily touch-based.)

Human factors

A discipline within design focused on optimizing products or systems for use by and interaction with humans.

Feedback

A response, such as a signal or cue that happens as a result of an action.

Feedforward

Similar to feedback, a special kind of a signal sent in in anticipation of an action, usually as a way of guiding users.

Kinesics

The study of how bodily movements such as facial and other gestures can communicate, whether intentionally or not.

Mental model

A representation of the way a person thinks about an object, event, or situation. That might include what that thing does, how it works, how it might interact, what the person can do with it, and relationships it might have with other things. The phrase may refer to a person's actual thought process, as well as representations or illustrations describing that process, such as those made by designers.

Modality

Patterns that shape the way people use sensory channels to inform their behaviors.

Mode

Device capabilities that drive the ways they interact with people, the world, and with each other. Because devices use senses to communicate with people, these often align with human modalities.

Multimodal

The use of several modes or modalities simultaneously or in sequence in order to affect an action or activity.

Neural adaptation

The way that the nervous system responds to long-term, non-painful sensations by lessening or losing perception of them, as with the lack of perception of comfortable shoes after a few moments wear.

Paralanguage

Non-language–based components of communication that can convey emotion, intensity, or other types of meaning, often in conjunction with spoken language, as with pitch, prosody, intonation. Paralanguage may be aware or non-aware.

Parity

The overlap between abilities and the way they support and inform each other, whether the abilities are within the same person, between a person and a device, or between devices.

Perception

How we sense physical information, become aware of it, organize it and interpret it.

Physical information

The practically unlimited state of the physical world and how it is understood, whether that means the sun is shining, there is a flat tire, the earth is the third planet from the sun, or that you are traveling 63 mph downhill on a roller coaster in Santa Cruz, California.

Prompt

A cue that signals a shift in agency, particularly in interactions that require turn-taking in communication, control, or activity.

Proprioception

The sense of bodily position, motion, and effort that is informed by nerves within the body as well as our vestibular sense.

Proxemics

The study of how space is used by people for communication and organization, as well as the effect that distance and crowding has on their perceptions, emotions, and interactions. Coined by anthropologist Edward T. Hall.

Umwelt

The particular sensory world that an individual or species lives within and that reflects what it understands can help it live, function, and flourish. Similar to the idea of affordances, but reflecting the idea that abilities to perceive helpful and nourishing things shape a being's worldview. This concept can be adapted to model a device's sensory world by grouping its sets of input and processing.

Range

The variation in a stimuli that can be sensed. Though our resolution in precisely detecting temperature is low, we can experience a range from between freezing up to about 140° or 150° Fahrenheit.

Resolution

The level of detail and amount of information within a stimuli. While vision has low dimension (only light), we can process a lot of detailed information using it.

Schema

In psychology, patterns in thought or behavior that organize experiences in order to understand them and how they relate to each other. Different categories of schema, such as perceptual, semantic, and conceptual, deal with different types of activity, thought, and perception. They are also created in order to handle new information and experiences effectively.

Substitution

The use of alternative senses when there is interference within a modality.

Synchrony

In multisensory integration, the way that sense abilities reinforce each other, and increase the ability to predict and correct each other.

System 1 and System 2

Psychologist Daniel Kahneman describes the brain working in two ways, System 1, which is intuitive, fast and sometimes even automatic; and System 2, which is slower and more deliberative.

Translation

A particular type of substitution that can map information to a relevant modality, when an experience lies outside of human perception or outside of practical means to obtain physical information.

Unimodal

Using one modality or mode.

[Index]

of touch, 68–70
understanding. *See* understanding
of vision, 60–62
human memory
  capacity of, 80
  implicit, 90, 121, 126, 226
  learning and, 88
  muscle memory, 162
  smell and, 74
  spatial, 109
human modalities. *See* modalities
Humanscale project, 93–95

I

iBeacon protocol, 157
Iberall, T., 98–99
Imazon (NGO), 2
immersive activities, 198–201
implicit memory, 90, 121, 126, 226
inferring versus designating intent, 99–101
information ecosystems, 214–215
ingestibles (IoT devices), 76, 129
input/output model, 243, 160
input triggers, 22
integrated mode, 243–244
integration
  design considerations, 164
  multisensory, 17–19, 114–115, 264
intent, inferring versus designating, 99–101
interfaces
  auditory, 64–65, 108
  examples, 11
  functional categories for devices, 131–133
  gestural, 70–72
  gustatory, 76
  haptic, 70–72, 108
  human factors, 21–25
  interaction with technology, 14–19
  olfactory, 74–75
  timeline of interface modes, 12
  visual, 61–62, 108
interruptions in modalities, 125–126, 163
IoT (Internet of Things)
  about, 129–130

assessing changes to existing product modes, 143–145
assessing user context, 142–143
assessing user needs, 139–142
beginning inquiry, 137–146
disruptive technologies, 134–137
embeddables, 129
hardware as service, 141
hearables, 129
ingestibles, 76, 129
key applications of, 130–134
workflow to identify opportunities, 138–146
iPhone (Apple), 42, 126, 48–49
Ishii, Hiroshi, 232

J

journey maps, 159

K

Kahneman, Daniel, 84–86, 122, 264
keyframes, 160, 178–180, 237
kinesics, 95, 126, 262
kinesthetic interface, 11, 108, 115
knowledge (understanding), 81–82, 150, 164
Kringelbach, Morten L., 87
Krug, Steve, 80
Kuechler, Heinrich, 91

L

learning
  acquiring proficiency, 119–120
  creating happiness through, 87–88
  cross-modal techniques in, 114
  driving cars, 106–107
  focus and engagement in, 161–162
  machine, 201–202
  styles of, 11
Lennon, John, 112
lidar system, 202
LIDAR system, 130
Lindsay, Peter, 88
logic flows, 243

M

MacBook (Apple), 36–37, 231
machine learning, 201–202
MacKenzie, C. L., 98–99
mapping applications, 137
mapping modal behaviors to modal technologies
  about, 196–197
  augmented or secondary activities, 199–200
  augmented reality versus augmented products, 200–205
  conversation and speech, 205–206
  creating haptic experiences, 205–206
  creating primary experiences with audio and speech, 202
  immersive activities, 198–201
  passive vision-based capabilities, 201–202
  personal sound experiences, 203–207
  social experiences, 204–206
  vision dominant activities, 197–198
Massachusetts Institute of Technology, 232
McCartney, Paul, 112
mechanical stimuli, 52–53
Meissner's corpuscles, 66
memory. See human memory
mental models, 43, 83, 167
Mercedes-Benz, 26–27
Meredith, M. Alex, 115
Merkel discs, 66
Midas touch, 32
mise en place, 79–80
mobile phones. See smartphones
modal focus, 54, 105, 109
modalities
  about, 9–12, 43, 45
  adding and augmenting, 145
  applying to design, 110–112
  attributes and abilities of, 109–110
  behaviors shared between users and devices, 156–157
  defined, xi, 10, 262
  design considerations, 161
  device modes and, 14–19

exercise, 103–104
  sensorimotor schemas and, 10, 81
  shaping our, 108–109
  types of, 108–109
  using our senses, 104–107
models
  about, 43–44
  experience, 167
  focus, 160, 169–170
  for multimodality, 158–160
  input/output, 243, 160
  mental, 43, 83, 167
  refining, 83–84
  semantic, 82
modes. See device modes
moisture (human factor of touch), 68–69
monitor functionality (devices), 131–133
motion sickness, 110, 149, 199–200
motivation, 87–88
Motorola StarTac phone, 135
movement
  about, 77–78, 89
  anthropometrics and, 93–95
  body language and, 36–37, 121, 126–127
  hearing and, 63, 150
  kinesics and, 96, 126, 262
  motion sickness and, 110, 149, 199–200
  precision versus strength, 97–98
  proxemics and, 96–97, 108, 263
  task performance and, 95
  touch and. See haptic interface; touch
  vesibular system and, 70, 77–78, 148
  vision and, 60–62, 77–78, 91, 149
multimodal design
  about, xi–xii
  alignment considerations, 157–158
  behaviors shared between users and devices, 156–157
  creating delight, trust, love, 30–35
  creating multimodal properties, 184–188
  ecosystems in. See ecosystems
  elements of, 147–154
  example maps and models, 168–178

[About the Authors]

Christine Park has designed products spanning fashion, furniture, print, exhibitions, and interfaces. From haute couture to healthcare, she is passionate about the way design can improve and transform our daily lives. She has helped companies like Intel, Microsoft XBox, Samsung, Nike, and many others to develop experiences for the screen, the living room, public spaces, and the body. Her work has won awards and patents, has been featured in numerous publications, and has been showcased at New York Fashion Week, the International Contemporary Furniture Fair, and the Cannes Lions Festival.

Currently, she is the Design Director of Livongo, creating new devices and services to improve the experience and quality of healthcare. In her spare time, she travels, plays video games, and is learning how to paddleboard with her dog, Barnaby.

John Alderman is a creative planner who helps companies develop and execute strategies for innovative brands, content, and design. He began his career as a writer and editor covering technology, internet, and culture at Mondo 2000, and *Wired*, and then worked as a creative director at Razorfish and The Barbarian Group. He writes about how technology, design, business, and culture shape each other, and transform how we live. He has previously written two books: *Sonic Boom* (a *New York Times* Notable Book) and *Core Memory* (a Design Observer Book of the Year), and has contributed to *Domus*, *Étapes*, *Rhizome*, *The Independent*, and *The Guardian*. He has been interviewed by BBC, NPR, CNN and many others. He likes to travel and play music, sometimes at the same time.

Learn from experts.
Find the answers you need.

Sign up for a **10-day free trial** to get **unlimited access** to all of the content on Safari, including Learning Paths, interactive tutorials, and curated playlists that draw from thousands of ebooks and training videos on a wide range of topics, including data, design, DevOps, management, business—and much more.

Start your free trial at:
oreilly.com/safari

(No credit card required.)